GCSE in Leisure and Tourism

Sue Donaldson

Anne Gray

Ranie Padayachee

Edited by **Jean Vranic**

D1439461

Hodder & Stoughton

A MEMBER OF THE HODDER HEADLINE GROUP

Orders: please contact Bookpoint Ltd, 130 Milton Park, Abingdon, Oxon OX14 4SB.
Telephone: (44) 01235 827720. Fax: (44) 01235 400454. Lines are open from 9.00–6.00,
Monday to Saturday, with a 24 hour message answering service. You can also order
through our website www.hodderheadline.co.uk.

British Library Cataloguing in Publication Data
A catalogue record for this title is available from the British Library

ISBN 0 340 85742 0

First Published 2003
Impression number   10 9 8 7 6 5 4 3 2 1
Year   2007 2006 2005 2004 2003

Cover illustration by Jacey at Debut Art
Digital artwork by Richard Morris
Figurative artwork by Pat Murray

Typeset by Fakenham Photosetting Limited, Fakenham, Norfolk
Printed in Italy for Hodder & Stoughton Educational, a division of Hodder Headline
Plc, 338 Euston Road, London NW1 3BH.

Contents

302262

302262

Acknowledgements

The authors and publishers would like to thank the following individuals and institutions for permission to reproduce copyright material:

Adwatch: 116; Airline Network: 71; Airtours Holidays: 63b; Anglia Railways: 232; Bar du Musée: 37; Blenheim Palace, by kind permission of His Grace the Duke of Marlborough: 49; Blockbuster Inc.: 35; Courtesy British Airways/Newscast: 149; British Airways Holidays: 54r; Broadcaster's Audience Research Board (BARB): 4, 17r; buzz airlines: 97–101, 116, 139; Charlton Toy Library: 33; The Commonwealth Games Federation: 48b; Corbis: 85, 118, Rolf Bruderer 107t, Michael Freeman 49, Martyn Goddard 47, Jason Hawkes 22, 58br, Robert Holmes 123br, Pawel Libera 179, Yang Liu 122, Lawrence Manning 16, Mug Shots 195, Palm Studio 143, Jose Luis Pelaez, Inc 214, Tim Page 187, Chuck Savage 206l, Paul A. Souders 12, Paul Thompson/Ecoscene 58tl, Paul Thompson/Eye Ubiquitous 58bl, Patrick Ward 169, Mike R. Whittle/Ecoscene 136; Courtesy Deep Pan Pizza Company/Red Carrot: 127t Dunston Hall, Norwich: 160–3, 166, 173, 175, 200, 212, 216t, 218, 219, 229; Courtesy easyjet.com: 127b; Eden Project: 21; © Edexcel: 92–4; Elmbridge Leisure Centre: 36; Elmbridge Lifestyle Magazine: 31; EMAP Active: 128t; English Heritage: 24; English Tourism Council: 20t, 244, 247–52; Evening Standard: 6r, 7, 9l,r, 14t Courtesy The Forum, Norwich: 155–7, 215, 220; Getty Images: 107b, 112, 132, 165, Larry Dale Gordon 235, Laurence Griffiths 120, Clive Mason 132, Photomondo 123bl, Gary M. Prior 11, Jeff Rotman 59, Stephen Swintek 206r, John Terence Turner 168; The Forum, Norwich: 155–9; *Global Magazine*: 62; *Hotline*, Virgin Trains 11; JMC Holidays Ltd: 56, 61t, 66; Leisure Estates International: 216b; Life File: John Cox 48, Aubrey J. Slaughter 62, Andrew Ward 67; London Underground Limited: 232; London Wetland Centre: 22b; Courtesy of Lunn Poly: 172, 223; Metro: 19t, 30l McDonald's: 115, 128b; Mirrorpix: 19b, 58, 59, 67r; © Microsoft: 19t; Motoring & Leisure/Gillian Thomas: 48t; © The National Maritime Museum, London: 39; © News International Syndication, London 2003: 47, 81, 82, 83, 85, 87; © OBSERVER: 81; Pleasurewood Hills, Lowestoft: 151–4, 164, 173, 200; Pool of London Partnership (www.pool)flondon.co.uk): 27; Ronald Grant Archive: 14; Robert Harding Picture Library: 58tr; Rugby Football Union: 40; Sainsbury's: 69; Shell UK: 133; Skyline Satellite: 18r; Snowdonia National Park Authority: 20b; © Sony: 19b; Courtesy of Superbreak Mini-Holidays Ltd. (www.superbreak.com): 60; www.tate.org.uk © Tate, March 2003: 70; Thomas Cook Tour Operations UK: 65; Thomson Faraway Shores: 53; Thomson Worldwide: 54t; Tografox: Robert Battersby 123tr, 124, 137, 138, 141t,b, 167, 181tr, bl,182, 227, Terry Jennings 152, 213; Top Notch Health Clubs: 45l; www.towersalmanac.com: 41, 114; Transport for London: 5r; The Wisley Golf Club: 32b; Unijet: 64; World Trade Organisation: 49, 50; Xscape: 102–6, 116, 121.

© Crown copyright material is reproduced with the permission of the Controller of HMSO and the Queen's Printer for Scotland: 6bl, 43, 245, 246.

Introduction

The leisure and tourism industries are major sources of income for many countries worldwide and they offer a vast and ever-increasing range of employment opportunities. It is estimated that in the UK approximately £2 billion p.a. is earned through tourism alone and the tourism industry employs about 7% of the workforce.

The GCSE in Leisure and Tourism has been designed to introduce students to the many different aspects of the leisure and tourism industries and develop students' knowledge and understanding of their structures. It is designed to provide a foundation for further study or to enter directly into employment.

The GCSE in Leisure and Tourism is a Double Award and is equal in size and demand to two GCSEs. You will find it appealing if you have a lively mind and are interested in the fast-moving pace of a vibrant industry. It is suitable for people who enjoy communicating with the public, enjoy challenges and like exploring new ideas.

This book has been designed to provide the underpinning knowledge necessary to meet all the requirements of the specification for the GCSE in Leisure and Tourism and offers opportunities for successful completion of the award at all levels.

There are three compulsory units for the award:

◆ Unit 1 – Investigating Leisure and Tourism
◆ Unit 2 – Marketing in Leisure and Tourism
◆ Unit 3 – Customer Service in Leisure and Tourism.

Unit 1 is externally assessed and Units 2 and 3 are assessed through evidence gathered in a portfolio. Unlike traditional GCSEs, this award is assessed primarily through coursework. All units carry equal marks.

The book has been divided into three sections – one covering each unit. Each section includes useful case studies and activities.

The activities throughout Unit 1 will provide underpinning knowledge and develop your understanding of the leisure and tourism industries as preparation for the final assessment which will be externally set and marked by the examination board. These activities will also help you to gather information useful for the other two units.

Unit 2 will look at the role of marketing in leisure and tourism. You will be required to carry out activities as preparation for your final portfolio assignment which will be internally set and assessed. You will need to investigate one organisation and report on how it markets its products or services and compare its marketing strategy with the strategy of another organisation. You will also need to produce a promotional item.

Unit 3 will introduce you to different types of customers and how organisations provide customer service in a variety of situations. You will also be offered opportunities to practise and be assessed on your own customer service skills through role play or simulated activities. For your final assignment, you will carry out an in-depth investigation of one organisation and report on the service it provides. This will also be internally set and assessed.

How to use this book

Each chapter has similar features to help with your learning:

This is to encourage you to share information and discuss issues with your colleagues.

Talk about...

THINK ABOUT...

This is to highlight points that need some consideration when preparing your work.

ACTIVITY

This will provide an opportunity to widen your understanding and possibly gather information for your final assignment.

Extension Exercise

This will widen your investigation and help towards gaining a high grade in the examination.

ASSESSMENT ACTIVITY

These have been written specifically to enable you to gather sufficient evidence to pass the portfolio assignment assessment and gain the award. You should, however, remember to check your work against the assessment specification provided by the examinations board.

WHAT YOU WILL LEARN ...

This section summarises the content of the unit and the essential aspects on which you will be assessed.

TEST YOUR KNOWLEDGE

These questions will act as revision for your external assessment.

Tips for Success

- ◆ Organisation! Make sure you present your portfolio in an orderly way, numbering pages, separating sections and using a contents page to show what you have included. Make it easy for the assessor to find the evidence you need to gain the award.
- ◆ Visits to different leisure and tourism organisations will enable you to gather lots of useful information for your examination preparation and your portfolio, but you should make sure that you enclose **only** relevant information for assessment. Do not include numerous leaflets or computer printouts. Assessors do not have time to hunt for information.
- ◆ Avoid dependency on the internet for all your information. Getting out to organisations and reading relevant trade papers is a much more valuable and interesting way to learn about very exciting industries. If you do not have suitable organisations nearby, there are many television programmes devoted to leisure and tourism activities, e.g. *Airport* and *Wish you were here?* These can further enhance your knowledge and are more interesting than reading a computer screen.
- ◆ You may like to investigate other forms of 'e-learning' such as interactive CD-ROMs. These will provide valuable insights into various leisure and tourism organisations and how they function. See the website list for sites to contact for these.
- ◆ It is useful to share information with your class colleagues, but the work you present must be your own and in your own words. You will need to get this confirmed by your assessor.
- ◆ Lastly, enjoy your studies – the world of leisure and tourism is changing every day and offers the widest possible variety of careers.

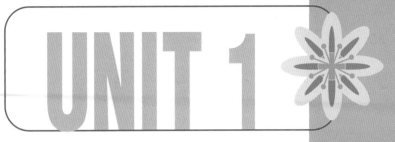

UNIT 1

INVESTIGATING LEISURE AND TOURISM

About this Unit

Taken from QCA specification guidelines, this unit is assessed externally.

For the purposes of this specification the United Kingdom shall be defined as the geographical boundaries of England, Scotland, Wales and Northern Ireland.

WHAT YOU WILL LEARN ...

In this unit, you will learn about the choices that people make about their leisure time and how they may be influenced by:

- ◆ age group
- ◆ culture
- ◆ special needs
- ◆ type of household, e.g. families, single people, couples
- ◆ gender
- ◆ social group.

Other factors also affect how people choose to spend their leisure time:

- ◆ Availability of local facilities
- ◆ Availability of transport
- ◆ Their interests
- ◆ Fashion
- ◆ The influence of family and friends
- ◆ How much money they have to spend on leisure

You will also learn about the tourism industry.

- ◆ The key components of the travel and tourism industry
- ◆ The types of holidays available
- ◆ The reasons why people choose to travel
- ◆ Employment opportunities in the industry

SECTION ONE

The Leisure Industry

Introduction

Leisure can be described as the range of activities that individuals undertake in their free time. Irrespective of age, all individuals undertake leisure activities and pursuits. Leisure has become one of the fastest growing industries in the UK. People are always looking for new ways to spend their time.

Figure 1.1   The United Kingdom

Figure 1.2

Leisure: leisure is the opportunity available to an individual after completing the immediate necessities of life, when one has the freedom to choose and engage in an experience which is expected to be personally satisfying.

Edexcel

Leisure activities are many and varied and examples of activities include reading, sport (participating and spectating), going to the cinema, disco or nightclub, going for a walk, watching television, listening to the radio, eating out, playing computer games or visiting a tourist attraction.

A number of factors have led to the growth of the leisure industry over a period of time. These factors can be summarised as follows:

◆ **An increase in leisure time due to the introduction of a shorter working week and a flexible working week**. Various industries operate a 'shift' working pattern. This has been fundamental to the emergency services, i.e. police, fire and ambulance service. Other sectors have operated a non-traditional working pattern due to the nature of their organisation, e.g. the catering and hospitality industry, the health service and the entertainment industry. The flexible style of work pattern allows people to manage their time effectively. They can undertake leisure activities when they desire, e.g. swimming, reading, and visiting attractions.

◆ **An increase in the duration of holiday time taken by people aged 16–60 plus**. People maximise the holidays that they are entitled to by participating in indoor and outdoor leisure pursuits. It is evident during public holiday periods that a number of cinemas, theatres and visitor attractions see an increase in their visitor numbers.

Country	Jan	Feb	Mar	Apr	May	June	July	Aug	Sep	Oct	Nov	Dec
Austria	1,6			15,16	1,24	3,4,14		15		26	1	8,25,26
Belgium	1			15,16	1,24	3,4	11,21	15	27		1,11,15	25
Denmark	1			12,13,15,16	11,24	3,4,5						24,25,26,31
Finland	1,6			13,15,16,30	1,24	3,22,23					3	6,25,26
France	1			15,16	1,8,24	3,4	14	15			1,11	25
Germany	1			13,15,16	1,24	3,4,14				3	1,25	25,26
Greece	1,6	26	25	13,15,16	1	4		15		28		25,26
Iceland	1			12,13,15,16,19	1,24	3,4,17		6				24,25,26,31
Ireland, Republic of	1		17	15,16	7	4		6		29		25,26
Italy	1,6			15,16,25	1			15			1	8,25,26
Luxembourg	1			15,16	1,24	3,4,23		15			1	25,26
Netherlands	1			13,15,16,30	5,24	3,4						25,26
Norway	1			8,12,13,15,16	1,17,24	3,4						25,26
Portugal	1			13,15,25	1	10,14		15		5	1	1,8,25
Russian Federation	1,2	23	8		1,2,9	12					7	12
Spain	1,6			13,15	1	3		15		12	1	6,8,25
Sweden	1,6			13,15,16	1,24	3,4,6,23					3	24,25,26
Switzerland	1,2			13,15,16	24	3,4		1				25,26
United Kingdom	1,2		17	13,16	7,28		12	6,27				25,26

Additional day holidays arise due to certain events, e.g. the Queen's Jubilee.

Figure 1.3 European holidays, 2001

ACTIVITY

1 Calculate the number of holidays that you will receive this year.
2 What do you do with your time?
3 Complete the table for your week's activities.
4 How much time do you spend at school/college?
5 What do you do with the rest of your time?

Activity	Monday	Tuesday	Wednesday	Thursday	Friday	Saturday	Sunday
Total hours							

What time is devoted to leisure activities over:
a) a day?
b) a week?

Talk about...

Fox Kids	w/e 30/09/01
Programme	**Millions Viewing**
1 Digimon (Tue 1657)	0.09
2 BraceFace 1	0.08
3 Digimon (Tue 1631)	0.08
4 Digimon (Thu)	0.07
5 Digimon (Sun)	0.06
6 Digimon (Mon)	0.06
7 Power Rangers (Tue)	0.05
8 Power Rangers (Sun)	0.05
9 X-Men	0.05
10 Power Rangers (Mon)	0.05

Source: Broadcaster's Audience Research Board (BARB)

THINK ABOUT...

Is retail activity (shopping) a leisure activity?

◆ **An increase in the number of people taking retirement at an earlier age.** When the opportunity arises people choose to take early retirement with a view to maximising the time spent on leisure activities. Leisure pastimes take on a full-time role, e.g. golf, swimming and 'do-it-yourself' (DIY). People are now more conscious of the need to develop a quality lifestyle.

◆ **An increase in the range and scope of home-based leisure activities.** Traditional home-based leisure activities still play an important part in a number of households. These activities include DIY, watching television, playing board games, and sewing and crafts, e.g. upholstery. New style home-based leisure has expanded with computerised leisure activities. Computer games, e.g. Playstation, Xbox, Game Boy Advance and internet access have further contributed to the revolution in leisure time. With the advent of satellite, cable TV and DVDs, television has focused on a range of interests, e.g. antique restorations, DIY, and gardening.

◆ **An increase in the amount of disposable income available.** People are now spending more money on entertainment, recreational activities, and on visiting places. People are finding ways to ensure that they have more disposable income and they budget for their leisure pursuits. The flexibility of credit cards and the ease of obtaining hire purchase facilities gives the individual a far more manageable way to budget their money and to ensure that their money goes further. Retail therapy continues to expand and is an activity undertaken by all age groups during their free time.

◆ **An improvement in transport, accessibility and mobility –
locally, regionally and nationally**.

1 Improvements in transport are evident and have contributed to the
growth of the leisure industry. Different modes of transport make
it easier for people to travel further afield and to enjoy a leisure
pursuit.

2 Air travel throughout the UK and to destinations abroad has
expanded. The airlines' flight paths are in constant competition
with each other.

3 The National Rail Network has shown improvements. Rail
networks cover the UK and allow people to travel the entire
country.

4 Bus services, coaches, taxis and cab companies allow people to be
more flexible in the travel methods they choose. Transport
terminals, interchanges and nodal points have developed into
unique travel hubs and are more user-friendly. Transport outlets
ensure that passengers enjoy travelling. Coffee shops, eating
places, public houses and other retail outlets now cater for the
average passenger.

5 Travelling now contributes to the ever-expanding leisure activities
available. People watching sports activities now travel to see the
events and are supported by the facilities and provisions. This is
part of the evolution in consumerism, and the growth and
expansion in marketing. Customer service is at the forefront of
most organisations.

5

How much television do
you watch in one day?
Which channels and
stations do you watch?
Do you think you are
spending less time
watching television than
you used to?

Talk about...

**THINK
ABOUT...**

Is the cinema less
popular with the
introduction of cable and
satellite television?

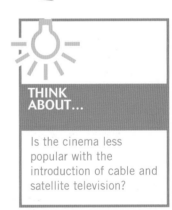

Figure 1.4   Tube access

Accessible toilets
Babycare
Bureau de change
Buses
Cash machine
Cycle park
Gentlemen
Information
Ladies
Left luggage
Lost property
Post box
Station reception
Stationlink buses
Taxis
Telephones
Tickets
Transport Police
Trolley point

Bakerloo, Northern
and Waterloo & City lines

Way out
South Bank

Way out
Waterloo Bridge

Way out
Tenison Way

Set-down

Way out
Station Approach

Stationlink buses

To Waterloo East
Station

Pick-up

Jubilee line

Way out
Waterloo Road

Way out
Westminster
Bridge Road

COSTA

Figure 1.5   Plan of Waterloo Station

ACTIVITY

Look at the plan of Waterloo Station in London. List the facilities that have been provided for:

a) the business traveller.
b) the family traveller.
c) the young single traveller.
d) the elderly traveller.
e) the person with specific needs.

THINK ABOUT...

Does London need another airport? What are the implications of the newspaper article in Figure 1.6?

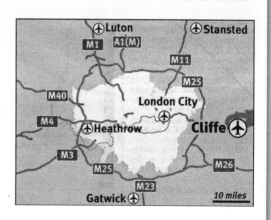

NEW AIRPORT FOR THE SOUTH

A HUGE new airport is being planned for the South-East to take the pressure off Heathrow, Gatwick and Stansted.

Controversial proposals would see a fourth London airport built on an environmentally-sensitive marshland site on the Thames Estuary in Kent.

Source: *Evening Standard*, 1 March 2002

Figure 1.6 New south London airport

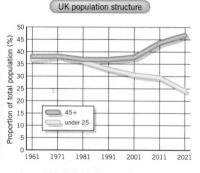

UK population structure

Source: Office for National Statistics, Government Actuary's Department, General Register Office for Scotland, Northern Ireland Statistics and Research Agency 1998

The over 45s will account for approximately 50% of the UK population by the year 2021. Conversely, the proportion of under 25s is projected to drop to just 25% of the population, a fall of 32% from 1961.

Figure 1.7 UK population structure

♦ **Changing social and demographic trends**. The UK clearly displays the characteristics of an ageing population. With advancements in medicine, research into lifestyles, diet and health, people are living longer and are paying more attention to their lifestyle patterns.

An ageing population has implications for the facilities and services provided in local areas. There is pressure on the government to provide additional facilities and leisure activities for the elderly through demand.

ACTIVITY

Look at your local area. Which activities are provided for the following age groups:

a) up to 18
b) 18–30
c) 30–60
d) over 60s?

Extension Exercise

a) What percentage of the population are 60 and over?
b) What types of leisure activities would the over 60s pursue?
c) The over 45s will account for approximately 50% of the UK population by the year 2021. How will this increase be accommodated in terms of leisure activities?

◆ **A Change in Fashion and Trends.** Changes in lifestyles have affected leisure and tourism provision. For example:

- ◆ Vegetarianism, veganism
- ◆ Healthy living policies
- ◆ Fitness regimes
- ◆ Increased awareness of leisure activities
- ◆ Holidays being considered beneficial
- ◆ Awareness of the effects of drug and alcohol abuse
- ◆ The effects of stress and employment demands

The government has taken an active role in raising the awareness of the population through supporting a range of campaigns for 'healthier lifestyles'. Health and safety policies have been updated constantly in the workplace and within organisations used by the leisure industry.

Changes in technology and legal policies have contributed to:

- ◆ A revolution in computer technology
- ◆ Improved methods of communication
- ◆ Developments in transport systems and regulations
- ◆ Changes in legislation and political policies

London is proclaimed the richest city in the EU

LONDON is the richest city in the European Union, a report shows today. The capital's economic output in 1999 was 2½ times the EU average, according to statistics office Eurostat.

London scored 242 per cent of the average, followed by Brussels (217 per cent), the Grand Duchy of Luxembourg (186 per cent) and Hamburg (183 per cent). Paris and Munich were fifth and sixth. The French overseas territory of Reunion in the Indian Ocean and Greece's Ipeiros came bottom of the poll with 51 per cent.

Source: *Evening Standard*

London is said to be the richest city in the EU.
What do you feel will be the implications of the Euro currency on the leisure industry in the UK?

Talk about...

Extension Exercise

Find:

a) Acts of Parliament which have contributed to the expansion of the leisure industry.

b) areas which are promoting 'car free leisure'.

c) how government policies affect funding, e.g. lottery grants/bidding.

d) the impact of the Access to the Countryside Act.

e) recent sport initiatives which are being promoted (Sport for All, Centre of Excellence).

f) the aims and objectives of the Department of Culture, Media and Sports.

Leisure is one of the fastest growing industries in the UK. People are always looking for new ways to spend their leisure time.

QCA

Leisure Activities

You will need to know what leisure activities are.

Leisure activities are many and varied, and include the following.

Reading

This has always been a popular pastime and has maintained the interests of all age groups, with charts showing which books are the 'best-sellers'.

Local libraries now provide other services to the general public, for example computer, internet and website access. Libraries are constantly updating their image. Local areas have libraries on wheels, which have a rotational schedule from area to area. Now the concept of the 'idea-store' is evolving. This will give the public an all-inclusive shopping experience – the supermarket library.

Glittering new design brings a blast of cool to libraries

THINK of public libraries and you don't think of glamour. Think of Whitechapel Road and you might think of the Krays or Jack the Ripper. Yet this is where David Adjaye, London's coolest architect, is to build a glittering new library.

It won't even be called a library but an "idea store", and it will be the flagship of Tower Hamlets' £30 million scheme to replace seven of its 12 libraries.

The plan is for centres that draw people to books as effectively as supermarkets draw people to cornflakes and baked beans. Located in shopping areas, cafes and dance studios will lure the punters in. "We have to compete with the best High Street shops," says ideas stores' programme director Heather Wills.

All over London, libraries have been closing and losing visitors; only 28 per cent of Tower Hamlets residents use theirs. One woman told researchers she "wouldn't be seen dead" somewhere so drab. It is hoped idea stores will reverse this decline.

The designs for the £6.5 million Whitechapel idea store, revealed today, show a sleek aluminium-and-glass box rising calmly from Whitechapel Road, raising the tone of a giant car park behind it. As in Paris's Pompidou Centre, an escalator will rise behind its glass facade. The top-floor cafe will enjoy views of St Paul's. A two-storey video wall will display information.

"You will walk into it just as you would into a department store," said Adjaye. Books will be electronically marked to stop theft and the venue will close at 10pm.

The concept is open to charges of dumbing down. Consultants Bisset Adams, which developed the idea, talk of "relaxed retail atmosphere", raising the spectre of encroaching commercialism.

But it is hard to find anyone with a bad word to say. Tower Hamlets should be "congratulated", says the Library Association.

The National Literacy Trust adds: "We've got to be totally in favour of it."

Source: *Evening Standard*, March 2002.

Love left on the shelf at London's libraries

Nationally, five of the 10 most borrowed titles are Cookson's but in London she only has one title in the top 10 – and that, The Thursday Child, ranks tenth.

Children's books and thrillers are most popular among London borrowers, according to Public Lending Right, which distributes library royalties to authors.

J K Rowling's Harry Potter books The Prisoner Of Azkaban and The Goblet Of Fire are in first and second place.

• London's new Women's Library opened today. Built with £4.2 million of Lottery money, it houses 60,000 books and leaflets dating from the 17th century.

Source: *Evening Standard*, February 2002.

WHSmiths, Waterstone's and Dillons have also contributed to the reading revolution. They have guest speakers and well-known authors signing books at launches, over a cup of coffee, glass of wine or beer.

WATERSTONE'S
The last word in books

Waterstone's first opened in Old Brompton Road, London in 1982 and is now the UK's leading specialist bookseller. By 1995 the company had opened its 100th store – in Reading. Waterstone's now trades from 204 high street and campus stores in the UK, Republic of Ireland and Europe.

Waterstone's flagship store in **Piccadilly, London** is the biggest bookshop in Europe and opened in 1999. Waterstone's in **Gower Street, London** is Europe's biggest academic bookshop. Waterstone's other superstores include Bridlesmith Gate **Nottingham**, Deansgate **Manchester**, High Street **Birmingham** and Sauchiehall Street **Glasgow**.

Waterstone's offers customers an unparalleled high street range of books and expert Waterstone's booksellers can provide recommendations and advice on every subject. Waterstone's stores aim to provide an enjoyable and welcoming environment in which to choose and buy books. Many stores have dedicated seating and browsing areas. Waterstone's opened its first coffee shop – an increasingly popular part of bookshop life – in Bath in 1988 and now offers cafés in 20 of its stores as well as a juice bar, restaurant and a licensed bar in its Piccadilly shop.

Source: Amazon.co.uk, March 2002.

Waterstone's Chart, March 2002
1. Lone Eagle
   ~ Danielle Steel
2. Harry Potter and the Goblet of Fire
   ~ J.K. Rowling
3. Harry Potter and the Prisoner of Azkaban
   ~ J.K. Rowling
4. Harry Potter and the Chamber of Secrets
   ~ J.K. Rowling
5. The Red Room
   ~ Nicci French
6. The House on Lonely Street
   ~ Lyn Andrews
7. A Minor Indiscretion
   ~ Carole Matthews
8. Blood Hunt
   ~ Ian Rankin
9. The Lord of the Rings Part 2: The Two Towers
   ~ J.R.R. Tolkien
10. Five Quarters of the Orange
    ~ Joanne Harris

ACTIVITY

1 List the facilities provided by Waterstone's for the avid reader.

2 Which age groups are catered for at Waterstone's, Picadilly, London.

Sports Participation: Active and Passive

People of all ages are devoting more time to active and passive participation in sports activities. From a very young age, children are encouraged at school to participate in a range of sporting activities. This is often taken further with after school clubs and local clubs. Local organisations arrange football matches, cricket fixtures, tennis tournaments and fun runs over the weekends and after working hours.

Passive participation involves people following sports events which they have an interest in watching. This could mean watching the event on television, listening to it on the radio or attending the event in person. The growth of cable, satellite and pay-per-view has led to a new generation of passive football supporters which has opened up a new marketing opportunity for clubs.

Participating and spectating in indoor and outdoor sports plays an important role in many households. Major sports have become more and more popular with the population, regardless of age group. Football, cricket, rugby, tennis, horse-racing, darts and ice-skating are a few of the sports from which a major industry has emerged. Sporting events have fan clubs of followers. Key players are now in the public eye and have developed celebrity status. Sports industries are linked to other industries, such as hospitality and catering for food and beverages, the media for sponsorship, and large organisations for marketing and advertising. The TV networks have developed worldwide coverage of sporting events. Dedicated fans and followers of a sport can follow their teams around the national, as well as the international, circuit. The revolution of satellite and cable television and DVD has ensured that sport is available at the 'flick' of a switch.

The football World Cup, held once every four years, has a massive impact on leisure time. Television viewing and actual spectating has a dynamic impact on various aspects of the industry:

◆ Television viewing figures increase
◆ Air travel to countries hosting the event increases
◆ Merchandising and souvenir sales rise

ACTIVITY

Look at the table on page 12 showing the FA Barclaycard Premiership 2002/2003 average attendances.

1 How many Premiership clubs have seen an increase in attendance figures?

2 Why do you think some clubs have experienced a decrease in average attendances?

3 What are the effects of attendance figures on merchandising for clubs?

Commonwealth City

The roar of a 38,000-strong crowd is a tremendous sound and one that will resonate around the magnificent new City of Manchester Stadium on the evening of the 25 July when the Queen's Jubilee Baton is borne into the stadium at the opening ceremony of the XVII Commonwealth Games. The jewel in the crown of the Games programme, the stadium is at the heart of Sportcity, next to the Indoor Tennis Centre and the National Squash Centre. Built to host all the track and field athletics events and the rugby sevens finals, it cost £110 million to build. After the games, it will become home to Manchester City FC.

The relay will signify the start of the Commonwealth Games which runs from July 25 until August 4 this year in Manchester.

Source: *Hotline*, Summer 2002

FA Barclaycard Premiership 2002–2003

No.	Club	Average	Games	vs '02	Highest
1	Manchester United	67.594	5	0,1%	67.645
2	Newcastle United	51.781	4	0,8%	52.181
3	Liverpool	43.420	5	0,1%	43.856
4	Sunderland	40.302	4	−13,8%	47.586
5	Chelsea	40.063	4	2,6%	41.541
6	Leeds United	39.986	4	0,6%	40.199
7	Arsenal	37.938	5	−0,3%	38.018
8	Everton	35.982	4	7,3%	40.120
9	Tottenham Hotspur	35.761	4	2,2%	36.082
10	Manchester City	34.718	4	5,0%	35.131
11	West Ham United	34.598	5	9,6%	35.550
12	Aston Villa	32.938	5	−5,9%	41.183
13	Middlesbrough	29.977	5	5,3%	32.155
14	Southampton	29.092	5	−5,0%	31.208
15	Birmingham City	28.576	4	30,0%	29.505
16	Charlton Athletic	26.203	4	8,4%	26.630
17	Blackburn Rovers	26.189	5	0,8%	29.207
18	West Bromwich Albion	25.908	4	23,9%	26.618
19	Bolton Wanderers	23.568	4	−6,1%	27.328
20	Fulham	16.092	4	−17,7%	16.757
Total		**35.278**		**2,5%**	**67.645**

Source: www.european-football-statistics.co.uk

Figure 1.8   Average football attendances in England

THINK ABOUT...

Can you think of any new style sporting activities? Which age groups are attracted to 'Extreme Sports'?
Why do you think people are attracted to 'Extreme Sports'?

Extreme Sports

New styles of sporting activities are constantly emerging, e.g. bungee jumping and 'gladiator' thrill-seeking sports. Many of these sports have been promoted on satellite television, for instance skateboarding.

Going to the Cinema

Cinema viewing has continued to be a popular leisure activity. Although in competition with video rentals, satellite and cable television, cinema going is marketed as an inclusive, all-in-one style package. Cinemas have become large multi-complex venues. They have fast-food outlets, as well as the more traditional products like tea, coffee, ice-creams, popcorn, souvenirs and programme guides. This is a marketing ploy to increase cinema viewing figures and to entice people back to the cinema. Big name brands, e.g. Odeon, Warner and UCI, continue to link their image to breakfast cereals, newspapers and confectionery. This marketing strategy provides vouchers and discounts to key cinema releases. People can choose to see some of the popular new film releases at a discount.

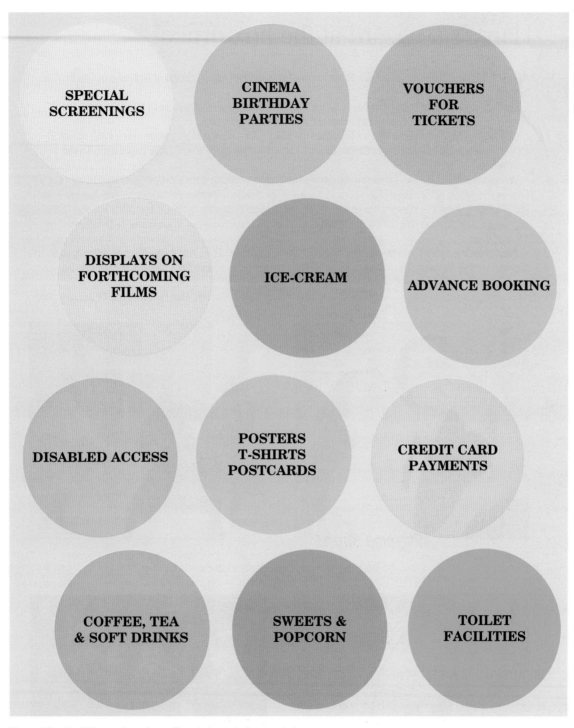

Figure 1.9 Facilities and services offered at most cinema chains

Brands have played an important part in film merchandising. Retail
outlets are filled with popular items advertising, e.g. Harry Potter
and Star Wars. Marketing strategies review the impact of the 4 Ps
(Product, Price, Place and Promotion) by constantly researching
methods to secure loyal customers and gain new customers.
Television advertising further highlights the effect on the population.

Harry's a wizard at the box office

HARRY POTTER And The Philosopher's Stone has soared to number four in the list of highest grossing films of all time.

The first of several projected films based on the runaway best-selling children's book by JK Rowling, Harry Potter And The Philosopher's Stone has entranced adults and children alike.

Last weekend's figures reveal that it has passed the £200 million mark and also made nearly £350 million in total international sales according to Screen Daily, the online edition of the British trade publication, Screen International.

Worldwide sales of the film stand at a staggering £562 million, making it the fourth biggest worldwide hit of all time behind Titanic (£1.3 billion), Star Wars: Episode I – The Phantom Menace (£639 million) and Jurassic Park (£637 million). The film's success has given a much-needed boost not only to the UK box office but also to the US box office, which was languishing at the end of a somewhat desultory year, made worse by the aftermath of 11 September.

Clearly, the big bucks are in fantasy and magic. The first episode of The Lord Of The Rings trilogy has taken an impressive £306 million worldwide since its post-Potter release as audiences flock towards movies offering maximum escape from the real world.

Source: *Evening Standard*, 11 January 2002.

Titanic: £1,270,291,000

Star Wars Episode I – The Phantom Menace: £638,832,000

Jurassic Park: £637,138,000

Harry Potter And The Philosopher's Stone: £562,000,000

Case study

Cinemas

The changing needs of customers, technological advances, persuasive marketing and modernisation have contributed to the revival of cinema.

Multiplex developments emerged in the late 1990s and currently account for 40 per cent of the UK's screenings and 50 per cent of customer visits. Multiplex cinemas are dominated by brand names such as Warner, Odeon, Virgin, UCI and ABC. They host a range of films for all age groups. The foyer area is usually large with a series of stalls selling a range of confectionery, hot and cold drinks, ice creams, food and souvenirs. Products and services include monthly and annual passes, gift vouchers, Internet booking, stadium seating, digital sound, convenience facilities and disabled access. This style of cinema is often associated with large, undercover shopping malls which complement the cinema experience by offering parking facilities, shopping, restaurants, fast food eating areas, leisure and health facilities and theatre performances.

Art house cinemas, which show non-Hollywood and non-mainstream productions, form a small but expanding part of the cinema industry. They appeal to a specific audience that enjoys films which follow an alternative approach.

The BFI London IMAX cinema was opened in 1994 in a prime location on the Southbank. It received finance from the Arts Council of England's Lottery Fund and provides state of the art cinema viewing. It accommodates 477 seats, a huge screen (20 metres high) and an 11,600 watt digital surround sound system. These features take the audience into a different world of cinema viewing, immersing them in larger than life images. The BFI London IMAX has a large foyer with a seating area for refreshments and snacks, a museum-style display of memorabilia, disabled access and convenience facilities. It screens both 2D and 3D films including *Cyberworld, Everest* and *Space Station*.

Picture House cinemas still capture cinema viewers. The Ritzy Cinema in Brixton, the Arts Picture House in Cambridge and the Stratford Picture House in East London provide the local community with a range of screenings including Saturday kids' films and Sunday matinees. The atmosphere is traditional, small and friendly. Typical films available include classics, independent films and foreign language films.

15

ACTIVITY

1 List the products and services available at your local cinema

2 How many different ways can you book and pay for tickets?

3 What do the different age restrictions mean?

Discos, Raves and Nightclubs

The attendance at discos and raves continues to expand, with nightclubs offering the best sounds with top DJs. This pastime attracts people across all age groups. Dance crazes include Salsa, Latin American, Ballroom, Butterfly, Moonwalk, Jerry Springer and Zip It Up.

Going for a Walk

Walking for exercise, pleasure or interest is popular with the young and the more mature age groups. Walking is associated with a healthy lifestyle and is often linked to an exercise regime that burns off calories. Walks can vary from the organised guided tour, to walks in the country along towpaths or through countryside and undulating landscapes. Leaflets with information and map directions are produced by local authorities and the Ramblers Association. Walks are often themed, bringing together groups of interested people, e.g. exploring the local history of an area. The Ramblers Association was founded in 1935. Its aim is to 'conserve the countryside and ensure that footpaths remain open'. Its website (www.ramblers.org.uk) provides information on walking, events, campaigns, contacts, groups, publications and how to become a member.

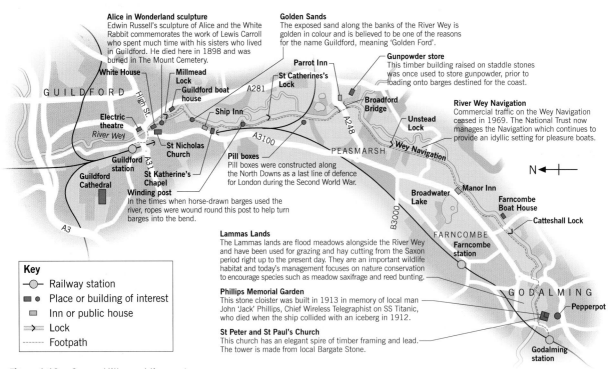

Figure 1.10   Surrey Hills rambling route

Key

Symbol	Meaning	Symbol	Meaning
——	Cycle route	▨	Woodland
------	Footpath	P	Car parking
–·–·–	Bridle Way	i	Information point

Figure 1.11   Esher Common cycle route

ACTIVITY

1 List the places and buildings of interest that can be seen along the Surrey Hills rambling route.

2 List the natural and non-natural facilities available for the cyclist on Esher Common.

Watching Television and Listening to the Radio

Watching the television and listening to the radio remain passive leisure pastimes. With the creation of satellite and cable television, and digital and interactive television, the range of programmes available to the viewer is impressive. Satellite and cable channels boast between 40 and 80 channels. Soaps, documentaries, films, cartoons, music, sports and shopping channels are available 24 hours a day. With the advances in technology, slimline and wide-screen viewing has created a mini cinema in many households. Video rental shops have also contributed to the revolution in television viewing, allowing the consumer to access the latest film releases within a relatively short period after major cinema releases.

Studio visits offer an opportunity to experience the viewing and making of television series. These visits have arisen from the expansion of television viewing. They are a relatively new style of leisure activity.

BBC4 Millions Viewing (Including Timeshift) – w/e **09/03/2003**

	Programme	Total
1	The Great War (Sat 2015)	0.14
2	Film: The Officer''s Ward (Sat 2213)	0.13
3	The Great War (Sat 1935)	0.13
4	Film: The Officer's Ward (Sat 2102)	0.11
5	Saddam Hussein: Profile (Sun 2142)	0.10
6	Video Nation (Sun 2138)	0.10
7	BBC Four World Cinema (Sat 2055)	0.09
8	A History of Iraq (Sun 2049)	0.08
9	Designer of the Year (Wed 2030)	0.06
10	Stalin: Inside the Terror (Mon 2100)	0.05

E4 Millions Viewing (Including Timeshift) – w/e **09/03/2003**

	Programme	Total
1	Friends (Thu 2130)	1.85
2	Friends (Thu 2059)	1.64
3	ER (Thu 2202)	0.99
4	Friends (Thu 2030)	0.44
5	Friends (Sun 2059)	0.34
6	Friends (Sun 2132)	0.33
7	Smallville (Tue 2059)	0.25
8	The Salon Live (Thu 1829)	0.23
9	ER (Sun 2202)	0.23
10	Smallville (Mon 2102)	0.22

MTV Millions Viewing (Including Timeshift) – w/e **09/03/2003**

	Programme	Total
1	The Osbournes (Wed 2159)	0.26
2	Suspect (Wed 2145)	0.15
3	Cribs (Mon 2257)	0.10
4	Making the Video (Mon 2340)	0.09
5	Dirty Sanchez (Wed 2243)	0.08
6	The Osbournes (Sun 2145)	0.07
7	The Osbournes (Tue 2142)	0.07
8	Road Rules (Wed 2054)	0.07
9	Dirty Sanchez (Thu 2159)	0.07
10	The Osbournes (Fri 2201)	0.07

Source: Broadcaster's Audience Research Board (BARB)

TEDDINGTON STUDIOS

STUDIO LOCATION & DIRECTIONS

TEDDINGTON STUDIOS

Teddington Studios are situated at Broom Road (off Ferry Road), Teddington Lock, Teddington, Middlesex. Enter Ferry Road at the junction of Twickenham road, Kingston Road and Teddington High Street, and bear right.

PARKING

Cars: Continue along Broom road and park beyond the yellow lines.

Coaches: At weekends we will endeavour to accommodate coaches in our company car park. Alternatively, due to a coach parking ban imposed by the London Borough of Richmond, passengers should alight at the main studio entrance and the coach driver is advised to use the Hampton Road, Hampton Hill lorry/coach parking facilities, approximately two miles from the studio.

TRAINS

From Waterloo to Teddington Station takes 28 minutes. On leaving the station turn right and walk along Teddington High Street. At St Alban's Church turn into Ferry Road and bear right into Broom Road. The walk will take approximately ten minutes. This is the most direct route. Alternatively, buses can be caught from Teddington High Street or opposite Hampton Wick Station (26 minutes from Waterloo).

BUSES

Numbers 281 and 285 can be caught from Hampton Wick Station, Teddington High Street or from Kingston (opposite Bentalls). Ask for Teddington Lock, alight here, cross the road, turn into Ferry Road and bear right into Broom Road.

Figure 1.12

Figure 1.13 Skyline satellite

> **Talk about...**
>
> Which television programmes are filmed in front of a studio audience?
>
> Which radio stations are popular with teenagers?

THINK ABOUT...

Since its arrival in 1982, Pret À Manger has revolutionised the eatery. As an organisation, it is said to be 'passionate about its people . . . and its food'. It offers career pathways with fun and subsidies, and bonus schemes for its employers. Do you know any similar organisations?

Radio listening has continued to capture people at home and at work. Soap themes and chat shows, in addition to documentaries have expanded the radio network. Popular DJs with game-show inputs keep audience listening figures high. Radio debates also continue to expand.

Listening to music on CDs, DVDs, minidiscs, records and tapes is a leisure activity that is often undersold, and underrated. Mobile music from personal stereos provides a pleasant atmosphere for the individual in a range of environments.

Eating Out

Eating out, whether for a social occasion, while shopping or on the way to a sports event, has continued to expand with the increasing network of franchises found at most popular locations. Coffee houses, fast-food outlets, restaurant chains, and the quick snacks purchased at shops or kiosks have made eating out an easy and pleasurable experience. The range of food items available provides the consumer with an array of traditional snacks as well as a range of foreign foods and delicacies. Disposable food packaging has contributed to the revolution in take-aways and in eating while travelling.

Playing Computer Games

The computer games and consoles available show technology at its very best. Sales of computer games and consoles continue to make record sales levels. Britain is the third largest computer market in the world. Computer games on the Playstation, Game Boy, Dreamcast and Xbox hold an ever-increasing market, with trade outlets such as Electronics Boutique, Game, Virgin and HMV. A second-hand trade in games has become popular and gives the consumer the opportunity to re-select games at reduced and bargain prices. In addition to playing on a game console, computer games are popular on the television, mobile phones and computers. This activity provides leisure in your own front room or bedroom, cutting out the cost of travelling or entrance fees for entertainment.

Game on as Xbox arrives in the shops

THE launch of the Xbox games console sparked a buying frenzy across Britain with industry experts predicting it could overtake Sony rival PlayStation 2.

Fans queued outside shops in London, Liverpool and Glasgow to be the first to buy the new Microsoft machine when it went on sale in the early hours of yesterday.

Nearly 1,000 were sold at the Virgin Megastore in London alone.

About 1.5 million consoles are being shipped to Europe but Microsoft believes they will sell out quickly.

Source: *Metro*, 15 March 2002

£1.6BN PLAYTIME

SALES of computer games and consoles reached record levels last year, figures out yesterday showed.

Players spent £1.6billion in 2001 – a 36 per cent increase on sales in the previous year.

The boom was partly fuelled by the launch of Sony's PlayStation 2 and a series of "must have" titles and sequels to popular games.

The computer games market in Britain is now the third biggest in the world, according to the European Leisure Software Publishers Association figures.

Only enthusiasts in Japan and America buy more. Roger Bennett of ELSPA said: "The industry has been growing for 20 years and these figures show that we are now in the realms of a mass market."

Source: *The Mirror*, 12 January 2002.

Visiting a Tourist Attraction

Visiting historical buildings, places of interest, areas of outstanding natural beauty, national parks, theme parks or leisure parks is another expanding leisure activity for all age groups. Visitor attractions are marketed to entice returning customers through various means, such as vouchers, discounts and new themes and attractions.

Major attractions in London

1 National Gallery
2 British Museum
3 British Airways London Eye
4 Tate Modern
5 Tower of London
6 Natural History Museum
7 Victoria & Albert Museum
8 Science Museum
9 National Portrait Gallery
10 Tate Britain

Major paid admission attractions in the UK

1 British Airways London Eye
2 Tower of London, London
3 Eden Project
4 Natural History Museum, London
5 Legoland, Windsor
6 Victoria & Albert Museum
7 Science Museum, London
8 Flamingo Land Theme Park and Zoo
9 Windermere Lake Cruises
10 Canterbury Cathedral

Major free attractions in the UK

1 Blackpool Pleasure Beach, Lancashire
2 National Gallery, London
3 British Museum, London
4 Tate Modern
5 Pleasureland Theme Park
6 Clacton Pier
7 York Minster
8 Pleasure Beach, Great Yarmouth
9 National Portrait Gallery, London
10 Poole Pottery

Source: English Tourism Council

Case study

Snowdonia National Park

Snowdonia is one of the twelve National Parks of England and Wales, created by the National Parks and Access to the Countryside Act of 1949.

The second largest National Park in the country, after the Lake District and the third to be designated, after the Lakes and the Peak District, in 1951, Snowdonia celebrated half a century as a protected landscape in 2001.

The National Park covers 840 square miles of the most beautiful and unspoilt countryside in north west Wales. Unlike 'wild' National Parks elsewhere in the world, Snowdonia is home to just over 26,000 people, who live and work in its towns and villages, and on its hill farms. An estimated 6 million holidaymakers visit Snowdonia every year.

Source: www.eryri-npa.gov.uk

Case study

The Eden Project, Cornwall

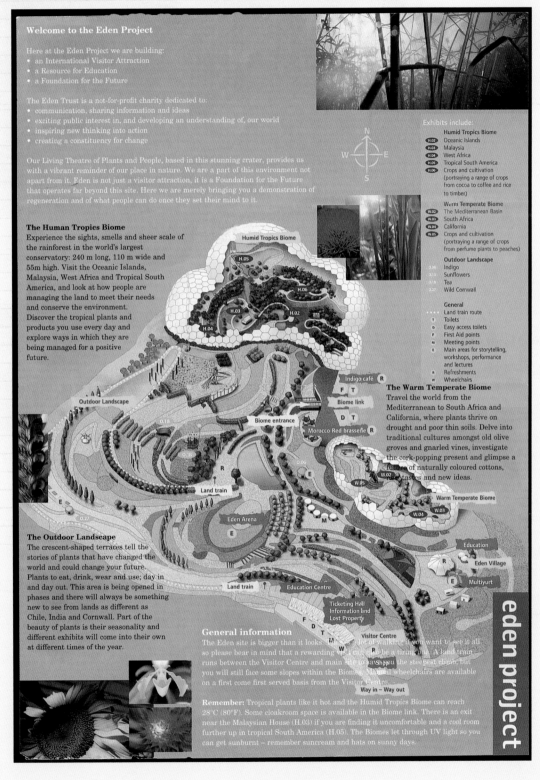

Welcome to the Eden Project

Here at the Eden Project we are building:
• an International Visitor Attraction
• a Resource for Education
• a Foundation for the Future

The Eden Trust is a not-for-profit charity dedicated to:
• communication, sharing information and ideas
• exciting public interest in, and developing an understanding of, our world
• inspiring new thinking into action
• creating a constituency for change

Our Living Theatre of Plants and People, based in this stunning crater, provides us with a vibrant reminder of our place in nature. We are a part of this environment not apart from it. Eden is not just a visitor attraction, it is a Foundation for the Future that operates far beyond this site. Here we are merely bringing you a demonstration of regeneration and of what people can do once they set their mind to it.

The Human Tropics Biome

Experience the sights, smells and sheer scale of the rainforest in the world's largest conservatory: 240 m long, 110 m wide and 55m high. Visit the Oceanic Islands, Malaysia, West Africa and Tropical South America, and look at how people are managing the land to meet their needs and conserve the environment. Discover the tropical plants and products you use every day and explore ways in which they are being managed for a positive future.

The Outdoor Landscape

The crescent-shaped terraces tell the stories of plants that have changed the world and could change your future. Plants to eat, drink, wear and use; day in and day out. This area is being opened in phases and there will always be something new to see from lands as different as Chile, India and Cornwall. Part of the beauty of plants is their seasonality and different exhibits will come into their own at different times of the year.

Exhibits include:

Humid Tropics Biome
H.02 Oceanic Islands
H.03 Malaysia
H.04 West Africa
H.05 Tropical South America
H.06 Crops and cultivation
(portraying a range of crops from cocoa to coffee and rice to timber)

Warm Temperate Biome
W.02 The Mediterranean Basin
W.03 South Africa
W.04 California
W.05 Crops and cultivation
(portraying a range of crops from perfume plants to peaches)

Outdoor Landscape
Indigo
Sunflowers
Tea
Wild Cornwall

General
•••• Land train route
T   Toilets
F   Easy access toilets
F   First Aid points
M   Meeting points
E   Main areas for storytelling, workshops, performance and lectures
R   Refreshments
W   Wheelchairs

The Warm Temperate Biome

Travel the world from the Mediterranean to South Africa and California, where plants thrive on drought and poor thin soils. Delve into traditional cultures amongst old olive groves and gnarled vines, investigate the cork-popping present and glimpse a future of naturally coloured cottons, new tastes and new ideas.

General information

The Eden site is bigger than it looks. There's a lot of walking if you want to see it all so please bear in mind that a rewarding walk can also be a tiring one. A land train runs between the Visitor Centre and main site to save you the steepest climb, but you will still face some slopes within the Biomes. Manual wheelchairs are available on a first come first served basis from the Visitor Centre.

Remember: Tropical plants like it hot and the Humid Tropics Biome can reach 28°C (80°F). Some cloakroom space is available in the Biome link. There is an exit near the Malaysian House (H.03) if you are finding it uncomfortable and a cool room further up in tropical South America (H.05). The Biomes let through UV light so you can get sunburnt – remember suncream and hats on sunny days.

eden project

Figure 1.14   The Eden Project

Case study

The Wetlands Centre, Barnes, London

Winner of the British Airways Tourism for Tomorrow Awards 2001

London life just got wilder...

A Truly Historic Site
Twenty-five minutes from Westminster in the heart of London, the Wetland Centre is unique in being the first created wetland habitat (105 acres) to have been developed in any capital city through the world. Designed by WWT's **Wetland Advisory Agency – WAS**, and built on the site of the former Barn Elms reservoirs, the area, designated as a Site of Special Scientific Interest (SSSI), had become redundant due to the building of the Thames Water Ring Main.

Over five years, the site has been transformed by WWT from 43 hectares of concrete reservoirs, into an impressively diverse wetland reserve and visitor attraction.

'An ideal model for how the natural world and humanity might exist alongside each other in the centuries to come.' Sir David Attenborough

Source: The Wildfowl and Wetlands Trust

ACTIVITY

Read the three case studies above and answer the following questions.

a) Locate the attractions on a map.

b) What are the major features that will attract people?

c) Why are these attractions popular with all age groups?

d) What are the products and services found in each attraction?

Hint: You may wish to look on the internet for further information

Extension Exercise

Complete the following table using information from the internet.

Attraction	Product/ Services	Admission cost	Usual travel mode	Age group of customers
Eden Project				
Wetland Centre				

The National Trust

The role of the National Trust is 'to act as a guardian for the nation in the acquisition and protection of threatened coastline, countryside and buildings'.

The National Trust was founded in 1895 by three Victorian philanthropists – Miss Octavia Hill, Sir Robert Hunter and Canon Hardwicke Rawnsley. Concerned about the impact of uncontrolled development and industrialisation, they set up the Trust to act as guardian for the nation in the acquisition and protection of threatened coastline, countryside and buildings.

More than a century later, we now care for over 248,000 hectares (612,000 acres) of beautiful countryside in England, Wales and Northern Ireland, plus almost 600 miles of coastline and more than 200 buildings and gardens of outstanding interest and importance. Most of these properties are held in perpetuity and so their future protection is secure. The vast majority are open to visitors and we are constantly looking at ways in which we can improve public access and on-site facilities.

We are a registered charity and completely independent of Government, therefore relying heavily on the generosity of our subscribing members (now numbering over 2.7 million) and other supporters.

Source: www.nationaltrust.org.uk

English Heritage

English Heritage operates a policy that 'the public should have a right to see the buildings to whose repair they have contributed'.

Visit Grant-Aided Properties

It has always been a condition of grant aid from English Heritage that the public should have a right to see the buildings to whose repair they have contributed. The extent of public access varies from one property to another; some public buildings are regularly open to all by virtue of their use. For others, especially those which are family homes or work places, access will need to be arranged 'by appointment' or they will be open an agreed number of days each year.

Source: www.english-heritage.org.uk

Countryside Agency

The Countryside Agency has the aim of 'working for people and places in rural England'.

Its work includes:

◆ enjoying the countryside
◆ land and economy
◆ protected countryside
◆ research
◆ rural communities
◆ special projects
◆ transport.

The Countryside Agency's website claims 'We achieve our work through research and advice, influencing others and demonstrating practical ways forward'.

Talk about...

What are the objectives of English Heritage and the Countryside Agency? You may wish to do some research on the internet to find out more information.

24

ACTIVITY

1 a) What leisure activities do you undertake?
   b) When do you undertake each of these activities?
   c) Where do you go for your leisure activities?
   d) How much do these activities cost?

2 Study local papers. Which of the following take place in your area?
   a) Car boot sales
   b) Antique road shows .
   c) Hobby fairs
   d) Short courses for hobbies
   e) Car rally events
   f) Caravan Show, Motor Show or Bike Show

The Key Components of the Leisure Industry

Children's Play Activities

Local authorities and local organisations promote a range of children's play activities. These include outdoor adventure playgrounds, indoor play schemes and toddler's clubs. Churches also provide children's clubs after the main Sunday service, providing teaching from the bible as well as board games, organised games and the use of play equipment. 'Tumble tots' have several centres which help promote the physical development of children, concentrating on balance and co-ordination. Facilities include climbing frames, playmats, swings, ropes and plastic balls. Department stores and shopping complexes provide crèche and play facilities so that people can shop with the reassurance that their children are in a safe, supervised environment.

Outdoor adventure playgrounds provide:

◆ sandpit areas
◆ climbing frames
◆ swings and ropes
◆ slides
◆ see-saws
◆ roundabouts.

The area provided for play activities is fenced off to provide a safe and secure environment for young children. The equipment used is made from material which is robust but equally environmentally friendly.

There are seven key components of the leisure industry and some examples of each are given below:

25

> Since the term leisure covers an enormous range of activities and facilities in a wide variety of situations, it is useful to divide the leisure industry into a number of key sectors (components).   QCA

> In any area there will be a variety of organisations and facilities that fit into each of these components.   QCA

◆ **Sport and Physical Recreation.** Hockey, football, gymnastics.

◆ **Arts and Entertainment.** Galleries, theatres, cinemas.

◆ **Countryside Recreation.** Walking, cycling, horse-riding.

◆ **Home-based Leisure.** Watching TV, gardening, DIY, computer games

◆ **Catering.** Pubs, cafés, restaurants.

◆ **Visitor Attractions.** Historic buildings, historic sites, theme parks.

◆ **Children's Play Activities.** Adventure playgrounds, play schemes, play centres/crèche.

1 Find a map of your local area.

2 Identify two examples of each component from your local area.

3 Locate these different facilities on the map of your area. Use a colour coding system to differentiate between the components.

4 What methods of travel would you use to get to each facility from your home?

What are the links within the components of leisure in the example given on the right? Manchester United offers stadium tours – linking leisure and tourism. Can you think of similar venues?

Can you think of other examples where the key components are interrelated in your local area?

Talk about...

Links

You will need to know that the key components of the leisure industry are often interrelated.

Links can be made between the components of leisure. Links have developed as the leisure industry has expanded and as people's leisure habits have evolved.

For example, football supporters use membership facilities of their football club to gain discounts on tickets, discounts at the club shop, priority booking facilities, allocation of designated seat areas and the club news letter. They can access the internet and club website for up-to-date information on the club and fixtures. They can use online services to buy tickets. They use rail, air or coach services to travel to home and away games. Supporters pay for travel, as well as for food and beverages for the journey. At the ground they can purchase a programme, refreshments and souvenirs. They will often be able to see the highlights of the game on television and read the main score draws in a range of newspapers. They can purchase merchandise related to their teams. Supporters can use hotel and bed and breakfast accommodation for away matches. They visit eating places and public houses after the match.

Horse-riding can be classed as both a sport and a countryside recreation – this shows how two key components of the leisure industry are interrelated.

1 You will need to contact the Tourist Information Centre for an area of your choice.

2 Find out how the leisure provision meets the needs of different people in your area, and how this provision has changed in the last 20 years?

3 Read the following case studies on the Pool of London and Birmingham and then complete the table below.

Area	Leisure provision Name of facility	Key Component
Birmingham City Centre		
Pool of London		

Case study   Pool of London

❶ SOUTHWARK CATHEDRAL

London's oldest Gothic church has been cleaned and restored. A place of worship for 1000 years, the cathedral contains the burial place of England's first poet, John Gower, and a memorial to William Shakespeare beneath a stained glass window showing scenes from his plays. Behind the effigy of Shakespeare there is a frieze depicting Elizabethan Bankside. The Harvard Chapel is dedicated to the founder of Harvard University, John Harvard, who was born in Borough High Street.

❶⑥ TOWER BRIDGE

Tower Bridge, built in 1894, was designed to enable ships to pass under it into the 'Upper Pool', and in its first year, opened 6000 times. Its impressive Victorian engines still work today, although openings are less frequent – only three or four times a week.

LONDON'S LARDER

Since Roman times, ships have sailed into the Pool of London laden with food, textiles and exotic goods. During the 1800s the Tooley St/London Bridge area became known as London's Larder as it was a key area for food-imports. You can visit the Borough Market that has been running for a thousand years – a must for food lovers.

LONDON BRIDGE

The first bridge was built by the Romans in about 50 AD, but was replaced several times over the years. On one notable occasion, King Ethelred the Unready pulled down the bridge to save the city from an army of Vikings, hence the nursery rhyme, 'London Bridge is falling down'.

❸ HAY'S GALLERIA

Hay's Galleria, originally a dock for clipper ships from India and China over 150 years ago, has been converted to provide a unique riverside venue with a mix of shops, restaurants, bars and craft stalls. A magnificent 18m kinetic sculpture, 'The Navigators', acts as a focal point. The Southwark Heritage Centre, which provides information on the history of the borough, is located here.

❶❶ POTTERS FIELD/CITY HALL

Potters Field is an excellent spot to relax and take in some of the finest views in London. It is located adjacent to City Hall, a landmark building designed by Sir Norman Foster, which was completed in Summer 2002.

❶⑧ THE TOWER OF LONDON

Following the Norman Invasion of 1066, William the Conqueror founded the Tower of London. The White Tower was built as a palace and fortress for the capital, and over the years, the walls and other fortifications were added by successive monarchs. Notorious for its bloody history, the Tower is now home to the world famous Crown Jewels and is guarded by the colourful 'Beefeaters'.

27

❶❾ ALL HALLOWS

The oldest church in the City of London, All Hallows by the Tower spans a history of over 1300 years. Visitors can view its Roman pavement, Saxon crypt and original parish records.

❹ LONDON DUNGEON

The London Dungeon is the interactive historic horror attraction, which dispenses fear and fun. Visitors can experience life in old London and encounter some of its gruesome highlights, including 'The Great Fire of London', 'Jack the Ripper Experience', and the 'Judgement Day' boatride down the River Thames through the legendary Traitors Gate where criminals used to meet their doom!

❾ BUTLERS WHARF

In the 19th century Butlers Wharf was one of the busiest docks in London, receiving cargoes of tea, coffee and spices from all over the world. The renovated warehouses still retain the character of the old days with the aerial walkways that were used to move the cargoes from the River to the warehouses. Butlers Wharf today offers great places to eat, drink and visit including art galleries and the Design Museum.

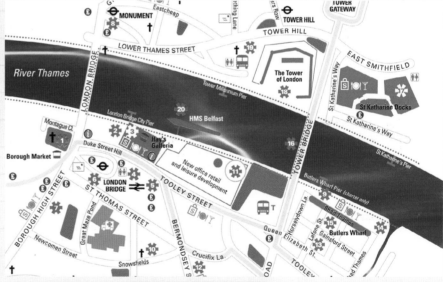

❷⓪ HMS BELFAST

The HMS Belfast, built in 1938 and saved for the nation in 1971, was one of the largest and most powerful cruisers ever built for the Royal Navy and saw action in the D-Day landings and the Korean War. She is Europe's last surviving big gun warship of the Second World War and today, visitors can view all seven decks.

❽ MONUMENT

The Great Fire of London in 1666 destroyed most of the old city on the north side of the Thames. In commemoration, the Monument was built by the great architect, Christopher Wren. It is 62m high and stands exactly 62m from where the fire began.

❶⑦ ST KATHARINE DOCKS

The St Katharine Docks was constructed in 1820 on the site where St Katharine's Church and hospital once stood. Today, the docks provide a peaceful setting for the hotel, shops and restaurants, which surround the picturesque yacht haven.

❺ BRITAIN AT WAR

The Pool of London received some of the heaviest bombing experienced by Britain during the Second World War. Winston Churchill's Britain at War Museum graphically recreates the horrors of the Blitz and later V1 and V2 raids.

Case study   Birmingham Attractions

28

R SAREHOLE MILL
Birmingham's only working watermill was the childhood haunt of 'Hobbit' author J.R.R. Tolkien. Flour was made here, and the mill was also used to roll and smoothmetal in the Industrial Revolution.

J SOHO HOUSE
Restored to its eighteenth-century appearance, Soho House is the former home of industrial pioneer Matthew Boulton.

A ASTON HALL
This splendid Jacobean mansion is filled with fine furniture, paintings and textiles. Explore the mixed fortunes of Aston Hall for yourself and see if you can spot the cannon shot damage.

B BARBER INSTITUTE OF FINE ARTS
With works by Gainsborough, Turner, Monet, Renoir, Degas and many others, this is one of the world's finest small galleries.

F CADBURY WORLD
Indulge your senses at this unique fun and educational multimedia attraction dedicated to Cadbury's chocolate.

E BIRMINGHAM NATURE CENTRE
A 2.5 hectare site in Edgbaston with otters, lynx and over 130 other species. Lilliput village is a specially created attraction for young children.

H MUSEUM OF THE JEWELLERY QUARTER
Enjoy a guided tour around a real jewellery factory which has been perfectly preserved from the day it opened in 1899.

G IKON GALLERY
Ikon Gallery is one of Europe's premier venues for new art. Alongside exhibitions by artists from Britain and abroad, Ikon organises talks, tours and special events, and has an excellent café and bookshop. Free admission.

I NATIONAL SEA LIFE CENTRE
Over 55 displays of marine life from shrimps to sharks. A full programme of feeding demonstrations, talks and special presentations.

M BLAKESLEY HALL
Throughout the year 2000, Blakesley Hall was redeveloped, to improve its services and facilities.

L BIRMINGHAM CATHEDRAL
A magnificent example of fine baroque design, including stained glass windows by Birmingham's own Burne-Jones. Watch out for the strange creatures masquerading as doorpulls! Guided tours available.

Q LICKEY HILLS COUNTRY PARK
Over 200 hectares of deciduous and coniferous woodland, marshy areas and heathland, with a rich variety of wildlife.

N CANNON HILL PARK
The ideal park for the family, with boating lakes, playgrounds, tennis courts, tropical greenhouses and nature conservation areas.

P KINGS HEATH PARK
Home to BBC Gardeners' World's gardens, this park is a must for all plant enthusiasts with its wide variety of prize-winning horticulture.

K SUTTON PARK – NATIONAL NATURE RESERVE
970 hectares of natural beauty. With woodland, heaths, wetland and pools attracting many species of wildlife. Facilities include visitor centre, cafés and restaurants.

O CASTLE BROMWICH HALL GARDENS
Beautiful formal eighteenth-century walled gardens, offering an oasis of tranquillity, featuring restored summer house, green house and holly maze.

D BIRMINGHAM MUSEUM AND ART GALLERY
This magnificent building is home to one of the world's finest collections of Pre-Raphaelite art and boasts a constantly changing and varied programme of exhibitions and events.

C BIRMINGHAM BOTANICAL GARDENS & GLASSHOUSES
Tropical, Mediterranean and desert glasshouses; National Bonsai collection; waterfowl and exotic birds; play area and gift shop – all within 6.5 hectares of beautiful gardens.

Extension Exercise

1 How are the two areas in the case studies similar and different?
2 Identify the leisure components, giving examples for each.
3 How are the components linked?
4 Select another area to compare with Birmingham and the Pool of London. Draw up a chart showing the components of the three areas.

THINK ABOUT...

Does the leisure provision in your area meet
a) your needs?
b) your family's needs?

Different customer needs

Different types of customer will require specific needs to be addressed depending on:

◆ age
◆ gender
◆ physical condition
◆ the type of service they are using.

Different groups of people require a different need to be satisfied by a facility or service within the context of the leisure environment. For example, teenagers using a leisure centre will expect to have the following needs met:

◆ car parking facilities
◆ reception and meeting area
◆ changing room and shower facilities with lockers
◆ restaurant, bar, and snack bars
◆ vending machines
◆ arcade machines
◆ pool tables
◆ squash, tennis, badminton, football facilities
◆ fitness centre
◆ swimming pool.

The challenges that face travellers with disabilities

ABLE-BODIED travellers who enjoy swapping airline and airport horror stories should be wary of discussions with disabled travellers. Their stories will top your just about every time.

Impossibly steep stairways, missing or damaged wheelchairs and airport staff who leave passengers stranded in corridors are just some of the adventures reported by travellers with special needs. All of that despite significant strides in providing better service over the past few years, notably in the United States. Many disabled travellers even report having to pay higher prices for tickets.

There's worse. "How many people can fly comfortably for up to 18 hours without using a bathroom?" asks Marti Gacioch, the founder of the Global Access Disabled Travel Network – *www.geocities.com/Paris/1502* – and a worldwide wheelchair traveller. "That's what we are often required to do, largely by watching our liquid intake."

Anyone who thinks these problems apply to only an unfortunate minority should think again. The community of disabled travellers is big and getting bigger as populations age in much of the developed world.

Source: *International Herald Tribune*, 15 December 2000

30

Hint for completion: Each group will have a different set of needs based on age and interests.

THINK ABOUT...

How has congestion charging affected the leisure and tourism industries in London?

How has leisure provision changed in the last 20 years in different areas?
What did your family do in its leisure time 20 years ago?

Talk about...

ACTIVITY

The table below shows a list of different user types. In discussion groups, complete the table to show what sort of leisure facilities might be popular with each user type. The first example has been completed for you.

User types	Examples
Business people	Leisure facilities within easy reach of organisation. Conferences held at hotels with leisure facilities, e.g. fitness centres, swimming pools. Venues within central locations of towns/cities, near to restaurants, cafés, theatres and cinemas. Long opening hours important to fit in with a busy schedule.
Babies and toddlers	
Teenagers	
Young adults	
Couples with children	
Single parents	
Couples without children	
Middle-aged people	
Retired people	
People with special needs	
People from different countries/religions	
People interested in culture, e.g. theatre, arts	

Passengers give buses big vote of confidence

LONDON'S buses are the real success story of the capital's public transport revival, with many more people using them.

But it's at night, where Transport *for* London – the body responsible for running the city's bus services – has seen the real popularity, with a 16 per cent increase.

Source: *Metro*, 22 February 2002.

How Has Leisure Provision Changed Over the Last 20 Years?

1 **Car ownership** has increased, which allows people to move from their immediate local area to other areas. This enables people to pursue leisure activities that their local area does not provide. It also allows them to move from rural environments to urban environments and vice versa.

2 **Increased mobility** has been possible as transport networks have become more

efficient and flexible, enabling more people to engage in leisure activities.

3 People are now experimenting with **new leisure activities** called extreme sports, e.g. bungee jumping, skydiving, highdiving. Many of these new activities are linked to fund-raising charities. Young people have supported skateboarding and the scooter. Skateboarding parks have been developed across the country.

4 **Home-based leisure has expanded**, catering for all age groups. Expansion of video rentals, take-away food and board games have played a dominant role in most households. Video rental shops, such as Blockbuster Video provide the opportunity to create your very own cinema at home. There are no constraints on viewing times, no travel expenses and this eliminates items that would have been purchased at a cinema or theatre.

Pizza Hut, MacDonalds, KFC and Chinese and Indian take-aways have helped home-based leisure. Relaxation and pleasure are supported by the ease of take-aways and their relative location in the local area. Home delivery has contributed to home-based leisure expansion. The image and popularity of cooking amongst certain age groups also eases the 'bain of cooking'. TV images of *Meals in Minutes* and *Ready, Steady, Cook* have been promoted and people now experiment at home. The sale of cook books has inevitably expanded.

Gardening continues to develop as a hobby with successful modern garden centres. Twickenham Garden Centre won the 'Garden Centre Association Award of Excellence' in 2001. This centre is the flagship of the Squire's Garden Centres. The shop has been redeveloped and offers the gardener a modern and comfortable shopping environment with garden products, houseplants, garden furniture, conservatory furniture, pet products and gifts. The Chelsea Flower Show and Hampton Court Palace Flower Show continue to be popular events with a range of age groups.

Board games have flourished. Traditional board games, such as Monopoly, Scrabble and chess are still popular. These games are marketed to stimulate audiences over and over again. Age groups are targeted by updating themes, e.g. *Pokemon Monopoly*, *Who's in the Bag?*, *The Weakest Link* and *Who Wants to be a Millionaire?*. Many board games have been recreated from popular television series and transferred into households through board games.

5 **Local councils** work with local organisations such as libraries, tourist information centres and other attractions to promote events in the community.

6 **Increased use of marketing and advertising** has raised the profile of leisure activities (see Unit 2).

THINK ABOUT...

How does your local council support leisure activities in your local area?
Which activities are organised by community groups?
Which age groups are targeted?
(**Hint** – check your local council's website)

Children's corner

It's holiday time again!

Half term week is looming, so be prepared by booking your kids onto one of the many courses run by Elmbridge Borough Council to keep 5–14 year olds entertained come rain or shine. Art, sport, woodland aventures, drama – there is bound to be something that appeals, but the courses do get booked up fast.

Source: *The Elmbridge Lifestyle Magazine*, February 2002.

7 **Increased awareness of internal and external customer needs** has affected leisure and service industries (see Unit 3).

8 **Flexible payment** with credit cards and direct debit has given more people the opportunity to take up club membership and access a range of leisure activities within organisations such as:

- tennis clubs
- golf clubs
- video rental shops
- computer shops
- restaurants.

An added attraction is the reward points system that many shops now operate. Clients build up points based on frequency of use of certain stores, e.g. computer shops, supermarkets. Points can be exchanged for goods or 'experiences' such as entrance to a theme park or a holiday.

9 **Meeting people**. Leisure environments have created the ideal location for people to meet and socialise, and to pursue similar interests. Cafés, snack bars, crêche facilities and health and beauty salons play an important part in the environment of leisure clubs.

10 **Educational value**. Watching television, listening to the radio and reading are activities which inform the public. Television is now said to educate and inform in a way that it has never done before. History series, arts series and documentaries, which provide views on contemporary/modern society all have good ratings. Regardless of age, people sense the educational value of raising awareness with the pursuit of new interests. Parents promote leisure pursuits, particularly sporting events and visiting places that have an educational dimension. Museums, galleries, working farms and cultural events can enhance development.

The Wisley Golf Club is one of the most successful private members clubs to be developed in the UK in recent years. The Club won instant recognition when it opened in 1991 and today presents unrivalled golf facilities to its cosmopolitan community of members. Wisley is a true private members club, consisting of 700 shareholders who own the full freehold of the course and clubhouse and with it, complete control of their asset and the future destiny of the Club.

Figure 1.15

Figure 1.16

11 **Technology**. The rapid development of computer technology has affected a range of industries, especially leisure and tourism. The internet and access to websites have all raised the profile of many leisure events and activities and made them more accessible. Some examples of popular online services are www.global4tickets.com and www.thisislondon.co.uk.

> The leisure industry has grown to meet people's leisure needs and is made up of a wide range of facilities. QCA

> **Facility:** this term is used in a leisure and tourism context to refer to equipment, buildings, structures or features of the natural environment which provide opportunities for leisure and tourism potential to be utilised. Facilities may be features of the natural environment which are perceived to have leisure use (e.g. lake or mountain) or be built structures and/or equipment (e.g. boating centre next to a lake).

Figure 1.17

Leisure Centres

Leisure centres have been developed to meet the needs of a range of users (customers). They promote a range of social and sports activities.

Leisure centres are promoted through advertisements in local papers. They are located in an environment which serves several local areas, and transport routes and transport methods are accessible to the user. Extensive car parking facilities are available.

A reception area provides an advance booking service, with a range of payment methods. The safety of personal items is assured due to the availability of lockers. Hiring and purchasing of equipment is a service that is provided.

34

A range of indoor and outdoor facilities is available:

Indoor
swimming pool
squash courts
badminton courts
basketball courts
table tennis
fitness centre
exercise classes
sauna/steam room
gymnasium
licensed bar
restaurant/snack bar
vending machines
arcade machines
smoking/non-smoking areas
party and event organising
children's clubs

Outdoor
football pitches
rugby pitches
outdoor play area
open field area
tennis courts

Case study

Elmbridge Leisure Centre

Drop-in Sessions		
Monday 25 March	**TIME**	**PRICE**
'Cool Cats' Under 5 years	9.30–11.00am	£2.20
Parental supervision is required for this bouncy castle & climbing equipment session.		
'Diddy Skating' 4–7 years	4.00–5.00pm	£2.20
Parental supervision is required		
Tuesday 26 March & 2 April		
'Fun House Rollerskating' 8+ years	4.00–5.00pm	£2.20
Wednesday 27 March & 3 April		
'Creepy Crawlies' Under 5 years	1.30–2.15pm	£1.80
Parental Supervision required for the bouncy castle & soft play session.	& 2.30–3.15pm	
The cost includes 1 adult and 1 child. £1 extra child		
'Football Mania'		
4–6 years	4.00–5.00pm	£2.20
7–9 years	5.00–6.00pm	£2.20
Friday 5 April		
'Cool Cats' Under 5 years	9.30–11.00am	£2.20
Parental supervision is required for this bouncy castle & climbing equipment session.		
'Creepy Crawlies' Under 5 years	1.30–2.15pm	£1.80
Parental supervision required for the bouncy castle & soft play session.	& 2.30–3.15pm	
The cost includes 1 adult and 1 child. £1 extra child		
'Diddy Skating' 4–7 years	3.45–4.45pm	£2.20
Parental Supervision required		
Saturday 23 February		
'Saturday Kids Club' 4–8 years	10.00–12noon	£5.20

Read the extract in the case study opposite.

1 What facilities are provided?

2 Which age groups are catered for?

3 List the facilities and services provided in your local leisure centre.

4 Are there any age groups not catered for in a leisure centre?

Health Farms

Health farms have been developed to provide people with a short break away from home, to be 'pampered'. Guests pay for a package deal with accommodation, all meals and full beauty treatments. Treatments include body treatments, facials and use of facilities, e.g. swimming pool, sauna, jacuzzi, steam room, gym and exercise and relaxation classes. At one time health farms were only used by rich and famous celebrities, however marketing departments in these organisations now target other client groups such as women's organisations.

Video Rental Shops

Case Study

Blockbuster Video

Our Mission

TO HELP PEOPLE **TRANSFORM ORDINARY NIGHTS** INTO BLOCKBUSTER® **NIGHTS** BY BEING THEIR **COMPLETE SOURCE** FOR **MOVIES AND GAMES**.

Background

Since Blockbuster opened its first store in 1985, the company has grown into the world's No. 1 video chain with more than 52 million U.S. and Canadian member accounts active during 2001, plus several million additional member accounts worldwide.

In 2001, an estimated average of more than 3 million customers walked into U.S. BLOCKBUSTER® stores every day.

According to research conducted for BLOCKBUSTER, the BLOCKBUSTER brand enjoys nearly 100 percent recognition with active movie renters in the U.S. In addition, Blockbuster estimates that 64 per cent of the U.S. population lives within a 10-minute drive of BLOCKBUSTER store. Generally, BLOCKBUSTER stores are open 365 days a year.

Blockbuster Inc., headquartered in Dallas, Texas, is a publicly traded subsidiary of a Viacom Inc. with more than 8,000 stores and approximately 89,000 employees, as of December 31, 2001, throughout the Americas, Europe, Asia and Australia.

In-Store Offerings

BLOCKBUSTER stores carry a broad selection of movie titles for rent, from the hottest new releases to a library of older titles. Blockbuster also is the leading renter of DVD, with the majority of the company's stores carrying hundreds of DVD units.

Blockbuster continues to explore ways to generate incremental profit through its store network. In September 2000, the company began marketing DIRECTV System equipment in approximately 3,800 of its U.S. stores. Through the success of this alliance, Blockbuster co-branded DIRECTV's pay-per-view movie service in June 2001, establishing the BLOCKBUSTER brand in the pay-per-view segment of the home entertainment industry for the first time.

Source: © 2002 Blockbuster Inc.

Cinemas and Theatres

Case Study

Prince Edward Theatre

BENNY ANDERSSON & BJÖRN ULVAEUS'

MAMMA MIA!

THE SMASH HIT MUSICAL BASED ON THE SONGS OF **ABBA®**

PRINCE EDWARD THEATRE
OLD COMPTON STREET LONDON W1

HOW TO GET YOUR TICKETS

BY PHONE

Prince Edward Theatre 020 7447 5400
Ticketmaster 020 7413 1708 24hrs, 7 days a week.
£1 per ticket booking fee for all performances.

ON-LINE

www.mamma-mia.com

IN PERSON

Prince Edward Theatre Box Office opens 10.00am Mon-Sat
Advance sales can be made up to 30 mins prior to
performances.
A maximum of 9 tickets can be purchased per person.
Or visit any Ticketmaster outlet (subject to booking fees)

HOTEL AND TICKET PACKAGES

Call the Radisson SAS Portman Hotel London on 020 7208
6146

PUBLIC TRANSPORT

Tottenham Court Road/Leicester Square

SOUVENIRS

Visit the official MAMMA MIA! shop at the Prince Edward
Theatre
(open Monday-Saturday from 10.00am) or
shop on-line at www.mamma-mia.com.

THINK ABOUT ...

Look at the information about Prince Edward Theatre. What services does your local theatre provide? Are they similar to those provided by Prince Edward Theatre?

ACTIVITY

Read the information about the video rental company and theatre.

1 List the services that are provided at each facility.

2 How have the two organisations catered for all age groups?

3 Draw up a table comparing the services offered for different age groups by similar organsations in your area.

Public Houses, Restaurant Chains, Hotels and Café Bars

Eating and drinking are necessities in life; they are also regarded as social pleasures.

Traditionally public houses offered people an environment where they could buy a drink and have a social chat after a stressful day at work. Darts, dominoes, crib and playing cards were some of the activities that were undertaken, however gambling laws have now prohibited some of these activities from taking place.

Public houses have changed their environments to cater for a wider client base:

- ◆ Families – gardens with outdoor play facilities
- ◆ Adults – theme nights
- ◆ Business clients – function areas, Christmas parties

Café bars, restaurants, internet cafés and hotel restaurants now provide a range of eating areas for all age groups catering for a range of functions.

Case Study

Bar du Musée

BAR du MUSÉE
WINE BAR & RESTAURANT

This warm and comfortable bar has been a feature at the heart of historic Greenwich since the 1970s. We have always prided ourselves on our service, wide range of wines and fine food.

Now the Bar du Musée has extended the dining area and we have a new chef offering innovative food in friendly surroundings. The intimate downstairs lounge is perfect for private parties, while the ground floor now features a large glass-roofed conservatory. The bar is close to Greenwich's many landmarks, such as the National Maritime Museum, Royal Naval College, Cutty Sark and the Royal Park.

ACTIVITY

1 Research and gather information on take-away food outlets in your local area.

2 What services do the outlets provide?

3 Which age groups and user types might be prevented from using the Bar du Musée and why?

Community Centres

Community centres host events for most age groups. They are usually owned by local authorities or churches. Community groups use local centres where the cost of hiring the accommodation and the use of the facilities is minimal. When staging an event, the organisers pay for the use of a large hall, cloakroom and kitchen facilities.

- Toddlers – mother and baby coffee mornings
- Children – birthday parties
- Teenagers – youth club facilities, e.g. pool, table tennis, table football, facilities for listening to music
- Adults – line dancing/salsa classes, bingo, antique and craft fairs, Christmas fairs, jumble sales

dance

BEGINNERS LINE DANCING: Wednesdays, 7pm to 8pm. Lavender Hill Methodist Church, Ewell Road (near fire station). ☎ 020 7399 4558.

ROCK 'N' ROLL CLUB DISCO: Every Friday, 8pm to 11pm. Beginners and intermediate dance instruction from 8pm to 9pm. Free style dancing, 9pm to 11pm. Sunshine Community Centre, Clapham. ☎ 020 7399 4558.

children

THE KANGA AND PIGLET CLUB: Richmond Community Centre, Parkfields Road, Richmond. Pre-school fitness and craft classes for two to five year olds, 1pm to 2.30pm. Classes last for an hour and a half. ☎ 020 8392 3455

MUSICRAFT: Church Hall, Avenue Rd, Clapham. Weekly music and art sessions for two and a half to four year olds. Tuesdays, 1.55pm to 2.55pm. ☎ 020 7390 3884.

exhibition

WANDSWORTH MUSEUM: Wheatfield Way, Wandsworth. Until November 2, Romance of the Roman Empire, this is the first public exhibition from Dorich House in SW17 of the Roman art collection of Richard Brown. ☎ 020 7546 5386. www.wandsworth.gov.uk/museum

PICTURE HOUSE GALLERY: Riverside, Hampton Wick. Dreamweavers: Contemporary Tapestries from the Coast. Until November 24. ☎ 020 7892 0221. www.hampton.gov.uk/depts/opps/eal/leisure/arts/picturehouse/

health/fitness

RUNNING: Leisure Centre, Lower Hoe Road, Hoe. Stragglers Running Club meets every Monday and Thursday, 7.30pm, ☎ Colin at 020 7404 7898.

JET-FIT: A fun, lively exercise class. Wednesdays, 8pm to 9pm, Church Hall, Molesey. ☎ Jo on 01932 880123.

CLAPHAM YOGA CENTRE: The Beacon, 42C Clapham Road (just one minute from the station). Daily healing yoga for all abilities. Gentle health yoga for illness and in pregnancy, beginners and advanced classes. £5 per class, deluxe yoga mats for £17. ☎ 020 7974 9866.

THE COMMON BADMINTON CLUB: Clapham Common. Mixed club has vacancies for more players. New season just started and runs for a full 12 months. Play every Monday evening, at 7.45pm to 10.45pm. ☎ David on 020 7399 1208.

comedy

THE JOKE: The Grey Horse, 46 Wandsworth Road, Wandsworth, October 20, Mark Smith, Rob Jones and Adam Brown. 7.30pm £5, £4. ☎ Barry 020 7188 8588. www.thejokecomedyclub.co.uk.

theatre/music

CLAPHAM THEATRE CLUB: The Main Theatre, Clapham Playhouse, 90 High St. The Tempest, from October 19. From October 29, Educating Rita. ☎ 020 7979 9499.

NEW VICTORIA THEATRE: The Ambassadors Centre, Battersea. Until October 26, Chicago. From October 27, London Mozart Players, at 7.30pm. ☎ 020 7654 3456.

CLAPHAM THEATRE: The Common, Clapham. Until October 19, Blood Brothers. October 23 and 26, The Cunning Little Vixen by Janácek, at 7.45. October 24 and 25, Don Giovanni by Mozart, at 7.45. ☎ 020 8940 0088. www.thetheatre.com/clapham

THE KINGS HEAD: 20 Lonsdale Road, Barnes, October 17, Dave Jones Affinity, £5. October 18, The Papa George Band, £6. October 19, The Peter King Quartet, £7. October 20, The Andy Roberts Blues Group, £5. October 20, The Ralph Lewars Band, £6. October 21, Friday Club features Wil Killeen, £5. October 22, The Red Stripe Band, £5. October 23, Touching Cloth featuring Chris Fletcher, £8. ☎ 020 7765 5241. www./thekingshead.com

Figure 1.18

ACTIVITY

Look at the range of advertisements that appear in a local paper. Make a table showing the age groups which would participate in each of the activities listed.

Museums and Galleries

Case Study

National Maritime Museum

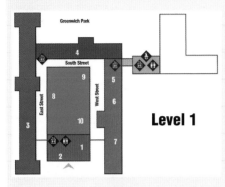

East Street Robin Knox-Johnston's yacht; a lighthouse lamp, a 1930s' speedboat
South Street Stern and figurehead of the 74-gun ship *Implacable*, which fought at Trafalgar; Prince Frederick's barge
West Street What do containers carry? Navigate the Straits of Dover; ship building and ship propulsion

1. **Shop**
2. **Friends Office**
3. 8 **Explorers** Sixteenth-century explorers; Franklin's voyage into the Arctic, underwater exploration – the *Titanic*; navigation
4. **Passengers** Mass migration in the twentieth century; travelling across the sea, for rich and poor
5. **Cargoes** How many ships does it take to make a car? Trade on the sea in the twentieth century
6. **The Submarine** Schools' room
7. **Lecture Theatre**
9. **Rank & Style** Naval dress – how climate and class affect uniform style
10. **Maritime London** The growth of London as a centre for maritime trade

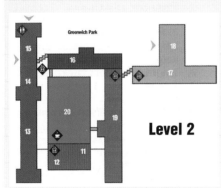

11. **Court Gallery** *Views from the edge*: temporary exhibition of National Trust photography
12. **Friends Room**
13. **Library**
14. **Search Station**
15. **Shop**
16. **Trade & Empire** Maritime trade and the British Empire; slavery; the tea trade and opium wars
17. **Seapower** The Navy and sea trade in the twentieth century, from the First World War to the first Gulf War
18. **Regatta Café**
19. **Art & the Sea** The role of the sea in visual culture; seventeenth-century Dutch marine art; twentieth-century film
20. **Future of the Sea** The sea covers 71 per cent of the planet. Global warming; the water cycle; oil exploration; pollution

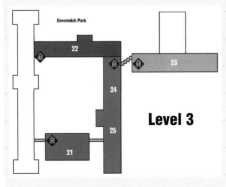

21. **The Bridge** Children's interactive gallery; sail a Viking longboat and take the helm of a paddle steamer
22. **Special Exhibitions** *South: the race to the pole* Scott, Shackleton and Amundsen race to the South Pole
23. **Nelson** Nelson's career and private life; the great sea battles; death and glory; the 'Nelson myth'
24. **Ship of War** The British sailing warship illustrated through ship models from the seventeenth and eighteenth centuries
25. **All Hands** Children's interactive gallery; send a signal; load a cargo; turn a valve under water; fire a gun at sea

Source: The National Maritime Museum
(www.nmm.ac.uk/traveltourism)

ACTIVITY

1 Outline the transport methods that are interlinked with the location of the National Maritime Museum.

2 Find out when the Government introduced 'free entry' to museums.

3 Describe the services available for

a) children with parents or school groups

b) people with special needs.

Sports Venues

Case Study

Twickenham Rugby Club

RUGBY FOOTBALL UNION

Match Day
- Bars & Food
- Corporate Boxes
- Debentures
- Facilities
- Hospitality Packages
- Parking
- Travel Info
- Twickenham Experience Ltd
- Twickenham Fixtures

Non-Match Day
- Banqueting
- Christmas At Twickenham
- Conferences
- Exhibitions
- Museum Of Rugby
- Stadium Tours

Facilities
1. England Rugby International Club
2. Players' entrance
3. Constituent Bodies Bar
4. North Tryline Restaurant
5. Obolensky's Restaurant
6. Museum of Rugby
7. Invincibles Restaurant
8. Cashpoint
9. RFU Offices
10. Wakefield's Restaurant
11. Rose Room
12. Ticket Collection
13. Police
14. Disabled Toilet
15. Toilets
16. First Aid
17. Bar
18. Fast Food
19. Wooden Spoon Bar
20. Lift
21. Lift to disabled areas
22. Escalator
23. The Rugby Store
24. Telephone
25. Enquiry Office

Source: www.rfu.com

QUESTION

1 What methods of transport can be used to travel to Twickenham Rugby Club?

2 What events take place at Twickenham Rugby Club?

3 Describe the services provided for different kinds of users.

Hint: Look at the website for more information.

Theme Parks

Case Study

Alton Towers

All the Alton Towers News, Reviews and Park Information You Could Ever Need

Attractions

Alton Towers is known throughout the world for its innovative attractions which push technology and the human body to its extremities.

Themed Areas

Alton Towers is divided into several themed areas, whether it be the mellow atmosphere of Merrie England, the African village called Katanga Canyon, or the thrills of X-Sector. Select which area you wish to visit, and find out about the area, and which attractions you will find there.

Towers Street

Whether it be sweets or ice-cream for the kids, a trendy jacket for dad, a cool brolly for mum, or whatever else you may fancy, Towers Street is where it's at.

Katanga Canyon

Here in an African colonial village you will find the Runaway Minetrain and the ferocious Congo River Rapids.

Merrie England

Traditional attractions including the Tea-Cups, 3D Cinema, and the well-loved Log Flume.

Gloomy Wood

Explore the forest cemetery before entering the most haunted house in the United Kingdom.

Forbidden Valley

Now the home of two world-class rollercoasters! Make sure you get to Forbidden Valley early.

Ug Land

Return to a prehistoric age with a visit to the land where fun began.

The Gardens

Take a walk around what are probably the most beautiful gardens in the United Kingdom.

Cred Street

Situated behind the Towers, Cred Street is family orientated. Here you will find peace and tranquillity, that is until Barney the Dinosaur makes an appearance.

X-Sector

Dare you enter the X-Sector, with the foreboding Oblivion, and coaster-in-the-dark, Black Hole?

The Towers

Explore the old mansion house, currently undergoing renovation, or try out Hex, and witness the legend of the Towers for yourself.

Storybook Land

A magical place dedicated to the young at heart.

Adventure Land

No Adults Allowed . . . . well that's what the kids would want anyway . . . .

Old MacDonalds Farm

Take a trip round the Riverbank Eye-Spy or drive a tractor on the Tractor Ride.

Source: www.towersalmanac.com

41

QUESTION

1   Locate Alton Towers on a map.

2   What services are provided for the following age groups:

    a) toddlers?
    b) children aged 5–12?
    c) teenagers and adults?

3   Suggest one way in which Alton Towers could develop a product or different service to meet the needs of

    a) groups from different cultures
    b) senior citizens.

Case Study

Odds Farm Park

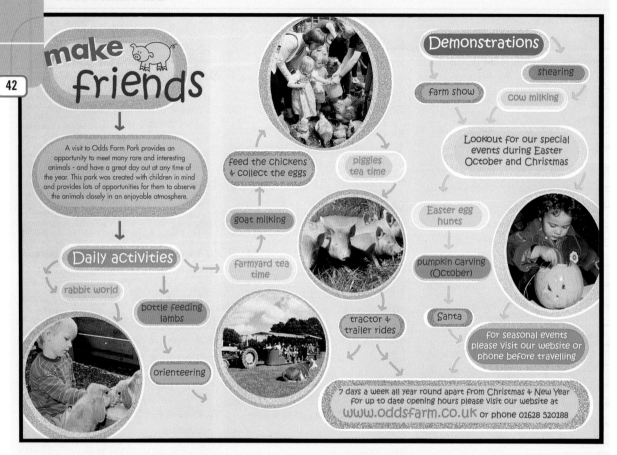

make friends

↓

A visit to Odds Farm Park provides an opportunity to meet many rare and interesting animals - and have a great day out at any time of the year. This park was created with children in mind and provides lots of opportunities for them to observe the animals closely in an enjoyable atmosphere.

↓

Daily activities

- rabbit world
- bottle feeding lambs
- orienteering

feed the chickens & collect the eggs

goat milking

farmyard tea time

piggies tea time

tractor & trailer rides

Demonstrations

- farm show
- shearing
- cow milking

Lookout for our special events during Easter October and Christmas

Easter egg hunts

pumpkin carving (October)

Santa

for seasonal events please visit our website or phone before travelling

7 days a week all year round apart from Christmas & New Year for up to date opening hours please visit our website at www.oddsfarm.co.uk or phone 01628 520188

THINK ABOUT...

Which products and services are offered at Odds Farm Park.

Facilities for home-based leisure are increasing in importance. According to recent research, home-based leisure has increased due to changes in social habits and the fact that this type of leisure has become so 'convenient' for all ages.

Shopping from home using the internet/online services and telephone shopping has increased. People are now shopping for groceries, clothes and household goods using websites and high street chain catalogues from stores including Tesco, Marks and Spencer, Sainsbury's and Next.

ACTIVITY

Identify which facilities are available in your local area to support home based leisure.

Home-based leisure	Named example
Take-away food	
Video rental shops	
Libraries	
Shops selling computer games	
Bookshops	

Another contributing factor to the increase in home-based leisure has been the high crime rates in the UK. This has made many people rethink their lifestyle, particularly in relation to their travelling patterns.

Total recorded crime by offence

England and Wales — Number of offences and percentages

Offence group	12 months ending		Change			
	March 2000	March 2001	Number		Percentage	
Violence against the person	581,036	600,873	19,837	(78,248)	3.4	(15.6)
Sexual offences	37,792	37,299	−493	(1,618)	−1.3	(4.5)
Robbery	84,277	95,154	10,877	(17,442)	12.9	(26.1)
Total violent crime	*703,105*	*733,326*	*30,221*	*(97,308)*	*4.3*	*(16.1)*
Burglary	906,468	836,027	−70,441	(−46,716)	−7.8	(−4.9)
Total theft & handling stolen goods	2,223,620	2,145,372	−78,248	(32,181)	−3.5	(1.5)
Theft of and from vehicles	*1,043,918*	*968,447*	*−75,471*	*(−33,808)*	*−7.2*	*(−3.1)*
Fraud and forgery	334,773	319,324	−15,449	(55,270)	−4.6	(19.8)
Criminal damage	945,682	960,087	14,405	(66,096)	1.5	(7.5)
Total property crime	*4,410,543*	*4,260,810*	*−149,733*	*(106,831)*	*−3.4*	*(2.5)*
Drug offences	121,866	113,458	−8,408	(−14,079)	−6.9	(−10.4)
Other notifiable offences	65,671	63,237	−2,434	(−2,036)	−3.7	(3.2)
Total all offences	**5,301,185**	**5,170,831**	**2130,354**	**(192,096)**	**22.5**	**(3.8)**

Change between 1998/99 and 1999/00 in brackets.

Figure 1.19

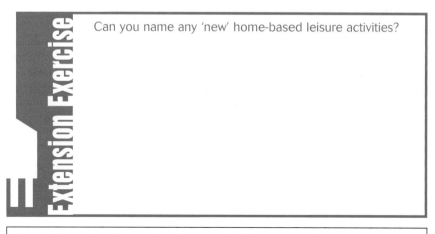

Extension Exercise

Can you name any 'new' home-based leisure activities?

You will need to know that leisure facilities provide a range of products and services.

44

> **Product/service**: the activities of many leisure and tourism organisations result in a product which may include goods and/or services to the customer. For example, a hotel may sell a weekend break as a product which also contains several services including meals, accommodation and entertainment.
>
> Edexcel

A leisure centre might provide:

◆ Sports activities including squash, badminton, tennis and football
◆ Lessons and classes for different groups of people including dance, step aerobics, keep fit, yoga
◆ Functions such as birthday parties, wedding receptions and conferences
◆ Restaurants, bars and vending machines
◆ Special rates for members and/or groups including family membership and promotional rates
◆ Purchase and hire of equipment such as lockers, sports equipment, squash and badminton courts.

Employment in Leisure

> Within the leisure industry there is a range of jobs available:
>
> ◆ Leisure assistant
> ◆ Fitness instructor
> ◆ Leisure centre manager
> ◆ Lifeguard
> ◆ Ground staff
> ◆ Park ranger
> ◆ Restaurant manager
>
> QCA

Few industries can match the leisure industry for the range of employment opportunities it offers, for example, the organisational chart below shows the variety of jobs available in a leisure centre.

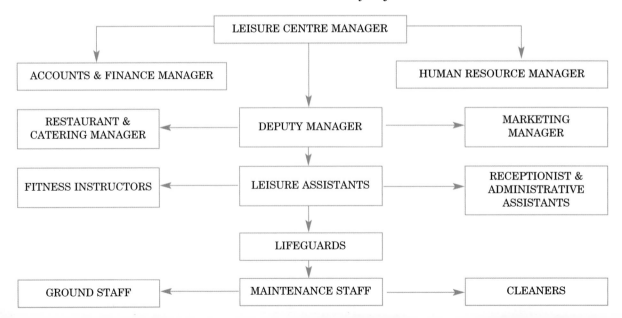

ACTIVITY

Select three jobs from the organisational chart and describe the responsibilities and duties that might be involved in each of these.

Figure 1.20

Figure 1.21

ACTIVITY

Above are two examples of advertisements for jobs in the leisure industry. Other advertisements can be found on the internet. Have a look at some theme park or local authority websites for job advertisements and answer the following questions for three different jobs of your choice.

1 What is the job title and which organisation has placed the advertisment?

2 What does the job involve?

3 What qualifications are needed?

4 Do you need any specific skills or experience to gain employment?

5 Which component does the job come from?

SECTION TWO

The Travel and Tourism Industry

Introduction

Leisure, Recreation and Tourism

It is necessary to clarify the interrelationship of leisure, recreation and tourism. When is leisure part of tourism and what is the link with recreation?

> Leisure time is my 'free time' when I am not working, studying, sleeping or carrying out other basic needs, e.g. paying bills, food shopping, going to the doctor, dentist, bank etc.

> Recreation includes the type of activities that I undertake in my leisure time, e.g. watching television, playing on the playstation, going to football, visiting a theme park or going on holiday.

> Tourism is when I travel away from my home and my workplace.

Tourism is a difficult term to define because it covers a broad area. However, basically tourism is temporary travel away from home or work. An essential part of tourism is the traveller's intention to return home afterwards. Tourism is the one activity that most people want to undertake. For a full understanding of the industry, a range of terminology needs to be explained.

Tourism: tourism is about the temporary short-term movement of people to destinations outside the places where they normally live and work and about their activities during their stay at these destinations. It includes travel for all purposes as well as day visits or excursions. An essential part of tourism is the intention of the traveller to return to where he/she normally lives, whether this is from a day trip, a holiday or a short business trip.

A tourist: a traveller, whose journey is due to leisure, business, visiting friends and relatives or taking a holiday.

Edexcel

ACTIVITY

Complete the boxes, writing down activities that could be undertaken for each heading.

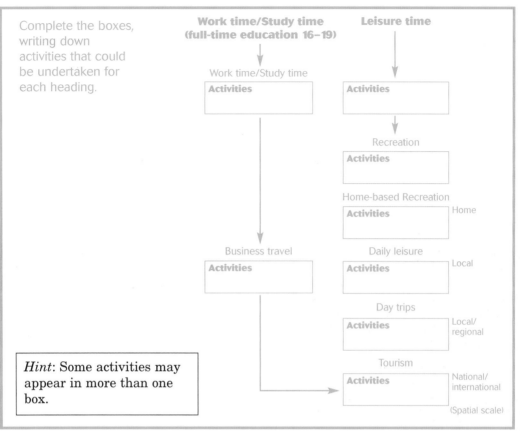

Work time/Study time
(full-time education 16–19)

Leisure time

Work time/Study time

Activities

Activities

Recreation

Activities

Home-based Recreation

Activities · Home

Business travel

Activities

Daily leisure

Activities · Local

Day trips

Activities · Local/regional

Tourism

Activities · National/international

(Spatial scale)

Hint: Some activities may appear in more than one box.

Case Study
Coastal location

Hint: For more information search the internet for websites on Blackpool.

Rock star

SEASIDE FAVOURITE IS VERY BEST OF BRITISH

SOME see Blackpool as a live version of a saucy seaside postcard and a mecca of candyfloss, fish and chips and heart-stopping fairground rides.

Others believe it can become Britain's answer to Las Vegas, a glittering strip of casinos, fabulous floor shows, smart restaurants and hotels.

But Blackpool, like its famous Tower, rises above the carping about its image and arguments about its future.

It's still the favourite resort of millions of Brits – an unpretentious paradise of sea, sand, affordale accommodation and thrills on the Pleasure Beach.

DESTINATION: Blackpool
GETTING THERE: There are 14,000 car parking spaces in Blackpool, so driving is the best form of transport.
STAYING THERE: During the Illuminations (Sept to Nov), the Queens Hotel's B&B tariff is from £32 midweek and £41 at weekends; three-night half-board breaks from £133, with discounts for children.
Call 01253 342015 or log on to www.thequeenshotel.freeserve.co.uk
OUT AND ABOUT: For more information on Blackpool, you can log on to www.blackpooltourism.co.uk

Source: *The Sun*, 12 January 2002.

Case Study

Kennet and Avon Canal

Hint: For further information look on the internet for websites on the Kennet and Avon Canal.

voyage on the
KENNET AND AVON CANAL

Who wants to steer? Who is getting off to do the next lock? And, most importantly of all, shall we moor at the next pub for a drink? Such decisions punctuated our weeklong voyage along the Kennet and Avon canal from Reading to Devizes.

Altogether the trip proved both relaxing and busy. With a top speed of 4mph – more would damage the banks – we could never be in a hurry. Even so we travelled about 90 miles there and back, negotiating each of the 45 locks, 14 swing bridges and a tunnel twice! Coming with relentless regularity, the locks certainly added to the fun, starting shortly after we had collected the boat from Reading Marine's base at Aldermaston. We soon worked out an efficient system of dealing with them. Two of us walked ahead along the towpath to lower or raise the paddles with a special key called a windlass and then, when the water became level, opened the gates. Afterwards one stayed behind to shut them again.

Driving proved simple, with a single lever for forward or reverse, but steering 69 unwieldy feet from the rear needs practice! You have to get used to a sluggish response to the tiller but moving it sharply soon results in embarrassing zig-zags. As

canals are narrow, there is little scope for error, as we certainly discovered inside the gloomy 500-yard Bruce Tunnel.

Consulting our Nicholson Waterways guide and Ordnance Survey maps, we made several forays ashore. We moored at Hungerford, another attractive old town, to go shopping for supplies and then spent the afternoon browsing in its antique market. On another day, while the others chugged on, I went off on my bike, cycling along the Vale of Pewsey through thatched villages and beneath a gleaming white horse cut into the hillside.

Source: *Motoring & Leisure*, February 2002.

Case Study

Manchester 2002 Games

Background to the Manchester 2002 Games

The XVII Commonwealth Games is a world-class event and the most significant multi-sport event to be held in this country since the Olympics of 1948. It will be the largest ever Commonwealth Games with athletes of the highest quality from 72 nations competing for Gold in 14 individual sports and three team sports from 25 July–4 August 2002.

Alongside a celebration of sporting excellence, the Games will provide the opportunity to celebrate multicultural, modern Britain at the start of the new millennium.

Manchester is fully committed to promoting and staging an 'inclusive Games', with equality of opportunity for competitors, spectators, volunteers and employees, irrespective of colour, race, nationality, ethnic origin, gender, religion, age, or disability.

The Games will involve more competitors from more Commonwealth nations than ever before. Women will compete across all sports with the exception of rugby 7s, boxing and wrestling and comprise 41 per cent of the athletes. Elite athletes with a disability will be included in the line up for many events.

Source: www.commonwealthgames.com

Case Study

Blenheim Palace

DIRECTIONS TO BLENHEIM PALACE
Blenheim Palace and Woodstock are 8 miles
north of Oxford on the A44 Evesham road.
London, Birmingham, Cheltenham, Stratford-
upon-Avon and Heathrow are all approximately 1
hour's drive away. Oxford Tube coaches depart
from London Victoria to Oxford daily (train
enquiries 08457 484950). Buses (No 20) run
from Oxford Bus Station to Woodstock, stopping
at the Park gate.

THE GARDEN AND PARK
Blenheim's gardens are renowned for their beauty
and range from the formal Water Terraces, Italian
Garden and Rose Garden to the natural charm of
the Arboretum and Cascade. Blenheim Lake,
created by 'Capability' Brown and spanned by
Vanbrugh's Grand Bridge, is the focal point of
over 2,000 acres of landscaped parkland.

Source: Blenheim Palace

ACTIVITY

Look at figures 1.22 and 1.23 (overleaf) and do some research
on the Internet to answer the following questions:

1 Which countries received over 18,000 visitors (international
   arrivals) in 1999?

2 What visitor attractions do these countries offer?

3 Are these countries part of the EU?

1999 rank	Country	Arrivals (million)		% change 1998/1999	1999 market share
		1998	1999		
1	France	70.0	73.0	4.3	11.0
2	Spain	47.4	51.8	9.2	7.8
3	United States	46.4	48.5	4.5	7.3
4	Italy	34.9	36.1	3.3	5.4
5	China	25.1	27.0	7.9	4.1
6	United Kingdom	25.7	25.7	0.0	3.9
7	Canada	18.9	19.6	3.7	2.9
8	Mexico	19.8	19.2	−2.9	2.9
9	Russian Fed.	15.8	18.5	17.0	2.8
10	Poland	18.8	18.0	−4.4	2.7
11	Austria	17.4	17.5	0.7	2.6
12	Germany	16.5	17.1	3.7	2.6
13	Czech Rep.	16.3	16.0	−1.8	2.4
14	Hungary	15.0	12.9	−13.8	1.9
15	Greece	10.9	12.0	9.9	1.8

Figure 1.22 World's Top Tourism Destinations, 1999

Source: WTO

	Visitors (thousands)	Av. Receipts per visitor		Visitors (thousands)	Av. Receipts per visitor
France	73,042	$431	Bulgaria	2,472	$377
Spain	46,776	$695	Finland	2,454	$618
Italy	36,516	$777	Cyprus	2,434	$772
UK	25,394	$796	Denmark	2,023	£1,820
Russia	18,493	$406	Lithuania	1,422	$387
Poland	17,950	$340	Malta	1,214	$556
Austria	17,467	$718	Slovak Rep.	975	$473
Hungary	17,248	$197	Estonia	950	$589
Germany	17,116	$977	Slovenia	884	$1,078
Greece	12,164	$722	Luxembourg	833	n/a
Portugal	11,632	$441	Latvia	490	$241
Switzerland	10,700	$723	Belarus	355	$37
Netherlands	9,881	$718	Monaco	278	n/a
Turkey	6,893	$755	Iceland	263	$863
Ireland	6,403	$530	Macedonia, FYR	181	$204
Belgium	6,369	$1,105	Yugoslavia, Fed. Rep.	152	$112
Czech Rep.	5,610	$541	Bosnia-Herzegovina	89	$236
Norway	4,481	$497	Liechtenstein	60	n/a
Ukraine	4,232	$756	Albania	39	n/a
Croatia	3,443	$724	Moldova	14	$143
Romania	3,209	$79			
San Marino	3,148	n/a			
Sweden	2,595	$1,501			

(Visitor arrival figures not available for Andorra, Channel Islands, Faroe Islands, Greenland or Gibraltar)

Figure 1.23 Visitors to Europe: International arrivals and average receipts, 1999

Source: WTO

The Purpose of Tourist Visits

There are many different reasons for tourism including:

◆ holidays
◆ sightseeing
◆ visiting an attraction
◆ visiting friends and relatives
◆ attending or participating in sports events
◆ business.

> **How has the outbreak of SARS affected tourism?**
>
> **Talk about...**

Holidays

> You will need to know that there are different types of holiday in the travel and tourism industry.

Flights up to five hours duration are classed as **short haul** and over five hours as **long haul** by the International Air Transport Association (I.A.T.A).

50

An essential part of the travel and tourism industry is when people go on holiday. This can be planned or unplanned. Households generally plan a holiday according to their individual circumstances:

◆ Amount of holiday time available
◆ Disposable income
◆ Interests
◆ Mode of transport available
◆ Age groups
◆ Opportunity

There are several types of holiday which play an important part in the UK travel and tourism industry:

◆ Package
◆ Independent
◆ Domestic
◆ Inbound and outbound
◆ Involving long and short haul fights
◆ Special interest
◆ Short breaks

Figure 1.24 UK travel and tourism destinations

PACKAGE HOLIDAYS

This is the holiday format which traditionally includes three main elements:

◆ Transport (coach, rail, air, car, sea)
◆ Accommodation
◆ Transfers

Package holidays incorporate these elements into one arrangement for an inclusive price. This includes the hotel accommodation, meal plan, transfers to the resort (where appropriate) and excursions. The package holiday is still very popular and can be taken within the UK or abroad. Popular destinations include the Lake District, Scotland, Glasgow, Edinburgh, Devon and Cornwall. European destinations include Spain, Greece, France, and Italy.

Common types of package holiday

There are common types of package holiday:

◆ Fly-drive
◆ All inclusive
◆ One centre
◆ Multi-centre
◆ Touring
◆ Active
◆ Cruise and stay
◆ Tailor-made

Groups of people have different requirements for a package holiday based on:

◆ age
◆ gender
◆ interests
◆ available income
◆ duration of holiday
◆ season of holiday.

Look at the following Case Study which shows a range of package holidays offered by Airtours, Hayes and Jarvis, British Airways, Thomson and JMC.

Read the descriptions of the package holidays and complete the table below.

Name of Brochure	Type of Package Holiday	Type of Activities/ Services
British Airways		
Hayes and Jarvis		
Thomson		
JMC		

ACTIVITY

Case Study

THOMSON ALL INCLUSIVE

Looking for an indulgent, carefree break? Then a Thomson All Inclusive holiday is exactly what you're looking for! With just about everything included in the price, you can simply relax and do as much or as little as you like.

Every Thomson All Inclusive holiday includes breakfast, lunch and dinner; soft drinks and locally produced alcoholic drinks (some time restrictions and age restrictions may apply, see the A-Z guide); and a variety of sports, daytime activities and evening entertainment.

THOMSON A LA CARTE

A la Carte hotels are chosen for their elegance and refinement. Whether you choose a modern or more traditional style hotel, each has it's own unique character and all offer the highest standards. Relax and unwind in the knowledge that every detail has been taken care of.

Other benefits include:
Service with a personal touch

■ A la Carte Guest Services Manager.
■ Individual appointment service.
■ 24 hour phoneline in resort.

Exclusive travel benefits

■ Private transfer and hotel porterage.

You may also receive

■ Increased baggage allowance if flying with Britannia.

ESCORTED TOURS

One of the best ways to get the most from your holiday has to be on a tour with the help of those who really know your chosen destination.

On one of our tours in Sri Lanka, we'll make sure that you get to see the finest sights, the most spectacular beaches and the best of local culture. And of course while you're enjoying them, we're making sure that all the logistics of your tour are taken care of, so that you don't have to.

TWIN CENTRE

If your idea of a dream holiday is a combination of sightseeing and relaxation, try a Thomson twin centre in Barbados, Cuba, Jamaica or the Maldives and Sri Lanka.

Combine a week in Barbados with either a week in Grenada – the most southerly of the Windward Islands, or a week in Tobago – just off the Venezuelan coast.

A twin centre in Cuba offers the chance to explore the history and culture of Havana combined with Cuba's leading resort, Varadero.

Jamaica offers Negril with its 7½ mile golden beach, twinned with Ocho Rios, a bustling market town.

Experience a once in a lifetime twin centre holiday with the wonderful rich culture of Sri Lanka combined with the amazing scenery surrounding the stunning islands that make up the Maldives.

Source: *Thomson* brochure

Case Study (cont.)

Self Drive Tour – South Africa

Ideal for those free spirits that like to be pointed in the right direction, our self-drive tour gives you the flexibility you want. Your stops along the way are booked and a suggested route is plotted. Staying two or three nights in one place gives you the ideal base to relax and to explore as much or as little as you want.

Winelands & The Garden Route

HERMANUS (1NT) – KNYSNA (3NTS) – OUDSTHOORN (1NT) – MONTAGU (1NT) – STELLENBOSCH (2NTS)

This self-drive tour gives you both independence and flexibility. Route planning, accommodation vouchers and suggested points of interest en route are taken care of in advance as are hotel reservations. Simply drive and enjoy.

Source: *Thomson* brochure

Dive and Stay

Warm crystal clear waters, interesting encounters, unforgettable memories.

Encounter weightlessness for the first time, glide with thousands of colourful fish, meet wonderful turtles, and be amazed by tropical coral reefs. Interested? Then take the plunge and let us show you a strikingly different world – all you need to be is fit and have a healthy sense of adventure!

- Dive in consistently warm water, with excellent visibility, in renowned dive destinations.
- Destinations ideal for both the recreational diver and non diver alike
- Great learn to dive destinations for the beginner
- Exotic and far flung 'must visit' dive destinations for the advanced and dedicated diver
- BSAC (British Sub Aqua Club) and PADI approved schools offering excellent standards of equipment, safety and tuition

Destinations include

- Red Sea
- Indian Ocean
- Micronesia
- Maldives
- Mediterranean
- Far East
- Caribbean
- Latin America
- Australia

Cruise and Stay

A new day, a new port

Cruising is an ideal way to relax and absorb the attractions of a region whilst enjoying the onboard facilities, as well as being convenient – no packing and unpacking, you take your hotel room with you. Cruise along the timeless Nile or journey through the waters of the Orient; travel at a leisurely pace through the Seychelles archipelago or the magical islands of the Galapagos. Our Cruise selection is displayed on pages 136, 202, 242–3, 284–5, 309 & 313

Source: *Hayes and Jarvis* brochure

Tailor Made Holidays

We recognise that no two customers are alike, and virtually every holiday we sell is individually tailored in some way. Perhaps you'd like to make a simple change in meal arrangements, choose an alternative hotel or fine-tune your holiday duration? On the other hand maybe you're interested in a 'mix and match' itinerary combining the Far East with a tour of India or you're tempted by a round-the-world trip of a lifetime. Our tailor made holidays specialists can draw on a wealth of knowledge and travel experience to prepare the best and most cost effective itineraries.

Source: *British Airways Holidays* brochure

Case Study (cont.)

Twin Centres, Safari & Stay and Tour & Stay Holidays

For a more flexible approach to your holiday, why not try one of our Twin Centre, Tour & Stay, or Safari & Stay options.

Choose from a week in Sri Lanka followed by an idyllic week or two in the Maldives, or experience Sri Lanka's natural beauty on a cultural tour followed by six days of pure indulgence on a beach in the Maldives. An alternative option is the Goa and Kerala Twin Centre. Enjoy a week relaxing on the fantastic beaches of Goa followed by a week of peace and tranquillity at a lake resort in Kerala, or combine it with a rice boat cruise along the magical backwaters. Alternatively combine a week in Goa with a tour of the southern tip of India.

For the more adventurous, why not combine the thrill of a safari mixed with the beautiful Kenyan coast. We offer three separate safaris of differing durations, plus a Select option for those preferring to say in tented camps.

The choice is yours and we have made life easier for you. Many of our tours (House Boats, The Essence of Kerala, Nature Trail, Wings over Masai Mara Safari, Safari Tsavo/Amboseli and Taste of India Tour) can be booked as a simple add-on to your holiday price, so you take the 7 or 14 night price and add on the supplement in the price panel of the hotel of your choice. The tour will be taken within the 7 and 14 night duration.

For all twin centre holidays, guests will spend seven nights in Sri Lanka or Goa and then six nights in the Maldives or Kerala. The last night will be at the beach hotel in Sri Lanka or Goa on the same board basis as your hotel in the Maldives or Kerala, ready for an easy transfer to the airport. Please note that if internal flights are re-scheduled, then this may change to seven nights in both destinations.

Prices include transfers to and from both resorts and return internal flights between Sri Lanka and the Maldives or Goa and Kerala. Your flight back to the UK will be departing from Sri Lanka or Goa.

Source: *JMC* brochure

Extension Exercise

Visit your local travel agent and research winter sports package holidays in various brochures.

What does the winter sports package holiday consist of?

Case Study

Winter Sun Destinations

✹ ✹ ✹
Hotel Honolulu
Majorca — Magaluf

Ideally situated between Palma Nova and Magaluf, the traditional and attractive Honolulu is an ideal choice for those seeking a hotel with a lively and friendly atmosphere.
Location
- In an elevated position, access is via a short but steep hill and 25 steps
- Magaluf beach is 400m away and Palma Nova beach is 160m away
- 280m away from a large selection of shops, bars and restaurants

Facilities
- Swimming pool; sun terrace; gardens
- Restaurant
- Lounge/bar; pub
- Reception

✹ ✹ ✹ ✹ PLUS
Athena Beach Hotel
Cyprus — Paphos

An impressive beachfront hotel, set in decorative gardens, the Athena Beach has an abundance of activities, and would suit couples and families alike.
Location
- On a sandy man-made beach
- Approx. 1.5km from the tourist centre of Paphos
- Only 2km from the harbour

Facilities
- Choice of free-form pools; indoor pool; sun terrace
- Pool bar serving food
- Gym; indoor and outdoor whirlpool; sauna; steam bath; hydro massage; facials; manicures and pedicures
- Pool table; games room with arcade machines
- Cocktail lobby bar with music
- Choice of restaurants

✹ ✹ ✹ ✹
  On S/C only
Aparthotel Paraiso de Albufeira
The Algarve — Albufeira

Stylish and well-maintained, this property provides a lively, friendly and relaxing atmosphere.
Location
- 1km from golden sand beach
- 150m to nearest mini-market and bars
- 350m to main nightlife, 250m to resort centre

Facilities
- Free-form swimming pool; sun terrace with sunloungers, parasols and pool bar
- 2 Indoor pools
- Main restaurant with buffet and waiter service
- Two lounges; bar with satellite TV
- Nightclub
- 24hr reception; money exchange facilities

✹ ✹ ✹
El Pueblito Beach Hotel
Mexico (Caribbean Coast) — Cancun

This hotel is built in 'hacienda' style, linked by winding pathways and well-kept gardens. Guest rooms are comfortable and spacious, furnished in traditional Mexican style. Staff are very friendly adding to the authentic charm and appeal of this lively property.
Location
- Situated directly on the beach front
- 7km to La Isla shops and nightlife, easily reached via the regular local bus service

Facilities
- Four freshwater pools cascading into a larger pool; sun terraces with views out to sea • Pool/swim-up bar; lobby bar • Three restaurants, main buffet restaurant; Mexican à la carte; snack bar • Shops; beauty parlour

Source: *JMC Late Holiday Dealz* brochure

ACTIVITY

1 Locate the winter sun destinations opposite on a world map.

2 Which destination is long haul?

3 Which language is spoken in each destination?

4 Compare the facilities and services offered in each destination.

Extension Exercise

Examine a wide variety of winter sun brochures and identify destinations that are suitable for:

a) families
b) young couples
c) over fifties.

Thomson Holidays, a tour operator, Lunn Poly, a travel agent, and the TV Travelshop, online booking, all have websites. This advancement in information technology and communications has changed the nature of booking a holiday. People need more efficient, faster ways of accessing information about holidays including availability and prices. With the internet revolution, people are now using online facilities more than the traditional methods of booking holidays.

INDEPENDENT HOLIDAYS
This type of holiday encompasses the tailor-made 'bespoke' arrangement. As more people become adventurous and their personal interests become part of their everyday lifestyle, people choose to create a more customised holiday. Hobbies and leisure activities are a vital ingredient to creating an individual holiday experience. The advantages of this approach are:

◆ Travel arrangements suit personal circumstances
◆ Accommodation and catering meet dietary requirements
◆ Flexibility of itinerary to suit personal schedule
◆ Cost suits individual needs
◆ Teletext or internet information readily available
◆ The number of budget airlines enables people to make their own arrangements

SHORT BREAKS
Short breaks have become popular for a range of client groups that choose to take a 'mini holiday' away from the monotonous routine of

work, usually at short notice. The introduction of last minute bookings by using the internet has greatly increased the short break market. Many tour operators offer short break programmes. These can be either international (usually short-haul) or domestic.

A number of operators provide short break holidays, which involve a range of destinations in the UK. *Leisure Times National* magazine promotes short break and UK holidays which capture the beauty of the landscapes.

The appeal of this type of holiday is:

◆ Short break away from work/normal routine
◆ A change of environment
◆ A period to rest and relax
◆ An opportunity to visit a new location with different attractions and activities

BLACKPOOL

Fun-packed, laugh-a-minute, great-value Blackpool – for a day, a weekend or a fortnight where the whole family can guarantee to have the time of their lives, morning till night, without breaking the bank.

For a free official brochure write to Blackpool Brochures, 1 Clifton Street, Blackpool FY1 1LY or call 0870 241 3315 calls charged at national rate e-mail: brochure@blackpool.gov.uk

WORTHING

A traditional seaside town situated on the attractive West Sussex coast, Worthing has so much to offer at any time of year. Superb theatres, excellent restaurants and great shopping. Close to the beautiful South Downs and 5 miles of award-winning coastline – the ideal base for your Sussex coast and countryside holiday. For our FREE brochure, please ring our brochure hotline: 08705 673086 (Quote ref 609/1)

SOUTH DEVON

Come and enjoy yourself in South Devon; an area full of contrast. Discover our spectacular coastline, superb beaches, great family attractions, historic towns, delightful villages, distinctive crafts, foods, mild climate and the beauty of Dartmoor. All the ingredients for a wonderful summer holiday or seasonal short break. With easy access by road and rail, it's so simple to get here.

Free holiday and short break guide – use the coupon or Tel (24hrs) 01626 215666 visit www.southdevon.org.uk or email tourism@teignbridge.gov.uk

NEWQUAY

Newquay . . . "Britain's favourite family holiday" Focal point of a breathtaking Riviera, where soaring cliffs alternate with sheltered coves and thundering surf, with soft golden sands stretching for seven miles over 11 superb beaches. There is magic in so much natural beauty. Call brochure line on 01637 854010 (24hrs) www.newquay.org.uk

Figure 1.25

Source: *Sunday Mirror*, 6 January 2002

HOLIDAY PARKS

A fun and exciting style of holiday, popular with families who are keen on an action-packed experience, with activities and entertainment laid on for them is one at a holiday park.

Case Study

Holiday Parks

Holidays 2002

GET YOUR KICKS

All-action breaks at Britain's holiday parks

A feast of fitness and fun is on offer this year at Britain's holiday parks. Throughout the UK the top locations present lots of action – with sports opportunities galore to improve your favourite game and activities to make your holiday memorable. It's all here from football training, archery and ballooning to sailing and scuba diving. DAVID KERR finds himself a piece of the action. . .

IF you're looking for activities guaranteed to keep you on your toes then **BRITISH HOLIDAYS** have the lot. And if access to swimming pools, tennis courts, multi-sports courts, golf courses and sailing isn't enough, now you can join in a whole range of organised activities too.

From swimming and scuba diving to professional football coaching – British Holidays also offer the Ian Rush Finishing School – every taste is catered for.

Budding Beckhams caught up in World Cup mania can improve their skills at selected parks during the summer holidays and go home with the exclusive "Rushie" certificate or maybe even the coveted Player of the Day trophy. You'll also be able to see all those important World Cup fixtures on widescreen satellite TV.

Holidaymakers of all ages will enjoy the extra activities in the swimming pools. Discover Scuba is a gentle introduction to scuba diving or you can learn lifesaving skills and body-boarding at the Wave Rider class.

Bubble Maker is a new and lively session of wacky family fun in the swimming pool. British Holidays (0870 242 444 or *www.british-holidays.co.uk*) have award-winning

parks all around the UK with a choice of fabulous coastal locations.

PARK RESORTS (08701 299 299 or *www.park-resorts.com*) offer the chance to find out about being a lifeguard with their new WaterResorts programme for 2002. Available at all 13 parks, set in coastal locations in England and Wales, the programme is aimed at all abilities.

If you prefer dry land there's plenty of other sports to choose from including football, archery, fencing, aerobics and golf.

WARNER HOLIDAYS (0870 601 6012 or *www.warnerholidays.co.uk*) specialise in holidays for adults, and operate six historic hotels, two character hotels and five classic resorts in country and coastal locations around the UK. Activities and sports vary and include tennis, golf, bowling, archery, clay shooting, swimming, cycling and ballooning.

And if all that leaves you exhausted you can revive yourself in the spa pool, sauna, or steam rooms.

Festival breaks are themed holidays. Shades of Country, for example, allows gusts to grab their stetson and re-live the Nashville dream. Other themes include Rhythm 'n' Blues, Big Band, Jazz and, new for 2002, a Jive Weekend.

HOSEASONS HOLIDAY LODGES AND PARKS (0870 900 9011 or *www.hoseasons.co.uk*).

At the Great Glen Water Park holiday village in Inverness a family of six can experience a week of white-water rafting, windsurfing and water-skiing in August for £585.

Accommodation is self-catering in a three-bedroom Loch Side Lodge.

Harcourt Sands on the Isle of Wight offers tobogganing, abseiling and archery. It costs £699 for a week in August in a Beech caravan that sleeps up to eight people. Return ferry with Wightlink is £65 for a car and passengers.

BUTLINS (0870 242 0870 or *www.Butlins.co.uk*) offer plenty of activity for the whole family with great-value breaks from as little as £32 per person.

Kids can enjoy the freedom of an adult-free zone packed with activities and music. There's something different to do every day of the week, with activities ranging from the Megazone Laser Challenge to the teen-only pool evening in Splash Waterworld. You can also try your hand at basketball and 10-pin bowling.

Younger children can enjoy Fox Kids Clubs and Noddy's Toyland rides. Parents can check out various live entertainment venues. Butlins also feature breaks for adults only, ideal for groups of friends.

Butlins Resorts are at Minehead, Bognor Regis and Skegness.

Source: *Sunday Mirror*, 6 January 2002.

DOMESTIC HOLIDAYS

Domestic holidays are taken within the internal boundaries of a country and involve travel arrangements by domestic carriers and agents. Most domestic holidays are arranged by the traveller on an independent basis. The flexibility to arrange transportation and accommodation without agents is key. Many people choose to travel in their own car which eliminates the need to arrange transportation. Furthermore, the opportunity to stay with friends and relatives removes the need to pay for accommodation.

Inclusive package arrangements in the UK are still not fully utilised by the majority of domestic holiday makers. This will inevitably be an area of change in the future. A number of tour operators have developed holidays within the UK, for example Superbreak and National Express Holidays. This style of holiday reduces the effort of researching travel and accommodation and provides set itineraries, often at a more economical price than independent bookings.

60

Hint: For further information, look on the internet for websites for each *Superbreak* location.

Case Study

Book a break with us and you'll enjoy the very best in service and quality. We'll help you choose a hotel that's ideal for your plans and your budget. You'll get great value for money thanks to our price guarantee. And because we're No.1 for Short Breaks in Britain you are assured quality, value and great service.

Contents

Top attractions to tempt you

NOW OPEN **Eden Project** *the living theatre of plants and people*	49
Alton Towers *excitement, thrills and surprises*	62
Beatles Story *feel the cavern beat*	77
Blackpool Pleasure Beach *the fun capital of Europe*	79
Britannia *the former Royal Yacht*	94
Camelot Theme Park *the magical kingdom*	80
Chessington World of Adventures *for a great day out*	40
Legoland *where the fun is always building*	36
Thorpe Park *featuring Europe's highest water ride*	40

Source: *Superbreak* brochure

INBOUND AND OUTBOUND HOLIDAYS

Client groups can travel into a country (inbound) and then travel out of a country (outbound). Many people travel to a country and then embark on a holiday away from their arrival point. This involves additional travel time. For instance, arriving in the UK and then travelling to the Isle of Wight, Isle of Man or Shetland Isles.

SPECIAL INTEREST HOLIDAYS

Leisure activities have increased both in popularity and in variety and form an important interest or hobby for people. Special interest holidays extend leisure activities into a holiday. Examples include snow sports, golfing and photography holidays.

Individual interests for both pleasure and business are now catered for by tour operators. Painting, drawing, architecture, history, culture, golfing, skiing, visiting health spas and fitness centres are some of the pastimes that appeal to a range of age groups. Client groups tend to concentrate on a certain style of holiday in a specific geographical location, for example, cooking in Tuscany.

Golfing Weekends

Get in the swing of things on one of our Golfing Weekends. These are suitable for all players, with or without club handicaps, and offer you the opportunity to play two rounds on some attractive courses against a variety of partners. The weekends are run as competitions but our experienced tournament organisers will ensure that, as far as possible, you are matched with players of a similar standard. And if you prefer your golf on a friendly basis, bring your own partner and we'll arrange a suitable tee-off time for you.

Summer Concert Breaks

An enchanted evening of glorious classics in stunning surroundings is the highlight of these breaks which are held in a number of hotels throughout the summer. Choose from the Last Night of the Proms in all its stirring splendour or the Fireworks and Laser Concerts, a real feast for all the senses. The package includes nights at a local hotel, transport to and from the concert, reserved seats and a pre-concert barbecue.

Racing Weekends

Enjoy the sport of kings on one of our Racing Weekends. The thrill of the race, the skills of the jockey, the beautiful setting of many of the courses and perhaps the odd flutter; all combined in a weekend to remember. Whether you're a seasoned punter or a complete novice, you'll have the benefit of your guide's years of experience. The weekend includes transport to and from the racecourse and entry to the members' enclosure. We'll even throw in a copy of the *Racing Post* so you can study form over breakfast.

Health Farm Weekends

Deserve some serious pampering? Well, why not try our Health Farm Weekends that invigorate as well as relax. The weekend starts with a full fitness assessment and you'll have plenty of opportunity to take exercise classes and use the gym. And, to help you look as good as you feel, pick up some tips from our resident beautician. Your meals throughout the weekend will feature delicious and health-conscious dishes prepared by our expert chefs.

Figure 1.26

Case Study

Isle of Wight Falconry Courses

The partnership between human and Hawk may be at least 4,000 years old, but it is still very much alive on the Isle of Wight today. Set in an area of outstanding natural beauty The Isle of Wight Owl and Falconry Centre based in the historic Appuldurcombe Estate, run courses in falconry so you too can participate in this noble sport. From the

sloping downland of the Isle of Wight, you can receive expert tuition in this ancient sport, and fly a number of trained Falcons, Hawks and Owls. The history, equipment, and the birds' behaviour, are all covered along with a good lunch!

The weekend can be either non-residential or residential, in one of their top quality, stone built holiday cottages on the estate. Non-participating partners are welcome.

So if you fancy learning more about this ancient art contact Appuldurcombe Heritage today.

Courses available all year	WHEN TO GO
Weekend Courses from £140, including lunch	COST
Appuldurcombe Heritage, Isle of Wight Owl and Falconry Centre Tel: 01983 840188, email: www.appuldurcombe.co.uk, website: UK@appuldurcombe.co.uk	CONTACT

Source: *Global Magazine*

ACTIVITY

1 Describe the type of holiday experience detailed in the case study above.

2 Which age group would take this type of holiday?

3 Look at the extracts from the 'Get Your Kicks' article and the *Superbreak* brochure.

a) Describe the different types of holidays offered.

b) Which methods of travel would be used by people to get to their chosen destinations?

HOLIDAYS INVOLVING SHORT HAUL AND LONG HAUL FLIGHTS

Short haul	Long haul
Cyprus	Brazil
France	Caribbean – Barbados, Jamaica, Dominican Republic, Antigua, St. Lucia
Greece	China
Italy	Cuba
Irish Republic	Ecuador
Netherlands	Malaysia
Portugal	Mexico
Spain	Peru
Turkey	South Africa
	Thailand
	United States of America – New York, Florida, California, New England

Figure 1.27 Popular long haul and short haul destinations   Source: Adapted from Holiday Trends, ABTA

Both types of destination are popular because they provide a different environment to the local one. Travelling abroad reached a peak in the 1990s when it became affordable for the average family to take a holiday outside the UK.

Case Study

Cyprus
ISLAND OF APHRODITE

Tucked away in the eastern corner of the Mediterranean and once a gift from Anthony to Cleopatra, Cyprus has everything from Greek temples and Roman remains to golden beaches, rugged mountains and all-action resorts that stay lively 'til dawn.

Cyprus is the island where, according to legend, the goddess Aphrodite emerged from the sea. With its sandy beaches, rugged cliffs, cool cedar forests, fragrant orange groves and meadows cloaked in wildflowers, she certainly chose a good place to come ashore. A treasure trove for lovers of history, art and culture, there are Stone Age ruins, Greek temples, Roman theatres and Byzantine churches scattered across the island, whilst the 466 miles of coastline offer superb conditions for swimming, sailing or just soaking up the sun. Good buys include delicately woven Cypriot lace and hand turned pottery, and in countless bars and tavernas you'll be welcomed in time-honoured style. Those in search of a more upbeat holiday are in for a treat too, with larger resorts like Ayia Napa now giving the Med's more traditional clubbing meccas a run for their money.

GET AN EYEFUL OF CYPRUS

Beach parties, jeep safaris, bar crawls and cruises ... we'll show you how to holiday in Cyprus! See our Top Ten for details, and book when you arrive. Hiring a car is always popular too – we can organise it for you.

IN THE KNOW

LANGUAGE Greek
CURRENCY Cypriot Pounds
FLIGHT TIME approx 4 hrs from the UK
EATING OUT Typical three course meal without wine £6.20 (salad, moussaka, dessert)
DRINKS Bottle of wine £4.20, glass of beer £1.10
CAR HIRE from £115
FLIGHTS from Gatwick, Luton, Stansted, Exeter, Bristol, Cardiff, Birmingham, East Midlands, Manchester, Liverpool, Leeds/Bradford, Humberside, Teesside, Newcastle, Glasgow, Edinburgh, Aberdeen

Source: *Airtours* brochure

Case Study

Barbados

Floating like an emerald gemstone between the turquoise waters of the Caribbean on one side and the surf-splashed Atlantic Ocean on the other, Barbados must be one of the most sophisticated holiday islands under the sun.

Barbados is an island of fantastic contrasts, epitomised by the difference between the calm, Caribbean waters of the west coast and the energetic waters of the Atlantic in the east. Barbados boasts small picturesque villages and larger, bustling towns dotted with elegant colonial buildings and pastel coloured "chattel" houses.

The north and east coasts are much less developed than the south or the west, with country lanes snaking between fields of sugar cane, and small villages basking in the Caribbean sunshine. The south, on the other hand offers excellent nightlife, with colourful bars and restaurants swaying to the beats of Reggae, Salsa and Merengue until the early hours of the morning.

Temperatures in the 80s year round ensure beautiful beach days and warm evenings, best enjoyed with an ice cold beer or cocktail and a local delicacy such as cou-cou, lobster or flying fish. And if you can tear yourself away from the idyllic beaches, why not treat yourself to a catamaran cruise up the west coast where you can swim with wild turtles, or even a day trip to the paradise islands of the Grenadines?

Local Interest

The local Jazz Festival takes place in January. The Holetown festival in February celebrates the arrival of the first settlers in 1627. March sees the gold Cup Horse Racing at the Garrison and the Holders Festival. The fish festival is over the Easter weekend and the congaline festival rocks through April. The Crop Over, celebrating the end of sugar-cane harvest and the Island's biggest festival, takes place from early July to August. Cricket is the national passion of Bajans and between March and May, Bridgetown can often see the West Indies hosting international test matches. Please contact the Barbados Tourism Authority (UK) for dates/fixtures.

Local Excursions

Unijet can offer a wide range of excursions purchased locally from your representative. Some of the most popular with approximate prices are outlined below:

Jeep Safari   c.£43pp

Explore the scenic interior and rugged coastlines by Land Rover and discover the island's best kept secrets.

Triple Delights

(with Atlantis, Harrison's Cave & Flower Forest)
                                                                 c.£74pp

Discover the wonders of nature with underground springs and natural waterfalls and then dive with the Atlantis submarine, before visiting the tropical flower forest.

The Grenadines

(full day, lunch and drinks included)   c.£215pp

A day like no other, sailing in the paradise islands of The Grenadines. You can also enjoy snorkelling and swimming in this idyllic location.

Catamaran Sailing/Snorkelling with turtles
(lunch and drinks included)   c.£45pp

Imagine yourself gliding across the waves, with the cool breeze on your face, the turquoise waters and turtles at your toes. This luxury cruise takes you along the 'platinum' west coast of Barbados.

Please note that prices are subject to change.

Important Information

Departure Tax: (subject to change). Currently BD$25 (approx. £8) per person payable locally when leaving Barbados.

Climate: For more information please ring Weathercheck on 0901 4 770009. Code: 1228. Calls cost 60p/min at all times.

Flights: Approximate Flight Time – 9 hours (non-stop).

Car Hire: Car Hire can be pre-booked in the UK with Unijet. We have negotiated special low rates to allow you the freedom to see more of Barbados which is ideally suited to car hire and daytime driving. Please ring Reservations for prices and booking conditions.

Time Difference: GMT –4 hrs. BST –5 hrs.

Please note: camouflage-style clothing is prohibited in Barbados.

Barbados Tourism Authority 0207 636 9448; e-mail barbadosuk@aol.com; website www.barbados.org.

Source: *Unijet* brochure

Case Study

Ibiza

Ibiza, the third largest of the Balearic Islands, has a deserved reputation for resorts offering hectic fun and lots of nightlife. But this can also be a wonderful place for a quieter holiday, with excellent beach resorts for all the family, and as much or as little entertainment and nightlife as you want. There are hidden coves tucked away down dusty beach-bound tracks, deep-green pine forests, and wide expanses of soft golden sand. Old Ibiza Town is surrounded by ramparts, with alleys running between old buildings which now also house local residents, bars, discos, boutiques and restaurants. The main beaches tend to have golden sand that shelves gently into the sea.

Fly from	
Birmingham	Liverpool
Bristol	Luton
Cardiff	Manchester
East Midlands	Newcastle
Gatwick	Stansted
Glasgow	

Resort Information

Language: Spanish

Currency: Euro

Time Difference: +1hr GMT

Average flight time: 2hrs 30mins

Prices from (approx): bottle of house wine £4.50, pint of beer £1.65, 3-course meal £7.50

Go and see:
• rocks of Formentera's headland
• Ibiza Town: Dalt Vila • San Miguel Caves
• The sunset in Cala d'Hort Bay

Best for:
Nightlife • San Antonio • Playa d'en Bossa
Tranquillity • Cala Llonga
History and Culture • Ibiza Town
Picturesque • Portinatx

For further information on Ibiza please contact the Spanish Tourist Office on 020 7486 8077.

Source: *Thomas Cook Tour Operations UK*

Read carefully the Case Studies on Cyprus, Barbados and Ibiza.

1 What type of holiday is advertised for each country?

2 What type of customers would be attracted to the holiday and why?

3 Of these three destinations, which are long haul and which short haul? How can you tell?

4 List the appeal of each country under the following headings:

a) natural attractions

b) built attractions.

✹ ✹ ✹ PLUS

Cidade de Goa

Central Goa — Vainguinim Beach

The Cidade de Goa offers a combination of elegance, true comfort and Goan charm. Its luxuriant gardens, separated from the beach by only a fringe of palm trees, overlooking the bay, is great for watching romantic sunsets across the Arabian Sea.

Location
- Situated directly on Vainguinim beach
- Complimentary shuttle service to Panjim (twice a day, morning & evening)

Facilities
- Attractive swimming pool; paddling pool; sun terrace; free towels and sunloungers • Miramar air-conditioned buffet restaurant; Alfama à la carte restaurant; open-air Fan Tan Chinese restaurant; barbecue restaurant; Lagoa Azul poolside coffee shop; lobby coffee shop • Lobby bar with sea-lounge; air-conditioned sports bar; poolside bar; flag service by pool and beach • Shopping arcade; Ayurvedic massage centre • 24 hour reception

✹ ✹ ✹

Maayafushi Island Resort

The Maldives — Ari Atoll

Maayafushi Island Resort is surrounded by crystal clear water and fringed by a white sandy beach. This traditional Maldivian style island resort offers good standard accommodation whilst maintaining a relaxed, informal and friendly atmosphere.

Location
- On the white sandy beach

Facilities
- Restaurant; main bar; coffee shop with TV
- Reception; souvenir shop

✹ ✹ ✹ PLUS

Dreams Beach Resort

The Red Sea — Sharm el Sheikh

Situated on the cliff of Ras Um El-Sid, the Dreams Beach Resort has clear views of Tiran Island. It has an international atmosphere and offers a good standard of accommodation.

Location
- Set above an artificial sandy beach area with sunloungers, parasols and beach bar (guests can only get into sea across a jetty to protect the shoreline coral); 7km from Naama Bay
- 5km from Sharm el Sheikh town and harbour
- Free shuttle to Naama Bay (4 times per day)

Facilities
- Five pools including diving pool; sun terrace; parasols; swim-up bar in main pool; whirlpool • Main buffet-style restaurant; poolside pizzeria • Fish restaurant on beach; Pub/disco; Beach bar; 'Love Boat' bar/restaurant; lounge area with bar • 24 hour reception; money exchange facilities • Egyptian shisha corner; shops; bank; aviary

✹ ✹ ✹ PLUS

Neptune Paradise Village

Kenya — South Mombasa Coast

The Neptune Paradise Village is a large complex composed of cottages scattered in 25 acres of tropical gardens. Situated just off the main coastal road, it is a lively property with a welcoming and relaxing atmosphere, which is popular with the European market & offers excellent facilities to cater for the needs of a wide range of holidaymakers.

Location
- On Diani beach • Restaurants and bars 500m away; discos and main nightlife 5km away; 7km to resort centre • 7km from Leisure Lodge golf course

Facilities
- Four swimming pools - two kidney-shaped, two free-form; sun terraces with sunloungers and parasols; two swim-up pool bars • Two main buffet restaurants; two grill restaurants • Two bars; small lounge with satellite TV • 24 hour reception; souvenir shop; boutique

Figure 1.28

Source: *JMC Holiday Dealz* brochure

ACTIVITY

1   Locate the destinations opposite on a world map.

2   Compare the facilities and services available at each destination.

Extension Exercise

Explain why some destinations isolate tourists from the local population.

67

Sightseeing

England
1. Arnside and Silverdale
2. Blackdown Hills
3. Cannock Chase
4. Chichester Harbour
5. Chilterns
6. Cornwall
7. Cotswolds
8. Cranbourne Chase and West Wiltshire Downs
9. Dedham Vale
10. Dorset
11. East Devon
12. East Hampshire
13. Forest of Bowland
14. High Weald
15. Howardian Hills
16. Isle of Wight
17. Isles of Scilly
18. Kent Downs
19. Lincolnshire Wolds
20. Malvern Hills
21. Mendip Hills
22. Nidderdale
23. Norfolk Coast
24. North Devon
25. North Pennines
26. Northumberland Coast
27. North Wessex Downs
28. Quantock Hillls
29. Shropshire Hills
30. Solway Coast
31. South Devon
32. South Hampshire Coast
33. Suffolk Coast and Heaths
34. Surrey Hills
35. Sussex Downs
36. Tamar Valley
37. Wye Valley (England and Wales)

Wales
37. Wye Valley (England and Wales)
38. Anglesey
39. Clwydian Range
40. Gower
41. Lleyn

Figure 1.29   Areas of Outstanding Natural Beauty

Some Lake it hot

MOUNTAIN peaks in crystal clear air filled the horizon and, between ancient woods and stone walls, I could see a sparkling lake from my picture window.

Windermere has a variety of local attractions and facilities for sports both on and off the water. There's sailing, canoeing, bowling, tennis and golf nearby. Windermere Lake Cruises offer a range of idyllic trips with services and connections to many local attractions.

The Lake District Visitor Centre at Brockhole is situated on the shore of the lake in landscaped gardens and has lots to see whatever the weather.

Source: *Mirror Travel*, 12 January 2002.

Sightseeing can be classified as:

a) taking a day trip to see an attraction/place.
b) taking a tour around an area which includes places of interest and sights, e.g. the Lake District.

Sightseeing can incorporate built attractions as well as natural attractions. The UK has a culture preserved in its history. This continues to be of interest to all groups of people, irrespective of age, gender or culture. The National Trust owns many historical properties.

What is the National Trust?

The National Trust was founded in 1895 to protect the best of our heritage for ever. It is not a government department, but an independent charity with a membership open to all. It relies on thousands of volunteers who help in every aspect of the Trust's work. Every visit you make to a National Trust property is a donation to the work of the charity.

Today the Trust protects 350 houses and gardens, over 580 miles of coastline and more than 275,000 hectares *(690,000 acres)* of countryside – all preserved for present and future generations to enjoy.

Ham House

Ham, Richmond TW10 7RS
Tel: 020 8940 1950. Email:
shhgen@smtp.ntrust.org.uk

* Outstanding Stuart house on the banks of the Thames, at the heart of Civil War politics and Restoration court intrigue.
* Lavish 17th-century interiors with spectacular and rare collections of original furnishings and paintings.
* Extensive and beautiful 17th-century formal gardens with famous Cherry Garden parterre.
* Delightful tea-room in 17th-century Orangery.

Open: House: 23 Mar to 3 Nov: daily except Thur & Fri 1–5. Garden: all year, daily except Thur & Fir 11–6 *(or dusk if earlier)*. Closed 25/26 Dec & 1 Jan. No dogs in garden please.

Admission: House: £6, family ticket £15. Garden only: £2, family ticket £5.

Location: On S bank of Thames, W of A307, at Petersham. *Station:* Richmond Mainline and Underground; *Bus:* 371 from Richmond Station; *Walk:* 1½ ml via Thames towpath.

Sutton House

2 & 4 Homerton High Street, Hackney E9 6JQ
E-mail suttonhouse@smtp.ntrust.org.uk
Tel: 020 8986 2264 *(information & admission)*

* A unique survival in London's East End, built in 1535 by Ralph Sadleir, a rising star at the court of Henry VIII.
* Although altered over the years, it remains an essentially Tudor house with oak-panelled rooms and carved fireplaces.
* An exhibition tells the history of the house and its former occupants.
* Changing shows of contemporary art, concerts, craft fairs and other events.
* Brick Place Café open most of the year.

Open: Historic rooms: (from 27 Feb 2002) Fri–Sat 1–5.30, Sun, BH Mon & Tues 4 Jun 11.30–5.30 (last admission 5pm). Shop, Art Gallery, Brick Place Café: Sun, BH Mon & Tues 4 Jun 11.30–5. Sun, BH Mons and Tues 4 June 2–5. Art Gallery opens as historic rooms.

Admission: £2.10, child 50p, family £4.70.

Location: At the corner of Isabella Road and Homerton High Street. *Bus:* Frequent services from central London (tel. 020 7222 1234). *Station:* Hackney Central ¼ ml; Hackney Downs ½ ml. Room for six cycles on railings outside property.

Osterley Park

Jersey Road, Isleworth, Middlesex TW7 4RB
Tel: 01494 755566 *(Infoline)* Tel/Fax: 020 8232 5050 *(Office)*
Email osterley@smtp.ntrust.org.uk

* Originally a Tudor mansion, Osterley Park House was transformed in the eighteenth century by Robert Adam into an elegant neoclassical villa for the founders of Childs Bank.
* The spectacular interiors contain one of Britain's most complete examples of Adam's work and include exceptional plasterwork, carpets and furniture.
* The magnificent sixteenth century stables survive largely intact and are still in use.
* Set in 300 acres of landscaped park and farmland with ornamental lakes, woodland walks and Pleasure Grounds.
* Contemporary art exhibitions in the Jersey Galleries open as house.

Open: House: 2–24 March: Sat & Sun; 27 Mar to 3 Nov: daily except Mon & Tues *(closed Good Fri but open BH Mons and Tues 4 June)*. Times: 1–4.30
Jersey Galleries: as House, Grand Stables: Sun afternoons in summer. Park & Pleasure Grounds: all year 9–7.30 or sunset if earlier.

Admission: House £4.40; child £2.20; family £11.
Park & Pleasure Grounds free. Car park £2.50.

Location: Follow brown tourist signs on A4 between Gillette Corner and Osterley Underground station *(access via Thornbury Road & Jersey Road)*; M4, Jn3. Cycle racks in stableyard. *Bus:* LT H28 Hounslow-Osterley, LT H91 Hounslow-Hammersmith, both not Sun, to within ½ ml *(tel. 020 7222 1234)*. *Station:* Syon Lane 1½ ml. *Underground:* Piccadilly Line, Osterley (turn left on leaving station ½ ml).

Source: The National Trust

ACTIVITY

Read the extracts on page 68 and complete the table:

Name of National Trust property	What is there to see?	How can you travel there?
Ham House		
Sutton House		
Osterley Park		

Visiting an Attraction

Case Study

British Airways London Eye

The world's largest and most awe-inspiring observation wheel. Situated in the heart of London, this beautifully designed 135 metre structure will take you on an unique experience. The capsules rotate smoothly through 360 degrees, providing spectacular views for over 25 miles in all directions* throughout the 30 minute 'flight'. (*Subject to weather conditions). **160 miles** – 2 adult admissions **120 miles** – 2 child admissions (5–15 yrs, under 5 yrs free). Children under 16 years of age must be accompanied by an adult over 18 years. Children under 5 years go free, but do need to be pre-booked – please mention if you have any under 5s in your group at the time of booking (see below for booking information).

PLEASE NOTE: Due to the popularity of this attraction, we strongly recommend that you pre-book your 'flight' to avoid disappointment by calling **0870 400 3040** in advance of your intended visit. A charge of 50 pence per person applies to this pre-booking facility and is payable on the day you visit this attraction. All bookings are subject to AIR MILES 'flight' availability. Once you have made your booking with the London Eye, it is non-changeable and non-refundable. The booking fee is also non-refundable. See Terms and Conditions at the back of this leaflet for pre-booking information. Attraction is closed on Christmas Day and New Years Eve, and 1–27 January 2002 inclusive.

ACTIVITY

Read the London Eye Case Study above.

1 What does the attraction offer to the visitor to see?

2 Which age groups would you recommend to visit the attraction?

Case Study

Tate Modern

Tate Modern is Britain's new national museum of modern art.

Housed in the former Bankside Power Station, Tate Modern displays the Tate collection of international modern art from 1900 to the present day, including major works by Dali, Picasso, Matisse, Rothko and Warhol as well as contemporary work by artists such as Dorothy Cross, Gilbert & George and Susan Hiller.

There is also a full range of special exhibitions and a broad public programme of events throughout the year.

Bankside Power Station has been transformed into Tate Modern by the Swiss architects Herzog & de Meuron. The former Turbine hall, running the whole length of the vast building, now marks a breathtaking entrance to the gallery. From here visitors are swept up by escalator through two floors featuring a café, shop and auditorium to three levels of galleries. At the top of the building is a new two storey glass roof which not only provides natural light into the galleries on the top floors, but also houses a stunning café offering outstanding views across London.

Source: Text taken from www.tate.org.uk © Tate, March 2003.

ACTIVITY

1 Where is the Tate Modern located?

2 What attractions are offered at the Tate Modern?

3 What facilities are offered at the Tate Modern?

4 Which age groups would visit the Tate Modern and why?

Guided tours are popular with sightseeing visitors and can be taken when visiting attractions of historical, economical, social, political or cultural interest. A number of organised guided tours may be available at an attraction. Overseas visitors are provided with guides or audio tapes when taking a tour.

Talk about...

1 Which ethnic groups are represented in your school/college?

2 Do these groups have friends and relatives in long haul destinations?

Visiting Friends and Relatives

This is an important part of many cultures. Visiting friends and relatives often involves travelling long distances. People who choose to visit friends and relatives often combine this type of holiday with a visit to local attractions. Many long haul flights have become dependent on the visiting friends and relatives market, e.g. flights from the UK to India, Canada, Australia, Middle East, China and Hong Kong.

Study the Airline Network advertisement.

1   Identify the short haul destinations.

2   Which long haul destinations are popular for the V.F.R. market?

Figure 1.30   'Airline Network' advertisement

Extension Exercise

1   Identify the ancillary services offered by the Airline Network.
2   How does the company offer consumer protection?

Going to a Sports Event as a Spectator or to Participate

Sports events are very much part of the leisure industry, but they now cover part of the travel and tourism industry. As a leisure pastime, people choose to spectate in a range of sporting events, for example:

◆ tennis at Wimbledon
◆ rugby at Twickenham
◆ horse racing at Aintree
◆ golf at The Belfry
◆ cricket at the Oval or Lords
◆ football at Cardiff Millennium Stadium.

People also participate in a number of sporting events during their leisure time. This participation inevitably involves travelling from one area to another on a temporary basis. Sporting events often take people outside the UK to long and short haul destinations, for instance to see the Grand Prix, Ryder Cup, World Cup or the Olympics.

ACTIVITY

Select one overseas sporting event and describe:

a) the choice of transport available to the venue

b) whether customers usually select the fastest or cheapest method to travel.

Business

Travelling for business, conferences and courses is an important part of a businessperson's job. Cities hold major conferencing events. Conference centres in hotels in London, Birmingham, Manchester, Glasgow and Cardiff, for example, are equipped to cater for the requirements of large business meetings and conferences. They have conferencing services and the facilities to cater for large numbers.

Case Study

Malaysia Airlines Business Traveller

A FIRST CLASS SEAT FOR A BUSINESS CLASS FARE

If you have already flown Malaysia Airlines Golden Club Class you'll know why the levels of service are renowned among business travellers. However, you now have the opportunity to experience our luxurious First Class service. All you have to do is pay for a full fare Golden Club Class ticket and travel before 31st March 2003 and you'll fly First Class all the way.

You'll enjoy all the benefits, including chauffeur drive to the airport, dedicated check-in, and await your flight in the comfort of our exclusive First Class lounge.

On board, you can stretch out on near-horizontal First Class sleeper seats, sample the vintage champagne, classic wines and some of the world's finest cuisine, or watch your choice of the latest films and TV programmes on your video-on-demand entertainment system. Or if you really must get down to some serious business our unbeatable in-flight 'Office in the Sky' includes fax and telephone facilities. All this plus the attentive service of our dedicated cabin crew – now proud holders of Skytracks 'Best Cabin Staff 2002' award.

Malaysia Airlines flies 21 times a week non-stop from the UK to Kuala Lumpur with fast convenient connections throughout the Far-East and Australasia.

So on your next business trip to Malaysia or beyond fly in a class of your own – choose Malaysia Airlines. **Going beyond expectations.**

Source: *Travelplus*

Case Study

British Midland Business Traveller

Flying transatlantic in the business

For passengers travelling in **the business**, the bmi experience begins the moment our dedicated team whisk you through the priority check-in and fast-track security to await your flight in the lounge. The business is quite simply in a class of its own. On board, you can look forward to the sort of service you might normally find in first class. And all at the normal range of discounted business class fares.

- access to business lounges in both the UK & US. The lounges offer complimentary drinks and a range of magazines and newspapers. The business lounges are equipped with a range of business facilities allowing you the flexibility to carry on working or to simply relax before your flight
- priority check-in & fast track security procedures
- a welcoming glass of champagne
- relax in luxurious, ergonomically designed sleeper seats with 60 inches of legroom and a recline of 160 degrees
- work (if you must) with laptop power, telephones, and dataports at each seat

And, when the work is done, sit back and enjoy our state-of-the-art entertainment:
- choose from 11 movie and nine television channels played through 9-inch armrest-mounted screens
- play the latest Nintendo games and classic PC games
- spin through sixteen audio channels
- or just shut out the world with our noise-cancelling headsets
- then take your pick from a full and varied selection of modern, international cuisine akin to the very best restaurant food, prepared by a fully qualified on-board chef
- on return to Manchester, come back to earth gently with a complimentary arrivals package of shower, gym, swim, coffee and croissant at The Radisson SAS Hotel, Manchester.

Since our early years, bmi british midland has provided business travellers with a service that is convenient, comfortable and cost-effective. By easing the travel process, we can help to improve the effectiveness of your working day. To make a booking, simply phone our Sales Centre or make your booking online. We appreciate the value of your time and the punctual departure of the aircraft is an integral part of our customer service. After safety, our priority is to get you to your chosen destination on time.

Lounges

Business lounge

Customers who present an International business boarding pass, regardless or what Star Carrier they fly, have access to all partners' designated business class departure lounges (guests are not permitted).

Star Alliance Gold card holder

Star Alliance Gold card holders and one guest have access to any lounge that is identified with a Star Alliance Gold lounge sign when departing on a Star Alliance flight.

Exclusive lounge facilities for diamond club members

Diamond club silver and gold card members may take one guest into bmi british midland lounges (subject to capacity), provided guest is travelling on the same bmi british midland flight. Third party executive lounges are not accessible to guests. We regret that children are not permitted in the diamond club lounges.

Source: www.flybmi.com

ACTIVITY

1   Read the case studies. List the facilities and services provided for the business traveller.

	Facilities	Services
Malaysia Airlines business traveller		
British Midland business traveller		

2   Investigate facilities available for business travel in a large hotel in your area.

Tourist generating areas: a tourist generating area is a country or location within a country from which tourists leave to travel to other locations. Examples of tourist generating countries in Europe are Sweden, Italy, France and the United Kingdom.

Tourist receiving areas: these are countries or destinations within countries that receive visitors. Examples of tourist receiving countries in Europe are the United Kingdom, Spain, Greece and Portugal.

Extension Exercise

1   Look at the diagram and provide an explanation.

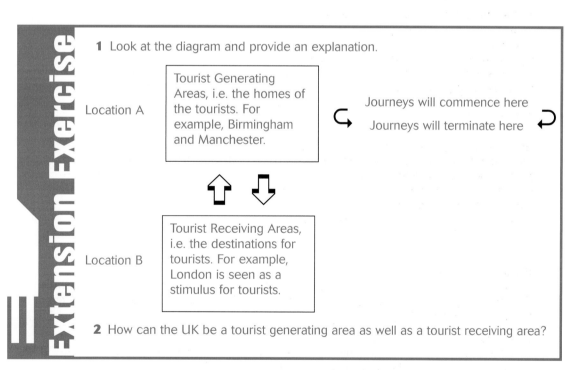

Location A — Tourist Generating Areas, i.e. the homes of the tourists. For example, Birmingham and Manchester.

Journeys will commence here
Journeys will terminate here

Location B — Tourist Receiving Areas, i.e. the destinations for tourists. For example, London is seen as a stimulus for tourists.

2   How can the UK be a tourist generating area as well as a tourist receiving area?

The Key Components of the Travel and Tourism Industry

Since the term 'travel and tourism' covers an enormous range of activities in a wide variety of situations, it is useful to divide the industry into key components that you will need to know about.

QCA

You will need to know that there are seven key components of the travel and tourism industry.

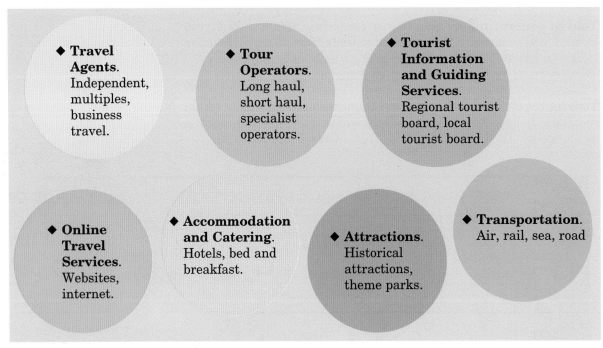

- **Travel Agents**. Independent, multiples, business travel.
- **Tour Operators**. Long haul, short haul, specialist operators.
- **Tourist Information and Guiding Services**. Regional tourist board, local tourist board.
- **Online Travel Services**. Websites, internet.
- **Accommodation and Catering**. Hotels, bed and breakfast.
- **Attractions**. Historical attractions, theme parks.
- **Transportation**. Air, rail, sea, road

Figure 1.31 Key components of travel and tourism

The UK travel and tourism industry is structured to embrace the following groups of people who travel:

- **domestic visitors:** the term domestic is applied to a person's own country. In the context of the UK population, domestic tourism is a UK resident taking a holiday or sightseeing trip within the UK. **Example:** Mr and Mrs Glyn and their children Daniel and Jacquita live in Hampton Court, Surrey and will be travelling to Bristol to visit their in-laws. They will also be taking in the sights at Cheddar Gorge and stopping off at Weston Super Mare to see the historic church at Uphill. As the Glyns are UK residents and travelling from Hampton Court, they are classed as domestic visitors and are undertaking domestic tourism.
- **incoming visitors** are those who choose the UK as a holiday destination and travel from countries outside the UK (countries in North and South America, Africa, Australasia, Asia and elsewhere in Europe) are known as incoming visitors as they are travelling into the United Kingdom.

Example: Isabel Elia from Pamplona, Spain will be spending Christmas in London and will be staying at the Savoy Hotel in London. As Isabel's main residence is in Spain and she will be travelling to London, she is classed as an incoming visitor and undertaking inbound tourism.

◆ **outbound visitors** are UK residents who take short haul and long haul holidays outside the United Kingdom are referred to as outbound visitors undertaking outbound tourism.

Example: Mr and Mrs Botham and Alex, 9, will be travelling to Florida during the Easter holidays. They are resident in the UK and will be undertaking a journey to a destination outside the UK. This is classed as outbound tourism and in this context, they are referred to as outbound visitors.

QUESTION

1 Which countries have the highest number of visitors to the UK from:
   a) Europe
   b) the rest of the world?

2 List the 5 most popular places to visit in
   a) London
   b) the UK.

Hint: Use the internet to search for answers

Principals are organisations providing transportation, accommodation and ancillary services:

◆ transportation i.e. air, rail, sea, road travel
◆ accommodation i.e. hotels, camp/caravan sites, guest houses
◆ guiding services, travel insurance, car hire

ACTIVITY

Complete the following table.

You will need to use the internet to find examples of principals operating in the United Kingdom.

Principal		UK Principal
Transportation	Air	British Airways
	Rail	
	Sea	
	Road	
Accommodation	Hotel	Thistle
	Guest Houses	
	Campsites	
	Caravan sites	
Ancillary Services	Car Hire	Hertz
	Travel Insurance	
	Guiding Services	

Key components

Tour operators provide a service for domestic incoming and outbound tourists. They provide a package holiday made up of accommodation, transportation and ancillary services. They usually advertise these in brochures. Customers can book either directly with the tour operator via telephone or the internet or through a travel agent.

Travel agents provide a service for domestic incoming and outbound tourists. They provide a service from many high street locations across the United Kingdom. They document the requirements of visitors and make suggestions on tour operators that may be used to fulfil the needs of the customer and book holidays for customers.

Tourist information and guiding services provide up to date information on tourist areas and tourist attractions. They hold information leaflets, maps, books, posters, slides, postcards and souvenirs and are also able to give information on accommodation and transportation.

Online travel services provide a service for people who have access to the internet and websites to gain information directly from tour operators as well as online travel organisations. Such a service is convenient for working people who are unable to get information through other means during office hours. Accessing travel services through an online facility can often reduce the cost of a holiday as up to date deals are available. Budget airlines have been particularly successful online.

Accommodation embraces a wide range of facilities. Some examples include hotels, bed and breakfasts, guest houses and caravan sites. Accommodation can be serviced (meals and a housekeeping service are provided) or self-catering (visitors cater for themselves).

Catering services provide a range of food and beverages. Catering outlets include fast food chains, cafés, bars, public houses and restaurants.

Attractions can be purpose built or natural attractions. The term has expanded in meaning to include a range of attractions in the retail and entertainment industries including retail parks, shopping complexes, multiplex cinemas and theatre venues.

Transportation includes modes of travel by road (bus, coach, taxi), air, sea and rail. Transport is a significant component within the travel and tourism industry.

1   List two examples of each component from your local area.

2   Which is the 'newest' key component of the travel and tourism industry?

3   Explain why this component has been added.

4   Complete the following table using the internet and/or travel brochures.

	Key component
Lunn Poly	
Going Places	
Superbreaks	
National Express Holidays	
Big Bus Company	
Evans and Evans	
London Tourist Board	
Cumbrian Tourist Board	
Concierge.com	
Ebookers.com	
Insight	
Thistles	
Novotel	
British Midland	
Virgin Trains	
Tower of London	

5   What is the relationship between the key components?

Modes of Transport

You will need to know that people use a wide range of methods of transport to get to their chosen destination. In addition, different types of transport are used to travel around the area visited.

There are relative merits, in terms of cost and convenience and availability, of each method of transport.

ACTIVITY

Method of travel	Examples	Relative merits in terms of cost	Relative merits in terms of convenience	Relative merits in terms of availability
AIR	British Airways British Midland Virgin easyJet buzz	Competitive	Quick Efficient Operational at most airports	Flights scheduled throughout the day
RAIL				
SEA				
ROAD				
a) Bus				
b) Coach				
c) Car				
d) Taxi				

Complete the above table. The first example has been completed for you.

Social, Economic and Environmental Impacts of Travel and Tourism

There are a variety of tourism destinations across the UK which are popular with both UK and overseas visitors. The social, economic and environmental impact of tourism needs to be considered so that tourist destinations may be developed in a sustainable manner.

For example:
♦ in harmony with the environment, preventing the degradation of landscapes, erosion and pollution of locations and the destruction of natural habitats
♦ to be socially acceptable to the needs of the host population so that conflict of interest is reduced
♦ to be beneficial to the local needs of people in terms of employment and generating income within the area.

Car-free tourism and leisure is being promoted to ensure that tourism is based on sustainable management. Ecotourism and green tourism are examples of sustainable tourism management.

The increasing demand generated by people for travel and tourism activity results in positive and negative impacts. Impacts can be social, economic or environmental.

Social: Positive Impacts

1 Increased investment in the local area improves the local infrastructure which benefits the local community through improved services, amenities and facilities.
2 Employment opportunities provide jobs with a regular income and improve the quality of life of the local community.
3 Visitors bring their norms, values and traditions raising awareness of other cultural and religious groups and resulting in shared understanding.

Social: Negative Impacts

1 Prices increase in retail outlets due to increase demand generated by the tourists.
2 Land values and house prices increase pushing local people out of the area.
3 The environment changes to meet the needs of the tourists, disrupting local communities.

Ban the extremists

Like extremists of any kind, the extreme traveller is the most selfish and despicable of all. Aid agencies in Afghanistan have complained that extreme travellers are taking up valuable resources – blagging their way on to aid planes and trucks to get around a country plagued by lack of infrastructure.

Maya Catsanis of Lonely Planet says the company has decided against publishing a guide book to the country because now is not the time to encourage tourists to go there.

'Extreme travellers are taking a big personal security risk and could be having a negative impact on the communities they visit. While they may simply be curious, their adventure could be sapping resources which are badly needed elsewhere,' says Maya.

Source: *Observer* 17 November 2002

Economic: Positive Impacts

1 The travel and tourism industry generates significant income to an area and to the country (through balance of payments).
2 Employment opportunities increase creating jobs for the local community and providing economic stability.

A belief in ethical travel is the guiding force behind Tribes Travel, which began in 1995 as nothing more than a name. Amanda Marks was then an overland truck driver with the tour operator Dragoman, and as she gazed out to sea on a holiday cruise, the name Tribes Travel popped into her head.

"I had no intention of starting my own tour company," she admits, 'but once the name existed, I began to wonder what kind of company I would have, if I had one. Where would it go, what would it do? Having thought about it some more, I handed in my notice and decided to give it a go."

Marks's passion was for "fair-trade travel", which quickly won Tribes a "Most Responsible Tour Operator" award from Tourism Concern in 1999. And later this month Tribes will be presented with the British Airways Tourism for Tomorrow award for tourism organisation of 2002. The BA awards recognise and encourage responsibility to community and environment in the tourist industry.

"The one complaint from people on overland trips was that you didn't get to know the local people," Marks says. "I decided that with Tribes the point would be that you did get to know them, and that I would only employ local people and only work with ground operators who respected local cultures, put something back into them, and paid fair wages."

Source: *The Times*, 16 November 2002

Economic: Negative Impacts

1 The seasonal nature of much of the industry can create instability. Some people employed in the industry find work severely limited in the winter months when visitor numbers can be low or attractions are closed.
2 A decline in visitor numbers due to terrorist attacks and other disasters can cause economic instability.

Environmental: Positive Impacts

1 A growing awareness of tourism management and sustainable tourism is evident.
2 The use of local raw materials, which are sustainable resources, for buildings.

Tourism with a conscience in Port Antonio, Jamaica

Mockingbird Hill hotel, which has won a string of awards for its environmental policies, was opened nine years ago by Shireen Aga and Barbara Walker. It has just ten rooms set in lush grounds on a hillside a few miles outside Port Antonio. My room was simply decorated, with bamboo rather than hardwood furniture, and had a fan but no air con, which I prefer. As well as the usual notes exhorting me to use as little water as possible and to switch off the lights, there was a basket for paper waste, which is recycled by a local co-operative into the hotel's stationery and menu cards.

Breakfasts are terrific: Shireen brought in four home-made preserves, including sour orange marmalade and tamarind jam, and warm breads: coconut, sunflower, wholewheat, plus banana scones. A huge fruit platter, perfect poached eggs and really good coffee (Jamaican, of course), had set us up for the walk that morning.

Shireen, originally from India, and Barbara, who's Jamaican, work with Valley Hikes, because, they told me, they are keen to encourage guests to get out of the hotel and explore the area.

They are forceful characters, much involved with the local community through projects such as improving adult literacy: "We're often perceived to be two crazy women on the hill," joked Barbara.

Their years in Germany, some of which Shireen spent working in the Body Shop, account in part for their environmental concerns.

"One of our biggest problems is plastic," said Shireen. "There's no proper recycling on the island for that. We ask our guests to take it home with them." Once a drinks manufacturer changes from recyclable glass bottles to using plastic, Barbara and Shireen stop using them.

Source: *The Times*, 16 November 2002

Environmental: Negative Impacts

1 The development of tourism has been badly managed in the past and has had detrimental effects on the landscape and historic and cultural sites.
2 The destruction and elimination of natural habitats through the development of tourism.

Greece told to clean up its act

GREECE is no longer the word, according to worried tour operators. Dirty beaches, overbuilding, price hikes, rape attacks and rave resorts are damaging the country's reputation, *writes Steve Keenan*.

Yet despite warnings, the Greek National Tourist office has said that the future of tourism is more big resort hotels.

The number of British holidaymakers to Greece levelled off this summer, and the country cannot afford to be complacent, according to Noel Josephides, managing director of Sunvil Holidays.

"This was the first summer in 30 years that we did not have a single incident of hotel overbooking. Nothing is ever full now."

Holidaymakers have a widening choice, said Abhi Dighé, a director of Kosmar Holidays, the biggest operator to Greece. He criticised slipping standards. "In Portugal and Spain, the beaches are raked overnight. People there still leave cans and rubbish – but in the morning they come back to a clean beach. This has to happen in Greece as well.

"People don't want to clear away rubbish and take it to an overflowing bin before they put their towels down. It is not luxury that people are looking for, just quality and safety."

One Kosmar client wrote to the company this summer describing Greece as "paradise – but paradise run down and uncared for".

Headlines about attacks on British holidaymakers in Corfu, and the excesses of rave resorts featured in television documentaries have added to the malaise, said Josephides. He called for the "ghettos" of Faliraki (Rhodes), Kavos (Corfu) and Malia (Crete) to be "fenced in".

Josephides told an audience of Greek tourism professionals that when he asked his staff to describe their image of the country, many still spoke of old women in black, donkeys, tavernas and blue water bays.

He also said that the World Tourism Organisation had urged European governments to halt investment in hotel development on the Mediterranean for three years.

The chairman of the UK office of the GNTO, Panos Argyros, said: "We have always to improve."

Source: *The Times*, 16 November 2002

ACTIVITY

1   Look at the case studies on pages 20, 41 and 47–9 and complete the following table:

Case study	Geographical location	Type of destination	Age group attracted	Potential social, economic and environmental impacts of the development of tourism in the area
Blackpool				
Snowdonia				
Kennet & Avon Canal				
Manchester				
Alton Towers				
Blenheim Palace				

2   Describe how tourism can damage an area's local environment.

3   Describe ways in which this damage could be prevented or minimised.

The Negative Impact of External Factors on the Travel and Tourism Industry

External factors and events that occur outside the industry itself, both nationally and internationally, can have an adverse affect on travel and tourism.

FOOT AND MOUTH

The outbreak of the foot and mouth disease in cattle in 2001 prevented many people gaining access to the UK countryside 'common' and park areas. Many attractions in rural environments also experienced closure. This has had an adverse effect on leisure activities, forcing people to seek alternatives. The effects have been:

- Businesses related to countryside or rural areas declining or closing
- No access by the general public

During last year's foot and mouth crisis, with images of burning cattle pyres on every news bulletin, attention focused first and foremost on the plight of farmers. Then, as footpaths and country attractions closed, the devastating impact on tourism businesses became apparent. In fact, the foot and mouth epidemic has affected every level of the rural economy, tourism and farming standing at the base of pyramiding networks of local companies providing goods and services, all of which have seen turnover plummet in the last 12 months.

The National Trust, which owns tenant farms as well as country houses, was forced to close many of its properties during the epidemic. This hit the Trust hard: at one stage a loss of £10 million for 2001 was predicted. 'We managed to claw things back with the help of visitors and members, so in comparison with someone running a small B&B we've not been as badly hit,' says Trust spokesperson Sian Evans. 'But whether our houses are open or not has a knock-on effect on the whole rural economy: for every one person we employ directly another nine local hobs depend on the house being open.'

In many ways the epidemic has only brought into focus much longer term problems with rural economies: 'We have to work hard to get visitors: 20 years ago there was nothing to do on a Sunday – plus there's the problem of how do you get to the countryside if you don't have a car?'

Source: *Marketingbusiness*, March 2002.

Figure 1.32 Marketing the countryside

TERRORIST ATTACKS

The events of September 11th 2001 cannot be underestimated. Four planes crashed after terrorist hijackings and all of the passengers and thousands of workers were killed. Two of these planes crashed into the World Trade Center in New York. As a result, the US and its allies declared war on terrorism and attacked the Taliban regime in Afghanistan. There were repercussions across the world, affecting industries throughout the UK and worldwide and the types of activities undertaken by people after this event.

These included:

◆ reduced travel on long haul and short haul routes
◆ visitor numbers to attractions decreasing
◆ the viability of some organisations becoming questionable
◆ people preferring to travel locally
◆ people travelling in small groups
◆ people travelling by car to avoid public transport.

PROFITS OF DOOM

AIRLINES

BA lost £48m in the week following the attacks. It axed 7,200 jobs and 10% of flights after transatlantic bookings slumped by a third. British Midland got rid of 600 jobs and eight aircraft to reduce capacity by 20%. Virgin Atlantic announced 1,200 job losses. More than 350 will go at GE Aircraft Engine Services.

HOLIDAYS

Bookings for winter and summer 2002 foreign hols are down by 30%. First Choice has cut 1,100 jobs. Its share price fell from £1.30 to 87p. Airtours axed up to 200 staff. Britannia Airways is set to lose 300. Thomas Cook will lose 370.

THEATRES

West End bookings are 13% down. The Lion King and The Graduate, usually sell-outs, had seats to spare.

HOTELS

Many hotels in the capital are barely half full. The Hilton group of hotels has cut 600 jobs after bookings fell by 20% during September. Shares fell 12% from 226p to 200p.

INSURANCE

The attacks will cost insurers over £100bn, much of that underwritten in London. Premiums for homes, and car policies could now rise. Many household names have lost value. Britannic shares, for example, fell from 872p on the day of the attacks to 774p yesterday.

TOURISM

The urge to stay at home will put 75,000 tourism jobs at risk. Overseas visitors were expected to spend nearly £13bn this year. It is now likely to be down 20% to £10.8bn.

LEISURE

FEWER people are eating out. Pizza Express shares fell from £8.70 on Sept 11 to £7.77 this week. Casinos are hit as high-rolling Middle East clients stay away. Cancellation of golf's Ryder Cup at The Belfry cost firms around Birmingham tens of millions.

Source: *News of the World*, 7 October 2001.

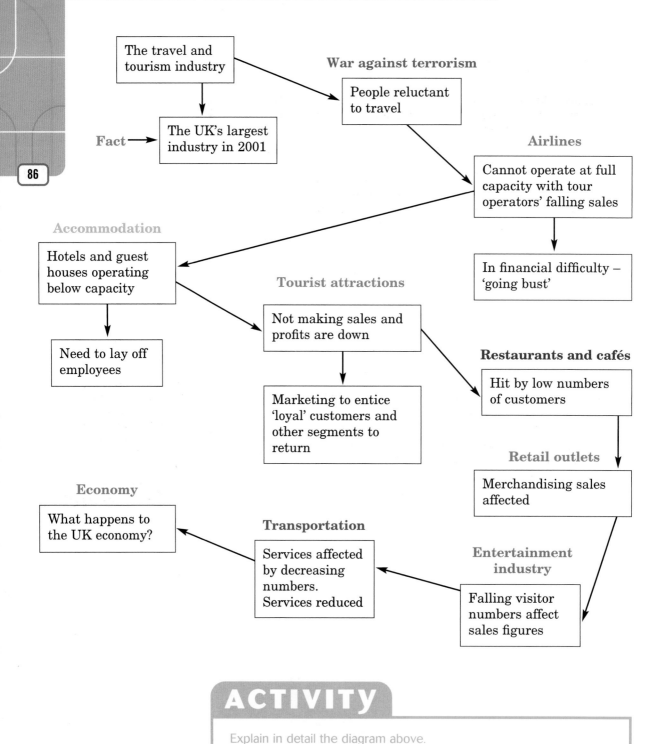

The travel and tourism industry

Fact → The UK's largest industry in 2001

War against terrorism

People reluctant to travel

Airlines

Cannot operate at full capacity with tour operators' falling sales

In financial difficulty – 'going bust'

Accommodation

Hotels and guest houses operating below capacity

Need to lay off employees

Tourist attractions

Not making sales and profits are down

Marketing to entice 'loyal' customers and other segments to return

Restaurants and cafés

Hit by low numbers of customers

Retail outlets

Merchandising sales affected

Economy

What happens to the UK economy?

Transportation

Services affected by decreasing numbers. Services reduced

Entertainment industry

Falling visitor numbers affect sales figures

ACTIVITY

Explain in detail the diagram above.

FCO sticks to its stance on Bali

TOURIST chiefs in Bali are urging the Foreign and Commonwealth Office to tone down its travel advice for Indonesia – which has recommended staying away from Indonesia since last month's terrorist attack, *Tom Chesshyre writes*.

Speaking at World Travel Market in London this week, Setyanto Santosa, executive chairman of the Indonesia Culture and Tourism Board, asked the FCO to re-think its travel advice.

"Please reconsider," he said. "Let the citizens of Britain decide if they want to come to Indonesia."

Igede Ardiea, Indonesia's Minister for Culture and Tourism, who said that security has been increased since the attack, added: "We believe that the Foreign Office should have a more flexible approach – and we hope this will happen soon.

"We don't want to separate ourselves from the rest of the world, but this is what the terrorists would like to see.

We should try to defeat terrorism. If everyone stays at home, we are letting terrorism win."

But the FCO says it is sticking with its advice. "We realise it is a very difficult time for Indonesia, but our number one priority is the safety of British nationals," a spokeswoman said. "Our advice is under constant review. It's not just something we stick on our travel website and forget about."

Insurance companies will not cover travel to countries on the FCO no-go list, which also includes Iraq, Burundi and Somalia. However, the FCO spokeswoman added: "People should remember our advice is just advice."

In January, Garuda Indonesia is suspending for three months the only direct service from the UK to Indonesia because of a drop in demand.

◆ FCO (020–7008 0232, www.fco.gov.uk)

Source: *The Times*, 16 November 2002

What happens to the UK economy when terror attacks and natural disasters take place? Mention which companies have an upsurge in business.

Talk about...

The 'war against terrorism' undertaken by the US in 2001 has taken a different perspective from earlier conflicts. The events of September 11th 2001 hit the headlines across the globe without any warning. The repercussions on the world's economy are paramount.

The visual impact, continuously televised, has left a vast percentage of the population lacking confidence in air transportation. It is a fact of life that in times of international tension, people stay at home where they feel safe. This has had an adverse affect on the airline industry and has affected all of the tourism sectors.

Tourist destinations in London experienced a downturn in business because American tourists chose not to travel to London.

Jobs Within the Travel and Tourism Industry

> You will need to know that the travel and tourism industry consists of a wide variety of organisations of different sizes and it offers many employment opportunities.

Within the travel and tourism industry there are a range of jobs available:

- ◆ Travel consultants
- ◆ Conference organisers
- ◆ Coach drivers
- ◆ Air cabin crew
- ◆ Tourist guide
- ◆ Resort representative

This successful tour operator, organising package holidays to Cyprus, Greece and Spain, has the following vacancies:

Resort Manager & Resort Supervisors

based in top Mediterranean destinations

Applicants must be able to work under pressure, use their own initiative and possess excellent communication and organisation skills. Must have a minimum of five years experience as a holiday representative with proven success in a senior role. Successful applicants must be able to work under pressure, use their own initiative and possess excellent team leadership skills. For the manager's role previous overseas managerial experience is essential.

For more details and/or application form, please contact Sarah on **01208 234 5678**
Mediterranean Holidays Ltd.,
7b High Street, Bayswater, London or
email sarahbooker@meditholidaysltd.com

Figure 1.33

Arnold Smith

London's luxury coach travel company requires the following personnel for its extensive UK day tour programme:

TOUR GUIDES

Excellent communication skills, the ability to give clear and concise commentaries with confidence. Pleasant personality, an aptitude for absorbing knowledge and be able to use your own initiative. A two-week training course will take place in May, the successful completion of which will lead to full time employment. If you believe that you have what it takes,
Call 020 7234 5432
WEEKEND AND BANK HOLIDAY WORKING IS ESSENTIAL

Figure 1.34

RockWorld

At Rock World, you can dance to the music or make your own. Where the people come first and rock and roll is second nature. If you like it loud, this is the place for you!

We are currently recruiting retail professionals at all levels for our store in Stratford including:

● **Supervisors**
● **Full & Part time Sales Assistants**
● **Stock Controllers**
● **Demonstrators**

We are looking for enthusiastic, fun loving, music loving individuals who posses a genuine passion for exceeding customer expectations

We provide full training and opportunity for advancement. So if you want to be part of a dynamic team, please ring between 9am – 5pm, Thursday 18th July on **0207–8234–5671** or e-mail your C.V. with your application letter to:
stratfordstore@rockworld.com

Figure 1.35

ACTIVITY

Look at the advertisements and answer the following questions.

a) What does the job involve?

b) What qualifications do you need?

c) Do you need any specific skills or experience to gain employment?

d) Which key component or sector do the jobs come from?

Extension Exercise

1 Research one job you would like to do.
2 What will you need to do to achieve this job?
3 Write an advertisement for each of the following jobs:
   ◆ Air cabin crew member
   ◆ Travel consultant
   ◆ Conference organiser
   ◆ Coach driver

Hints: a) What does the job involve?
         b) What qualifications are required?
         c) What specific skills or experience are needed to secure employment?

Links between Leisure and Tourism

Leisure and tourism industries are generally considered separately. However, there are many links between the two, for example, accommodation and catering, attractions and transportation. Both industries are dependent on each other for customers.

◆ A family day out at a visitor attraction is a leisure activity but also involves travel and tourism
◆ Travelling to an away football match could be considered as both leisure and tourism
◆ Going on holiday and many of the activities undertaken while on holiday could be considered as both leisure and tourism
◆ Going to the theatre and staying in a hotel overnight are both leisure and tourism activities

The local Tourist Information Centre provides details of both leisure and tourism facilities and activities.

Transport providers operate services to places of interest for both the leisure market and tourists.

QCA

Leisure industry: key components	Travel and tourism industry: key components
Sport and physical recreation	Travel agents
Arts and entertainment	Tour operators
Countryside recreation	Tourist information and guiding services
Home-based leisure	On-line travel services
Catering	Accommodation and catering
Visitor attractions	Attractions
Children's play activities	Transportation

The table shows the key components for the Leisure industry and the key components for the travel and tourism industry. The 'lines' represent similarities between the key components for each industry.

ACTIVITY

1   Explain the links between the components.

2   Can you think of any other links?

3   Investigate and research **one** of the following:
    a) Restaurant or catering organisation
    b) Leisure centre or health club
    c) Caravan site or guest house
    d) Special interest package or weekend break
    e) Conference
    f) Short haul or long haul destination
    g) Area of natural beauty or National Park.

4   Outline the main facilities and services offered. Which of these belong to the travel and tourism industry and which belong to the leisure industry?

5   Which key components are evident in your research?

6   Are there links between the travel and tourism industry and the leisure industry within the place you have researched?

Extension Exercise

1   In what ways can the leisure industry and the travel and tourism industry work together to create improved products and services for all user types?
2   How can the two industries link together to improve facilities and fulfil the needs of users?

External Assessment

An external assessment is taken by students under examination conditions. You will need to recall information under time-constrained conditions.

It is important that you are able to apply the information in this chapter to the examination questions set.

You will *not* be required to produce a portfolio of work, although this may help you in your revision.

How to Tackle the External Assessment

1 The syllabus covers key points which must be understood. These are covered in the 'You will need to know' sections.
2 There are several statements endorsed by QCA. These are prompts and they should get you thinking.
3 You will need to describe and analyse situations (Why? Where? What? When? questions).
4 The case studies should help you to understand the key objectives (points) in the syllabus.
5 You will also need to understand your local area and to use examples from your local area.

How to Revise for the External Assessment

1 You must cover *all* of the syllabus. All questions are related.
2 You need to know that there are distinct differences between the leisure industry and the travel and tourism industry.
3 You must be able to provide examples of all the components in the Leisure Industry and in the Travel and Tourism Industry.

Exam Hints

1 Collect information from your local area, for example leaflets, maps, bus and train timetables.
2 Use the websites/internet to research destinations and organisations.
3 Study trade journals and keep relevant articles in your folder.

Sample Exam Questions – Edexcel

1. There are many different types of organisation in the travel and tourism industry. The industry is divided into components.

Look at the components in the left- hand column below. Link each component, using a straight line, to the correct organisation the right-hand column below. Each component should be linked to **one** organisation only.

Below is an example of what to do. Note that lines may cross over each other.

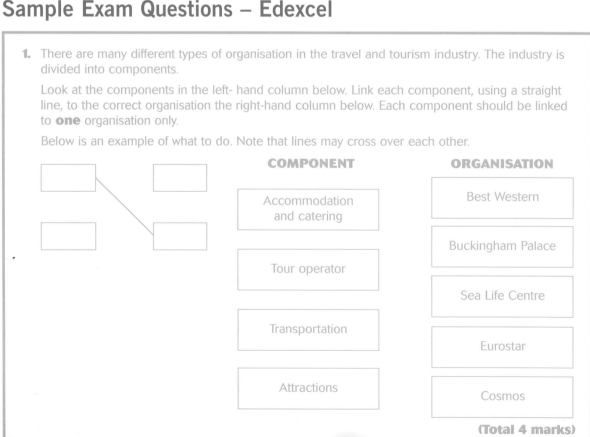

COMPONENT	ORGANISATION
Accommodation and catering	Best Western
Tour operator	Buckingham Palace
Transportation	Sea Life Centre
Attractions	Eurostar
	Cosmos

(Total 4 marks)

2. There are many different leisure activities. These are divided into components. They are available in different facilities or venues.

Look at the different components in the table below.

a) Link each component with **one** facility or venue from this list

- ◆ **A video rental shop**
- ◆ An outdoor activity centre
- ◆ A theme park
- ◆ A café
- ◆ An adventure playground
- ◆ A cinema
- ◆ A swimming and leisure centre.

b) For **each** component and linked facility or venue, suggest **one** leisure activity that people could take part in.

The first one has been completed for you as an example.

Component	Facility OR Venue	Activity
Home-based leisure	*Video rental shop*	Hire out a video to watch at home
Sport and physical		
Recreation		
Arts and entertainment		
Countryside recreation		
Children's play activities		

(Total 8 marks)

3. There are many employment opportunities within the different components of the leisure and tourism industries. Some of these are listed below:

Overseas Representative	*Dancer*	*Hockey Coach*
	Travel Consultant	*Librarian*
Coach Driver	*Restaurant Manager*	**Tourist Guide**
	Park Ranger	*Museum Curator*

Complete the table overleaf by matching a job from the list above to the most relevant component given. Each job can only be used one.

The first one has been completed for you as an example.

93

Component	Job
Tourist Information and Guiding Services	*Tourist Guide*
Travel Agents	
Sports and Physical Recreation	
Transportation	
Catering	
Home-based Leisure	
Countryside Recreation	

(Total 6 marks)

4. There are many links between the leisure and tourism industries. For example, both industries rely on each other for their customers.

   a) Explain the links between leisure and tourism in **Situation 1** given below.

Situation 1

A rugby team from Erith in Kent who need to stay overnight in Kendal, Cumbria in order to play in a sporting event the following day.

(5)

   b) Explain the links between leisure and tourism in **Situation 2** given below.

Situation 2

Mr and Mrs Falstaff are travelling from Germany to the UK for a short break. They will drive to the UK and stay just outside London. They plan to visit Buckingham Palace, and the National Gallery, in Trafalgar Square. They also want to go and see a musical in the West End.

(5)

(Total 10 marks)

5. A leading football club recently conducted a survey of its season ticket holders. The responses indicated that many fans are unhappy with their stadium, saying that it is not up-to-date.

The survey also provided information about their season ticket holders. Explain **one** way that the football club could develop a product and service to meet the needs of **each** of the types of customer given below:

   i) Female season ticket holders **(3)**

   ii) Season ticket holders from outside the local area **(3)**

   iii) Adults and children season ticket holders from the same address **(3)**

(Total 9 marks)

Source: Specimen Paper, © 2001 Edexcel

UNIT 2

MARKETING IN LEISURE AND TOURISM

Introduction

Every time you discuss a television advert with your friends, or you make use of a discount or a 'two-for-the-price-of-one' offer, or you fill in a customer comment sheet in a leisure centre or restaurant, you are taking part in the marketing campaign of an organisation.

You may have wondered why travel agencies display their brochures the way they do, why cinema complexes are located where they are and how tour operators decide which destinations to sell. These are the results of marketing decisions made within organisations.

Successful leisure and tourism companies use very sophisticated marketing and promotional activities to ensure that they sell their products and services – they have to in order to survive.

WHAT YOU WILL LEARN ...

Marketing is about understanding the customer, anticipating their needs – now and in the future and providing the products or services to meet these needs.

This unit focuses on the marketing process. This involves looking at:

- The customers that different organisations target with their marketing
- The market research that organisations undertake
- How organisations choose their products, and then decide where to sell them, how to promote them and what price to charge for them
- How an organisation uses strengths, weaknesses, opportunities and threats
- How organisations run promotional campaigns

The two case studies outlined on pages 97–106 introduce the marketing activities of two leisure and tourism organisations – buzz airlines and Xscape. Try to familiarise yourself with them because they are often referred to in this unit.

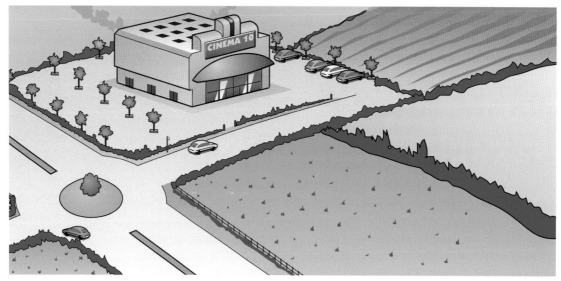

Figure 2.1

Activities

The activities throughout this unit link with your study programme and help develop evidence for assessment.

The Marketing Assignment in Section 10 brings together all these activities and could be used as the final assessment for your portfolio.

ACTIVITY

Do you ever argue with your parents about the type of holiday you want to go on? Are your needs the same as those of your Mum or Dad?

a) List three leisure and tourism needs you have when you go on holiday.

b) Now list three leisure and tourism needs you think adults aged 35–50 may have.

c) Use these notes to take part in a group discussion. The aim of the discussion is to develop a new holiday product aimed at meeting the needs of everyone in a family with teenagers.

Case Study buzz

WEBSITE – http://www.buzz.co.uk

What is buzz?

buzz is a low-cost airline that flies to a wide range of business and leisure destinations in Europe. All flights depart from London Stansted.

Marketing Mix

The Product

buzz is an example of an organisation that sells an 'intangible' product. It is not a product you can pick up and take away. It cannot really be examined or experienced before you pay for it. Really the products that buzz sells are a range of services. buzz's main service is access to an aircraft seat and a journey to an agreed destination.

Other services they offer are:

♦ Food and beverages from Café buzz, the trolley service operated by the flight attendants during a journey.

Case Study (cont.)

◆ Executive lounge access for customers travelling on business or leisure who want to get away from the stress of the airport. There are non-alcoholic drinks, snacks, newspapers, laptops, a fax and telephones available.
◆ Three Airport Plus packages which each offer fast-track security clearance, entry to the VIP lounge and special shopping, eating and foreign exchange offers.
◆ E holiday finder, part of the buzz website, which provides flyers with the opportunity to book both catered and self-catered accommodation throughout France.
◆ Accommodation line which can book hotel accommodation for customers.

All of these services can be bought at an additional cost to the basic flight. buzz also has associated partners, including:

◆ Budget Car Hire
◆ Airbus
◆ Freedom Rail
◆ Ace Insurance

These partners all offer products that complement those of buzz.

Price

buzz operates a 'one way' pricing policy. Seat fares is sold for one-way journeys, inclusive of tax. Yield revenue management controls the prices. This means that prices start at the lowest price and, depending on the demand for the flight, the seats sell out at increasingly higher prices until the flight is full. Fares start at the cheapest price of £19 one way and rise to approximately £150.

Place

London Stansted is a good base for buzz. It is a growing airport with good road and rail access to London. It is relatively accessible for people from central and north London, Hertfordshire, Cambridgeshire, Essex, Suffolk, Norfolk and many parts of the East Midlands. There is a large population base within two and a half hours driving time of Stansted.

Case Study (cont.)

In addition, landing costs are not as expensive as other London airports, e.g. Heathrow and Gatwick, and it is easily accessible to mainland Europe. Stansted is a good base for buzz.

In terms of where you can buy buzz products, these are available online from the buzz website, http://www.buzz.co.uk. There is also a call centre for those who prefer to book on the phone. Flights can be purchased from the buzz sales desk at the terminal at London Stansted.

All the travel, accommodation and insurance optional extras can be booked and purchased online. Executive lounge access is bought at check-in and Café buzz food is available on board every flight.

Promotion

buzz is involved in a great deal of promotional activity.

Advertising

buzz undertakes much poster advertising at railway stations and bus shelters. Moreover, buzz uses TV and radio advertising, as well as major newspaper and magazine advertising.

The marketing campaigns are scheduled quarterly and each has a different theme, for example, 'more action', 'more me', and 'more pleasure'. These themes are supported by promotional offers, cheap seat sales or special packages all offering an increased incentive to fly.

By advertising in specialist magazines, buzz tries to increase awareness in the more niche markets. For example, by targeting ski and snow, golfing and food and drink publications, buzz hopes to make the readers more aware of the destinations it travels to. buzz hopes people will realise that they could ski, golf and so on, at these destinations. buzz also has a stand at all the big travel and holiday exhibitions and shows. This ensures that potential flyers, who are not already familiar with the company, become more aware.

You know where chic Parisians head to for 'le weekend'?

We fly there.

buzz.co.uk

Sales Promotion

Past promotional activity includes a recent two-for-one seat offer in *The Times* newspaper. Passengers collected tokens and booked flights online to gain their two-for-the-price-of-one flights.

buzz has also been involved in promotional partnerships, e.g. The Ski Club of Great Britain. In this promotion, flyers were offered a free day of skiing with a Sky Club of Great Britain representative.

Other examples of promotional partnerships include packages that involve a leisure event at a buzz destination. For instance, free entry to Futuroscope in Poitiers, a free round of golf in Jerez or a free tour of a vineyard in Bordeaux.

Public Relations

buzz works alongside UK and European-based PR agencies. They work together to plan and monitor press release and

Case Study (cont.)

activity. buzz also organises inbound press trips – journalists based near buzz's European destinations come to London on a buzz flight and the airline arranges for them to see the sights of London. The emphasis is on the sights and benefits of London – the aim is to get potential customers from the European airports to travel over to London.

Direct Marketing

buzz's direct marketing consists of Club buzz – a kind of customer loyalty club. Flyers are given the opportunity to join Club buzz and then receive regular updates, via e-mail, which give them prior notice of forthcoming deals, offers, promotions and buzz news.

Market Research

1 When customers join Club buzz they have to fill out a short questionnaire. From this questionnaire, buzz is able to find out about its customers' travel needs, where they live, their life stage and lifestyle, how far they travel and so on. buzz can then tailor its promotional offers to suit different groups of people. Club buzz segments its members into the following categories:
   ◆ Business users only
   ◆ Leisure users
   ◆ Price sensitive (early bookers)
   ◆ Non-price sensitive (later bookers)

2 buzz also makes use of secondary research. When deciding which new airports to fly to, it will investigate how many potential customers live within a two to three hours' drive time of the airport. It will do this by finding out the population of people aged 18–54 in the area. It will also look at the businesses in the area to see if they are likely customers. buzz will want to know the general prosperity of the area. If a place has high unemployment and little industry it is unlikely that there will be sufficient customers there for buzz.

The Target Market

buzz has identified two target markets:

1 **Broad base**. This consists of men and women aged 18–54 who fall within the socio-economic grouping ABC1 (see table on page 108). They may live up to three hours' drive from Stansted.
2 **Core target**. The more regular flyers fall into this category. They consist of men and women aged 25–40 who fall within the socio-economic grouping ABC1. They live within two hours' drive of Stansted.

Case Study (cont.)

SWOT Analysis

Strengths	Weaknesses
◆ Great range of business and leisure destinations (21) ◆ Distinctive UK brand ◆ Good quality service ◆ Award winning website ◆ Strong partnerships with large companies (Budget) ◆ First airline to offer domestic flights within a mainline European country (four routes in France) ◆ Good relationship with out of house design and PR agencies ◆ Give personal responses to customer e-mails (Club buzz, Ask buzz) ◆ Low-cost, short haul flights have been more successful since events of 11 September 2001	◆ Low brand awareness in Europe and in other markets ◆ Perceived as the weakest of the five main low-cost airlines ◆ No recognisable public face or voice of z buz ◆ Not an independently-run company
Opportunities	**Threats**
◆ Low-cost airlines have sustained business since events of 11 September 2001 ◆ Increased traffic from traditional airline routes ◆ More business travellers from business sector, no longer flying with traditional airlines ◆ New technology (Interactive TV, 3rd generation phones) ◆ French domestic routes	◆ Competition from other four main low-cost airlines ◆ Competition from traditional airlines which have increasingly lower seat sales ◆ Further distrust in air travel ◆ Takeover of Go by easyJet

On 31 January, 2003, buzz's parent company, KLM Dutch Airlines, announced that it had signed an agreement for the sale of buzz to Ryanair.

As more competitors entered the low cost arena, air prices fell and buzz found it increasingly dificult to survive alone. Ryanair 'will significantly rationalise buzz's operations by closing a number of high cost, unprofitable routes and operating the remaining routes at increased frequency, lower fares and much lower costs. buzz's BAe-146 fleet will be replaced by more efficient Boeing 737s.'

This latest takeover provides more evidence of the 'cut throat' environment airlines work in today.

Case Study Xscape

WEBSITE – http://www.xscape.co.uk

What is Xscape?

Xscape is a large building dedicated to
leisure, retail and entertainment. In fact,
Xscape promotes itself as 'the ultimate leisure, retail and entertainment destination'. The
first operational Xscape is in Milton Keynes with two more opening in Castleford near
Leeds in Autumn 2002 and Braehead near Glasgow in 2003. More Xscapes are planned.

Marketing Mix

The Product

The Xscape building houses a large number of different products:

The Snozone, which Xscape is most famous for. This consists of three giant indoor ski
slopes covered in real snow. Customer can ski all year round and a range of ski and
snowboard lessons are offered as well as sledging parties. The whole area is kept at a
temperature of $-2°C$ and it 'snows' conveniently every night when the customers and staff
have gone home!

City Limits has a number of entertainment and leisure facilities including:

- Mid City Lanes, a bowling alley which includes 24 lanes and glo-bowling, a café area
  and dance floor
- State Fair, an amusement arcade featuring a host of electronic interactive games and
  rides
- First Base, the pool table bar with dance floor and a stage for live acts
- a range of function and meeting rooms for banquets and corporate events.

Old Orleans is a themed family restaurant serving a choice of American-style dishes,
including typical creole catering.

Esporta Health Club, a state of the art gym with two studios for classes, a swimming
pool, sauna and jacuzzi. There is also a creche.

Silver Trek Climb Zone, in which there are two climbing walls. A taster session with
experienced staff costs £7.50. All equipment is included.

A 16-screen Cineworld Multiplex

Restaurant outlets including McDonald's, KFC, O'Neills, ASK, Nando's, Bar Citrus and
Toad.

Retail outlets including O'Neill, Swatch, The Designer Room, Trespass, Smart Cars,
Nautica and Action Bikes.

Case Study (cont.)

An internet café called Clicknetic.

Oceana: two night clubs, four bars and one restaurant – all themed to represent different countries.

These products can be divided into those that attract the local population mainly and those that attract an interest from a wider geographical population.

The cinema, ten-pin bowling, Esporta Health Club, retail outlets, restaurants and internet café will mainly attract the local population – people will not drive further than their nearest cinema usually to view a film.

The Snozone and Silver Trek Climb Zone will attract customers from much further away. They are such unusual attractions that people will be prepared to travel further to use them.

Price

The price obviously varies according to the product being purchased. Below you will find some examples

- Climbing taster session £7.50, standard session £4.90
- Snozone – lessons range upwards from £20 per child
- Recreational sessions range from £15–£20 per adult and around £50 for one hour for a family of four
- Customers can buy monthly and six monthly season passes to reduce the cost of recreational skiing.

Place

The first Xscape was located in Milton Keynes. Because this type of leisure and entertainment complex is very expensive to set up, the geographical location is very important. Xscape carried

Case Study (cont.)

out research to ascertain how many people live in the immediate area of Milton Keynes and how many live within two hours' drive time. It checked the road and rail links to ensure that large numbers of people could travel easily to Xscape. It needed enough space for the building and for car parking. There is no point attracting large numbers of people by car if there is not enough parking for them.

In addition to checking the size of population within a two-hour journey time of Milton Keynes, Xscape checked the type of population. It needed customers who have the money to spend on leisure pursuits. It asked questions about the demographics of the population. For example:

◆ How many professional, managerial and skilled workers are there in the population?
◆ Is unemployment high or low?
◆ How many young people are there?
◆ Milton Keynes has a very low rate of unemployment – less than 2 per cent, one of the lowest in the country. It also has a high percentage of people under 35 in its population.

Xscape is now expanding to Castleford near Leeds, and to Braehead near Glasgow and Edinburgh. These two venues both have large populations within a two-hour drive time with good rail and road routes.

Promotion

Xscape does not use TV advertisements. However, it does advertise on local radio and in specialist magazines, e.g. those dealing with winter sports. When Xscape does special Christmas, Easter and Valentine's Day campaigns it will use the local and regional media to advertise these.

Xscape also distributes leaflets through hotels, the local library and Tourist Information Centres.

Due to its unique selling point – Snozone – Xscape has many public relations opportunities. For example, the slopes are used for fashion shoots and pop videos.

Blue Peter has broadcast twice from the site. BBC's *Look East*, Anglia TV and Radio Northampton have used the venue as an example of exciting leisure pursuits. A number of national papers including the *Daily Express* and *Daily Mail* have sent journalists to Xscape to learn how to ski and snowboard and to write an article about their experience. The Winter Olympics also increases people's interests in winter sports. Xscape has supported a number of athletes including Sam Temple, Chemmy Alcott, Alain Baxter and Great Britain's women's downhill racing team.

Direct Marketing

Xscape has used postal mailshots to both individual customers and to business organisations to encourage them to use Xscape for corporate events. In addition, 20 internal plasma screens and the huge LED screen on the front of the building can be used to advertise products.

Case Study (cont.)

The complex offers great opportunities for selling activities and there are 'Red Letter Days' to both businesses and to individuals. These are days sold as a package, sometimes as gifts, where people have the opportunity to experience something they have never done before, for example, learning to snowboard in a day.

For the future, Xscape will use e-mail marketing and it is looking at mobile phone SMS text messaging.

Market Research

1 In order to undertake effective direct marketing, Xscape needs a large database. Many of their activities are geared towards obtaining this. They use competitions and invite feedback in order to gather information about their present and potential customers.
2 As stated under 'Place' Xscape uses secondary research to look at the demography of the population in areas they are thinking of expanding into.

The Target Market

Xscape's main market is wide ranging. Its many different products mean that it targets both families with young children, men and women aged 18–35 and ABC1s within a two-hour drive time in Milton Keynes. Snozone particularly targets families with young children – from the age of three – if they are 'hooked' young they remain customers for decades.

Other target groups include the over 50s who come at off-peak times and specialist groups, such as companies, school and university students.

Case Study (cont.)

SWOT Analysis

Strengths

- Xscape has a unique selling point – it is the first one of its kind
- There are currently no direct competitors
- The company has a high profile Chief Executive – P Y Gerbeau who ran the Millenium Dome and Disneyland Paris, continuously promotes Xscape
- The building has won design awards
- Xscape is not reliant on one product – it has snow slopes, climbing, bowling, a cinema etc.
- Location, the local population and the transport routes
- Proximity to London
- 95,000 people pass through Xscape each week in peak season
- It is a winner of the Best Major Leisure Scheme and Best Innovative Concept 2001 LPF award

Weaknesses

- Relatively low awareness of the brand nationwide
- Lack of hotel and conference facilities for corporate events
- Confusion about what Xscape is – it is more than a snow slope
- The market for winter sports is relatively small
- Xscape is dominated by Snozone which means the venue can be seen as seasonal – the peak time is weekends in the winter months
- Winter sports retailers are dependent on Snozone and can be very quiet in the summer.

Opportunities

- Expansion of the product to other destinations in the UK and Europe
- Ability to extend or change products and services offered to respond to a changing market, e.g. if climbing becomes unpopular that space could be filled with a skateboarding park; Castleford Xscape will include an ice climbing wall – the only one in the country
- The growth in the leisure market
- Snozone's year round snow – global warming means European ski resorts continue to lose snow and their season becomes shorter and therefore the slopes are very crowded – Snozone offers the enthusiast the opportunity to continue skiing and snowboarding throughout the year
- Links to the travel industry – the winter sports market continues to grow and expand with the availability of cheap flights
- Cross cooperation between Xscape tenants, e.g. a loyalty card could be introduced giving discounts, such as a free McDonald's meal with each ski course booked
- An increasingly active older generation – people not only live longer, they are active for longer and this section of the population is growing rapidly in number
- Sponsorship opportunities as PR increases and it is seen as a 'cool' venue to be connected with – soft drinks companies, computer games, electrical companies could all be interested

Threats

- Economic recession – people spend less on leisure
- The growth in competition, e.g. Becton Alp has recently been updated from an artificial slope to a real snow slope and because Becton Slope is in London, this is a real threat to Snozone
- Complacency!

SECTION ONE

Target Marketing

Target marketing involves deciding which customers you want to attract to your product or services, and then making sure that your advertising and promotions are placed where these customers will see them.

107

Whereas in the past customers were offered, in many instances, the same goods and services, organisations now realise that different customers have different needs, wants and tastes. For example, in the holiday market today, the accommodation offered ranges from 'the fully inclusive package', which includes food, snacks and most beverages, to the self-catering option – simply offering accommodation and the independence to decide where you want to eat.

Generally, up until the mid 1950s, teenagers did not exist as a separate market. People in their teenage years wore similar clothes to their parents and everyone aimed or aspired to be 'grown up'. How times have changed! Now the teenage market is vast. You have your own clothes, music and leisure activities. All 'grown ups' aspire to look young again!

> 1 If someone wanted to promote a new product or service aimed at you, where would be a good place to 'catch' you?
> 2 What newspapers or TV programmes do your Mum and Dad follow? Where would be a good place to promote a product for them?

Talk about...

Figure 2.2   Teenagers now and in the 1950s

Market Segmentation

Market segments are groups of customers who are similar in certain ways and therefore tend to have similar needs. The task of an organisation is to produce and supply different products or services to suit the different market segments.

The main market segments that tend to be used, divide customers according to their:

- ◆ Age
- ◆ Gender
- ◆ Social group
- ◆ Lifestyle
- ◆ Ethnicity

Figure 2.3   Market segmentation

108

Age

Large tour operators can use market segmentation to differentiate between their various products by age. For example, Thomas Cook has Club 18–30 and Thomson has Club Freestyle. Saga Holidays are sold exclusively to the over 50s, while Club 18–30 tells you the market segment it is targeting in its name!

New products have been developed to meet the different needs of men and women. Golfing holidays in the Algarve and southern Spain have been popular for many years. However, unless both partners in a relationship are keen, there is always one left behind – usually the woman. Now golf and spa holidays have been launched to meet the needs of both customers.

Social Group

Social group segmentation divides the population according to the type of job they do. This can cause many difficulties.

SOCIAL GRADE	SOCIAL CLASS	TYPICAL OCCUPATIONS
A	Upper middle	Higher managerial, admin. and professional (e.g. judges, surgeons)
B	Middle	Intermediate managerial and admin. (e.g. lawyers, teachers, doctors)
C1	Lower middle	Supervisory, clerical, junior management (e.g. bank clerk, estate agent)
C2	Skilled working	Skilled manual workers (e.g. joiner, welder)
D	Working	Semi- and unskilled manual workers (e.g. driver, postman, porter)
E	Those at lowest level of subsistence	Pensioners, widows, casual workers, students, the unemployed

THINK ABOUT...

Does any market exist today where segmentation does not take place?
Can you think of a product or service within the tourist industry that meets the needs of more than one social group?

One problem is that a student is classified as Group E. However, he or she could be supported by a parent who is a Managing Director, earning a six-figure salary.

Teachers are placed in the same category as lawyers and doctors, but currently do not have the same income and cannot afford the same products and services.

Generally this socio-economic classification is regarded as old-fashioned. Various other methods have been developed over recent years. One of these is the life cycle classification.

Table 15 Life cycle classification

CATEGORY	CHARACTERISTICS
1 Bachelor stage	Young singles, reasonable level of disposable income, which is mostly spent on entertainment, such as pubs, discos, CDs, computer games.
2 Newly-weds/ living together	Maybe slightly higher income spent on eating out, clubbing, cinemas.
3 Full nest 1	Young couples with child under six years. Main leisure pursuits would be related to family outings.
4 Full nest 2	Young couples with youngest child over six years. Less disposable income to spend on leisure.
5 Full nest 3	Older couple with dependent children, possibly students. Little disposable income.
6 Empty nest 1	Childless couple or children left home. Disposable income has increased, likely to pursue more frequent holidays, active leisure pursuits, such as golf, tennis.
7 Empty nest 2	Older couples. Chief earner retired. Entertainment home-based.
8 Solitary survivor 1	Single/widowed working person. Mostly home-based entertainment.
9 Solitary survivor 2	Retired single person. Little disposable income for leisure purposes.

This classification suggests that newly married couples spend money on eating out and entertainment, such as cinemas and clubs/pubs, whereas young couples with young children spend money on renting videos, subscribing to Sky and eating in. While some of this is undoubtedly true, it does not provide the full picture.

Tour operators and Xscape, a leisure company in Milton Keynes, both report increasing business from parents who have children living at home.

In the early 2000s, people in employment in Britain have more money to spend on leisure activities. Mortgage rates are low, the cost of borrowing money is low and the exchange rate of the £ is high, meaning that we get more foreign currency for our money.

None of these factors are taken into consideration with either social group classification or life cycle classification.

Lifestyle

This market segment generally refers to four classes of people:

- **Mainstreamers** who represent 40 per cent of the population. They are the traditional 'backbone' of the country. They stick to well-known brands like Sony and Thomson Holidays and they have conventional leisure pursuits such as gardening, reading or walking.
- **Aspirers** are led by acquiring the latest 'must have' gadget, e.g. plasma PCs, flat wide-screen TVs, the latest mobile phone. Leisure pursuits usually involve the latest adult toys – motorbikes, hang gliders and snowboarding.
- **Succeeders** are people who have 'made it' and no longer show off. They like quality but will not necessarily stick to well-known names and brands to get it. They entertain, socialise and take frequent holidays.
- **Reformers** are the group least likely to be seen in the latest tourist destination or playing with the latest piece of technology. They tend to be into recycling and they provide their own entertainment in their leisure time. They favour activities like camping and cycling.

110

ACTIVITY

If you were trying to sell the following products, which lifestyle grouping(s) would you target your marketing at? Justify your answer.

a) The latest opening of a McDonald's restaurant.

b) A new ride at Alton Towers providing the biggest thrills ever.

c) The latest football boots as worn by David Beckham.

d) A trip to the Eden Project in Cornwall.

e) A holiday on the exclusive island of Mustique.

Ethnicity

Different ethnic groups must be recognised in marketing. For example, some types of promotion and advertising may cause offence to some cultural groupings. Showing the soles of your feet in public is regarded as very rude in some Far Eastern countries.

Talk about...

What factors should a restaurant in a hotel consider when arranging catering for people from different religions and cultures?

SECTION TWO

Market Research

In the last section we learned that marketing can help organisations to develop products and services that meet customer needs. But how do organisations decide what these needs are? The simple answer is through market research.

Methods of Market Research

There are two main ways that organisations can carry out market research:

1 **Primary or field research**. If an organisation carries out the research itself by interviewing or phoning people, sending questionnaires to their customers, carrying out observations, then this is primary research. Primary research is sometimes called field research. For example, buzz airlines might conduct interviews with its Club buzz members to find out what they think of the food in Café buzz or the transport links to Stansted Airport.
   The main types of primary market research are:

◆ **Postal surveys**. This is where a questionnaire is sent through the post. The advantages of this technique is that it is cheap, and for this reason almost one-quarter of all surveys use this method. The disadvantage is that it has a very low response rate.
◆ **Telephone questionnaires**. This is becoming more popular because it is convenient for both the interviewer and the respondent. However, many people do not like being contacted in this way and the number of people refusing to take part is on the increase.
◆ **Personal surveys or face-to-face surveys**. The advantages of this method are that interviewers can measure body language and facial expressions as well as what is being said. More accurate data is collected because the interviewer can clarify any questions the respondent does not understand. However, the disadvantages are that this method is expensive and time-consuming.
◆ **Observation**. This involves looking at the way customers behave. Places like Alton Towers can use observation to work out how most people travel around the park and theme park can place shops and eating places accordingly.
◆ **Internet**. This is rapidly growing in popularity because it is perhaps the cheapest way of obtaining information. Organisations place a questionnaire on a website, using the internet. Anyone can answer the questions directly on the web page and the information is logged by computer at the host site. This method of collecting information is likely to grow quickly.

2 **Secondary or desk research**. If the organisation makes use of information gathered by people unconnected to the company who are not researching with that company specifically in mind, then this is secondary or desk research. Obvious advantages of secondary methods of research are that they are cheap and quick to do.

buzz, when deciding on a new destination, might undertake secondary research by investigating the number of passengers currently flying to the destination. They might undertake this research by looking at data published by the airport, or by competitor airlines. They might look at government statistics that detail the population living within two hours driving time of the airport. Xscape might look at tour operator statistics that give the number of people booking skiing holidays and where they live. They might use external statistics that detail the areas of the country where the population spends more money on leisure pursuits in order to consider whether to open there.

For your GCSE in Leisure and Tourism you should concentrate on primary forms of market research.

Analysis of market research can help a company to identify its target market, the types of promotion which are likely to be successful and the costs involved.

Figure 2.4   Market research

What Can Market Research Investigate?

You should now understand the methods of market research, but what information are organisations trying to find out specifically?

♦ **Who their potential customers are**. For example, buzz knows from its Club buzz registration process which of its members to contact when advertising new business services
♦ **Gaps in the market**. buzz could use this information to decide which new destinations to start flying to.

◆ **The likely demand for a new service**. Xscape is a new leisure concept and the company would have undertaken extensive research. In order to obtain enough customers for the Snozone (the indoor snow slope) to make a profit, they need to locate themselves near a large population base. Milton Keynes has the road and rail links, plus a large population base within two hours driving time.
◆ **Competition**. All organisations are interested in what their competitors are up to. buzz, as a low-cost airline, needs to ensure its fares reflect this, especially because it currently shares its home base of Stansted with the low-cost airline Go. Now easyJet has bought Go, this might change.
◆ **Level of current customer satisfaction**. Particularly in the leisure and tourism sector, much use is made of customer satisfaction questionnaires or comment cards. Some public leisure centres put the comments on the notice board along with an outline of the action they are going to take.

ASSESSMENT ACTIVITY

Now you are ready to do some research towards your assessment evidence for this unit. Choose an organisation you know well and one which you will be able to investigate in detail because you will be undertaking much of your assessment using this organisation. It should preferably be a medium-sized or large organisation.

Identify the primary research methods the organisation uses to identify their target markets. Show how all market research methods could be used by the organisation to identify their target markets.

SECTION THREE The Marketing Mix

The marketing mix is sometimes called the 4 Ps:

Product	The goods and services an organisation offers.
Price	How much the goods and services cost.
Place	Where the goods and services are offered.
Promotion	How organisations tempt people to buy their goods and services.

THINK ABOUT...

Using either the buzz or Xscape case study (see pages 97–106), identify the research methods the organisation uses to identify its target markets. Show how all methods can be used to identify target markets. For example, a postal survey could include a question asking where the customer has been on holiday over the last few years. buzz could use the answers to find out if the customer goes on holiday near one of their destination airports and Xscape could see if they have recently been on a skiing holiday.

The marketing mix provides a useful way of looking at the marketing of products. Organisations need to create a successful mix of:

◆ The right product or service
◆ Sold in the right place
◆ At the right price
◆ Using the most suitable method of promotion

All four elements in this marketing mix are important in their own right. However, for a product to reach its full potential all four aspects should work together.

Case Study

Alton Towers

Alton Towers has a huge leisure product – thrills and entertainment for all the family in a fun-packed day out. Theme parks need to attract large numbers of customers to ensure that they stay in business. You will find that they are based largely around London or in the Midlands between Manchester, Birmingham, Leeds and Nottingham, where large numbers of the population of England live.

Research shows that people are happier to pay a one-off price at the gate, rather than for each individual ride. A newer innovation is to charge people a premium to pre-book a time slot for the more popular rides and so reduce the queuing time. This also ensures that people have more time to wander around experiencing the shops and the restaurants!

Promotion is normally carried out through leaflets placed at Tourist Information Centres and sometimes special offers promoted in newspapers. Schools are targeted after exams have finished, through mailshots for 'special treat days out' with free places for teachers.

Figure 2.5   Alton Towers

TEST YOUR KNOWLEDGE

Using the same organisation as you did for market research methods in Section Two, briefly explain how the organisation uses the 4 Ps (the marketing mix) to sell itself. Use the information in the case studies on buzz and Xscape to help you.

SECTION FOUR

Product

Within the leisure and tourism industry, the product is often a service. This means that the product is 'intangible', – you cannot see or hold it, e.g. a Snozone lesson, a holiday or gym session.

The problem with intangible products is that, because they cannot be seen, it is only after the customer has bought the product that they can try it out. Therefore, descriptions of the experience that the product offers must be accurate to avoid misleading the customer.

Figure 2.6 'What does he think he has bought?'

Service products have many different parts, all of which contribute to the experience offered to the customer. For example, when selling someone a ticket to visit a tourist attraction, the facility will be offering:

◆ Entrance to the attractions
◆ Accessibility to all of the facilities, including rides, exhibits, catering, toilets
◆ A type of environment – lively, peaceful, safe, exciting
◆ Delivery of service by qualified staff – guides, ride operators, caterers, first-aid assistants
◆ An identity or 'brand' that is recognisable, e.g. Disneyland, Alton Towers, or Center Parcs

THINK ABOUT...

What are you buying from buzz airlines? Name all of the services.

The Brand Name

A brand can be a name, a symbol, or a logo, which is used to identify a product and to make it stand out from its competitors. For instance, McDonald's has the 'Big Mac'. This is a very powerful brand name. Other organisations can produce various types of beefburgers but none can claim to be the 'Big Mac'.

Creating a brand is very important in marketing. Often people will buy the product because of the brand name, as much as for the product itself. They associate the name with various images or emotions that they are also trying to buy. These may include security, power, 'coolness' and quality, to name a few.

Large organisations are very protective of the power of their brand. They often spend many millions of pounds to build and maintain it, and they are determined that nothing will damage it.

TEST YOUR KNOWLEDGE

Identify two or three brands of products in the leisure and tourism market. Explain what image that brand is trying to sell through its product.
How do they achieve this image? Is it through the personality they use to promote the product, the packaging or where they advertise the product or service?

Think of ten accessories you use in your leisure time. These could be trainers, mobile phones, leisure clothes. Note the brand and prepare for a group discussion on why you chose these brands over others in the marketplace.

Talk about...

The After-Sales Service

The word 'intangible' was used earlier to explain many leisure and tourism products and services. If you buy a 'tangible' product, such as trainers or a stereo system, these are usually covered by some form of guarantee from the manufacturer, and consumer laws state the goods must be 'fit for the purpose'. For example, electrical goods must work and work safely, and trainers should not fall apart the first time they are worn.

However, with intangible products it is more difficult to ensure that a service is 'fit for the purpose'. One person's expectations of a holiday will not be the same as someone else's, and a customer would find it difficult to take a holiday back if it is not 'working correctly'. Therefore, any company offering services has to consider what they will do if things go wrong. This should form part of the marketing and promotion strategy because it helps to build up trust in a service.

Tour operators display their after-sales service policy in the section of the holiday brochure covering booking conditions. Some companies call this section a 'Fair Trading Charter', and it sets out the responsibilities of the customer and the tour operator, including the steps to take if there is a complaint.

Figure 2.7 Holiday brochures

Compare different types of holiday brochures and how they offer after-sales service. Look at both large organisations like Thomsons and smaller independent companies.

Product Life Cycle

The life of a product is the period during which it appeals to customers. There are many goods that everyone wanted at one time but that have now gone out of fashion, for example Pokemon cards, Tamagotchis, Transformers and Pogs.

There are many products that are overtaken by newer versions – mobile phones, Playstation 1 and video players. You cannot identify the possible life expectancy of any product. Some last and others do not.

When a product is first introduced to customers, it starts with a sales performance of zero – no one has bought it because it has only just arrived. As it goes through the introduction stage, growth is low and sales are low due to a limited awareness of the product. Sales then rise rapidly during the period of growth. Towards the end of this stage competitors enter the market and promote their own products and this affects the growth of sales of the original product. Now that competitors are around and growth is slower, this stage is maturity. Various strategies, such as introducing new colours and new shapes will occur at this stage. At the next stage – saturation – some stronger brands may force competitors out of business. Eventually the market for the product may decline and reach a stage when it becomes unprofitable.

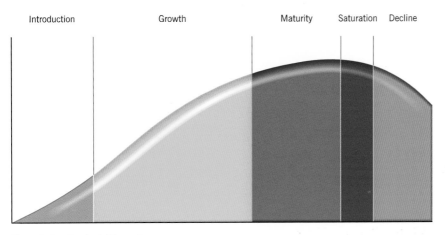

Figure 2.8   Product life cycle

Case Study

The Airline Industry

The airline industry is a good example of the product life cycle to look at. British Airways, until very recently, flew regularly from Heathrow to Belfast International. The airline flew every two hours in peak times from Monday to Friday. The only major competitor was British Midland. Both of these airlines had reached the late growth early maturity stage in the product life cycle. Competition from other modes of transport, such as ferry companies was declining – more people were flying.

Then easyJet, the low-cost airline based at Luton, launched a new service to Belfast International with fares that were easily half the price of British Airways or British Midland. Growth for easyJet was rapid. The customers liked the cheap fares and wanted more. Two other low-cost airlines became involved: Go flying Stansted to Belfast International and Ryanair flying out of Dublin. This led to lower fares. British Airways found it difficult to compete. British Airways has now withdrawn from the Heathrow to Belfast International market. British Midland now flies to Belfast City and Belfast International airports.

easyJet has taken over its rival Go, and this may have implications about whether both Go and easyJet continue to fly to the same destinations.

Figure 2.9   British Airways plane

Extension

As companies see their products moving into maturity, they may try
to extend the product's life cycle. This can be done in various ways:

1 Updating the product – Playstation 1 replaced by Playstation 2.
2 Providing different destination points – a tour operator introducing
  a new destination.
3 Changing prices to reflect competitive activities – the airline
  industry.
4 Changing the style of promotion – perhaps two-for-the-price-of-one.

ACTIVITY

In groups, with each group looking at two components of the
leisure and tourism industry, identify different types of products
and services and give a presentation on their features. Draw a
product life cycle on a flip chart. Choose five of your products
and identify where they are on the product life cycle. Explain
why you have placed them where you have.

SECTION FIVE

Price

The Actual Selling Price

Various factors need to be taken into
account when deciding on price,
including:

Figure 2.10

◆ The cost of producing the product or service
◆ Development and marketing costs
◆ Competitor prices
◆ What the customer would be prepared to pay – there is fierce
  competition in the travel industry and customers expect discounts
◆ Profit

Within both the leisure and tourism industries there are 'peaks and
troughs' in demand. During school holidays there is an increase in
tour operator prices as demand grows. Similarly, January to March
have the lowest prices because demand is low.

Often in the leisure industry prices go up at the weekends and
evenings – look at Xscape's pricing policy (page 121). Other types of
pricing strategies are:

◆ **Concession fares**. This is when lower charges are made for
  students, senior citizens, children or family groups.
◆ **Discounts** are often used as a marketing tool to sell products that

are not in demand. This may be due to the time of year or the time of day. Discounts can also be given to encourage people to book products and services. Travel agents often use this promotion to encourage customers to book their summer holidays in the months from September to January. The slump in travel after the tragedy in America on 11 September 2001 meant that there were many discounts on flights and holidays in the following months. In fact these discounts were amongst the highest the industry had ever experienced.

◆ **Group discounts** are also a common pricing strategy. For example, theme parks encourage school groups to visit after their exams but before the start of the school summer holidays.

◆ **Season tickets**. Regular customers to facilities such as tourist attractions or football stadiums can often purchase tickets at a cheaper rate that allow them access for as many times as they like over a set period of time.

◆ **Yearly or lifetime subscriptions** to organisations such as The National Trust.

Not all leisure and tourism products are priced to make a profit. Many prices are set at a level which is only sufficient to cover the costs of providing the service. For instance, many leisure activities do not make a profit, such as youth groups or amateur dramatic groups. Some organisations may be subsidised by the local authority, e.g. a museum or a leisure centre.

Figure 2.11

THINK ABOUT...

Can you think of any other leisure and tourism companies that offer credit terms?

Credit Terms

Not all leisure and tourism services are fully paid for when purchased. For example, when you book a holiday you normally pay a deposit immediately and then pay the balance eight to ten weeks before you are due to travel. As a customer, this ensures that you get the holiday you want at the time you want it, without having to pay for it all at once.

Travel companies often make very little profit per passenger and therefore the deposit and money they take ten weeks before their passengers travel are very important to them. They can put this money in the bank and earn interest on it. A large company like Thomson Holidays will make a reasonable income from this.

LESSONS

Take advantage of our wide range of lessons. Our fully qualified instuctors cater for skiers and boarders of all ages and abilities, in groups (no more than 10) or individual lessons.

For further details. Including lesson times, please contact the Info Desk

(ski & snowboard)

age	hours	max people	price per person
Adult (16+)	1	group of 4	1 @ £45
10 – 15	1	group of 4	2 @ £35
6 – 9*	1	group of 4	3 @ £30
3 – 5†	1	1	4 @ £25

*Snowboard boots & equipment must be supplied by customer.
†Ski only. Pease note minimum child boot size is 8½ .

Introduction to snowboarding.

age	hours	max people	price
Adult (16+)	1	group of 6	£25
10 – 15	1	group of 6	£20

Introduction to skiing.

age	hours	max people	price
Adult (16+)	1	group of 10	£25
10 – 15	1	group of 10	£20
6 – 9	1	group of 6	£20
3 – 5*	1	group of 4	£20

*Sundays only.

For beginners/intermediate/advanced (ski & snowboard).

age	hours	max people	price
Adult (16+)	1	10 ski / 6 board	£25
10 – 15	1	10 ski / 6 board	£20
6 – 9	1	6 ski only	£20
3 – 5	1	4 ski only	£20

over 5 weeks (ski & snowboard).

age	hours	max people	price
Adult (16+)	5×1	10 ski / 6 board	£100
10 – 15	5×1	10 ski / 6 board	£80

Weekdays 9am – 5pm.

age	hours	max people	price
Adult (16+)	8*	group of 8	£100

*inc. rest periods but not refreshments.

Sat & Sun, 9am – 5pm.

age	hours	max people	price
Adult (16+)	8*	group of 6	£100

*inc. rest periods but not refreshments.

over a 7 day period.

age	hours	max people	price
Adult (16+)	5×1	10 ski / 6 board	£100
10 – 15	5×1	10 ski / 6 board	£80

(ski & snowboard)

age	hours	max people	price
Adult (16+)	3	10 ski / 6 board	£65

Intermediate (snowbaord only).

age	hours	max people	price
Adult (16+)	3	group of 6	£65

Beginners (ski only).

age	hours	max people	price
3 – 5	1	group of 4	£20
6 – 9	1	group of 6	£20

Sno plough turner (ski only).

age	hours	max people	price
3 – 5	1	group of 4	£20
6 – 9	1	group of 6	£20

Turner improver (ski only).

age	hours	max people	price
3 – 5	1	group of 4	£20
6 – 9	1	group of 6	£20

Racing snow plough turns (ski only).

age	hours	max people	price
3 – 5	1	group of 4	£20
6 – 9	1	group of 6	£20

(ski & snowbaord)

age	hours	max people	price
up to 16	1	10 ski / 6 board	£100

SNOZONE CLUB

Are you a keen skier or snowboarder? Why not join the Snozone Club? Benefits include reduced rates on recreational slope use and lessons, at all times, and concessions on some additional activities eg Kids Holiday Club, Adult Toboggan Parties.

All Snozone Club members receive a club newsletter and invitations to special events and activities some of which are exclusive to members.

membership category	Annual fees
Adult individual (16+)	£85
Adult couple	£130
Junior individual (3 – 15 yrs)	£50
Family A (1 Adult + 2 juniors)	£130
Family B (2 Adults + 2 juniors)	£160
Additional junior individual	£30

Sun 7 pm – 11pm.

age	hours	price
Adult (16+)	1	£10
3 – 15	1	£5

For details please call 01908 680820.

Figure 2.12   Xscape's rates

Other leisure and tourism companies which offer credit or monthly terms could include gyms, who often allow members to pay their annual fee on a monthly basis.

Profitability

The majority of companies in the leisure and tourism industry are private companies, which means that they need to make a profit to survive.

From the mid-1980s the large companies in the travel industry, both travel agencies and tour operators, have competed fiercely on price. In many instances they sacrifice profit and use their size to take over smaller companies. Their objective is to 'increase market share' rather than to 'maximise profit'. To increase market share means that they want to increase the number of customers. Ultimately, if a few large companies take over the smaller ones then there is less competition and customers have less choice. Organisations with a large market share are more likely to be profitable.

In the travel industry, the larger tour operators such as Thomson Holidays, Thomas Cook and Airtours can 'bulk buy' airline seats and accommodation to keep their costs down. They may own airlines and hotels, which means that the company has total control over costs and, therefore, prices. The next few years should see whether the large companies continue to increase their market share or whether they decide to increase their prices.

TEST YOUR KNOWLEDGE

Explain why market share is an important marketing objective for many organisations. Can you think of any leisure and tourism organisations in your area that sometimes introduce special offers to increase customer numbers?

SECTION SIX

Place

The Type of Outlet or Facility Used

In simple terms 'place' in the 4 Ps means where the product or service is sold. With regards to leisure and tourism there are various outlets or facilities used:

- Travel agents
- Leisure centres
- Gymnasiums
- Cinemas
- Hotels and restaurants

- Airports
- Call centres – many leisure and tourism organisations have special departments dedicated to telephone business
- The Internet

The internet is fast developing as a major outlet where travel services are sold. The low-cost airlines sell the vast majority of their tickets over the internet. easyJet and buzz both have elaborate websites which give plenty of information about their products and services, and even about anticipated problems with travel to the airport. In addition, websites have easy booking procedures to allow customers to book online. This enables the companies to keep costs down because they do not need to employ many reservations staff.

123

Increasingly other providers, such as hotels and car hire companies, are developing their own websites. Sportswear can be imported directly from the US at half the UK price.

Other web operators sell discounted books and CDs. Amazon.co.uk is a prime example of an operator which offers such goods for sale at much lower prices than in many high street stores. However, WHSmith and Ottakars are hitting back with lower prices as the internet revolution impacts on prices in the high street.

ACTIVITY

Choose a European destination and research the cost of getting there through the internet, through a traditional travel agency and on teletext.

Figure 2.13

The Location of Outlets and Facilities

Organisations will locate where large numbers of people have access to their products and services. As discussed earlier, Xscape, the leisure park containing Snozone, chose to locate in Milton Keynes because this area has a large population with very good road and rail networks. More people from further away can travel there relatively quickly.

In the 1980s Thomas Cook planned its new agencies as close to Marks & Spencer shops as possible. This was because Marks & Spencers always attracted many people to its stores and often was the focus for customers in shopping centres. Lunn Poly, in turn, tried to open its new shops as close to Thomas Cook as it could. This was because they hoped that customers would find it easy to compare their prices and services with that of the competition. In fact, frequently in town centres you will find a number of travel agencies situated close together.

Figure 2.14 Travel agency

However, this is only part of the story. With travel agencies, airlines and tour operators there are several 'places' where the sale occurs. There is the place where the service is sold (internet, telephone or high street), there is also the departure airport, and, of course, the destination the businessperson or holiday-maker is going to.

buzz airlines made Stansted its base because it is close to London. Most low-cost airlines use the smaller airports within the UK to set up base.

Not only are these airports smaller, they are also cheaper to fly from than airports like Heathrow and Manchester, and they are much less busy. This means that 'turnabout times' for aircraft are shorter.

'Turnabout time' is the amount of time that an aeroplane spends on the ground after arriving from one destination and before departing for the next one. The short 'turnabout time' means more flying time, which means more money is earned.

In addition, Stansted is still expanding and provides easy access to the European destinations that buzz flies to.

Another low-cost airline, easyJet, long associated with London Luton, is now the second largest scheduled airline at London Gatwick. The company expanded to Gatwick because it believes that London has two separate catchment areas. easyJet's main operating hub at Luton attracts people from central and north London, but Gatwick is more convenient for people living in south London and the surrounding counties.

In terms of destinations, tour operators are always looking for new hotels and resorts to tempt the holiday-maker. Meanwhile the low-cost airlines increase the range of their destinations almost weekly. New destinations for buzz include their internal French flights, for example Brest to Marseilles and Bordeaux to Toulon. Ryanair are now flying from London Stansted to Newquay, and easyJet are flying from Gatwick to Barcelona.

Identification of Distribution Channels

Distribution channels are the means by which a product or service gets from the principal (tour operator, airline, hotel, etc.) to the customer. So, for example, a hotel room can be booked in a number of ways:

◆ Ringing the hotel direct
◆ Through a travel agency
◆ Via a website through a hotel booking agency
◆ Through a tour operator as part of a package holiday
◆ Via the Tourist Information Centre

buzz airlines allows customers to book:

◆ through the buzz website, www.buzz.co.uk
◆ via a call centre for those who prefer to make the booking on the phone
◆ at the buzz sales desk at the London Stansted terminal.

Thomas Cook Holidays and jmc (John Mason Cook) can be booked:

◆ through travel agencies
◆ direct via Thomas Cook Direct, a contact centre.

British Airways and other scheduled airlines have numerous distribution channels:

◆ Direct over the phone
◆ Via the British Airways website – www.britishairways.com

125

◆ Through travel agencies
◆ Through tour operators as part of a package holiday
◆ Through consolidators – organisations which specialise in selling cheap flights to the public
◆ Via BA miles – a programme aimed at people who travel frequently on British Airways. Travellers are awarded points every time they fly with the airline, and they can collect enough points for a free flight anywhere.
◆ Via Air Miles. Air Miles can be collected in a variety of different ways usually as part of loyalty programmes (see page 133). Tesco, NatWest and Shell all have loyalty cards that allow people to collect points. British Airways is one of the airlines that accepts points.

You can see that some organisations have very complicated distribution channels, with a variety of ways to get their product or service to their customers.

ACTIVITY

In pairs, choose three different leisure and tourism companies and investigate what distribution channels they use for their products or services. A good place to start may be the relevant websites. Compare the different methods used and discuss which you feel are the most successful.

ASSESSMENT ACTIVITY

At the beginning of Section Three on the Marketing Mix, you briefly identified how your chosen organisation uses the marketing mix to sell itself. Now you need to expand your answer.

◆ The full range of products and services must be described and should include the features of key products and services, together with outline details of all other products and services.
◆ The complete range of prices available should be detailed including basic prices, special offers, concessionary rates (cheaper rates for children, senior citizens, etc.) and discounts if used.
◆ You also need to explain fully how products and services are made available to customers and how they are promoted.
◆ Now you must describe how the 4 Ps work together. To do this you must first describe the objectives of the organisation.
◆ Now you have shown how the 4 Ps work together, explain how this allows them to meet the organisation's objectives. For example, a public leisure centre may have an objective to give access to as many people as possible. If it is placed in a popular location with good public transport links and free car parking spaces and it provides good concessionary fares during off-peak times for old age pensioners and the unemployed, there is an interrelationship between two of the 4 Ps that helps the leisure centre to meet its objective. How does your company meet its objectives through the 4 Ps?

SECTION SEVEN

Promotion

Different Types of Promotional Techniques

The term promotion describes all the methods that an organisation uses to tell customers about, and to persuade them to buy, its products and services. The different types of promotional techniques that a leisure and tourism organisation can use include:

◆ advertising
◆ direct marketing
◆ public relations
◆ personal selling
◆ displays
◆ sponsorship
◆ demonstrations and visits
◆ sales promotions.

Advertising

Advertisements are messages sent through the media intended to inform or persuade the people who receive them. There are many possible locations for advertising:

◆ Newspapers, magazines and leaflets
◆ Television and radio
◆ Cinemas
◆ Hoardings
◆ Buses, taxis, trains
◆ On the internet

Even well-established companies need to advertise in order to retain customer loyalty, repeat business and their share of the market. Fierce competition makes it necessary to advertise. If one travel company starts an advertising campaign, all the other tour operators and travel agencies do the same.

After Christmas and through to March is the peak time for holiday travel advertising on TV. Leisure centres and private gyms also advertise widely in local newspapers after Christmas – they try to encourage those feeling guilty from overeating to get into better habits.

Printed Material

Newspaper and magazine adverts are by far the most popular media. There are about 9000 regular publications in the UK that can be used by advertisers. These range from national newspapers, such as *The Sun* and the *Daily Mail*, which allow companies to advertise to a very large audience, through to magazines like *The Travel Trade Gazette*, which allows the advertiser to communicate with people in the travel

industry. Organisations can use specialist magazines to advertise their products and services to people with an interest in that area. For example, magazines on fishing or golfing should have a readership who will be receptive to hearing about new fishing and golfing holidays.

The benefit of advertising in newspapers and magazines is that long detailed messages are acceptable and the advert may be read by many people over a long period of time (think of GPs' surgeries and dentists' waiting rooms).

Broadcast Media

This includes TV and radio adverts. Television is accessed by 98 per cent of households and viewing figures for some programmes can exceed 20 million. Television advertisements are expensive, however, and are only on for the 20–30 seconds. With the introduction of Sky, the number of opportunities for television advertising has greatly increased.

The types of advertisements chosen by companies are usually determined by the budget available. Charity event organisers are likely to place small advertisements in local papers, shop windows, schools and on posters, whereas large sportswear companies can afford to place their advertisements on TV, in cinemas and in the press.

External Agencies

Large companies will usually employ an advertising agency to handle all of their promotional work. For example, McDonald's uses the advertising agency Leo Burnett to design and place its advertisements.

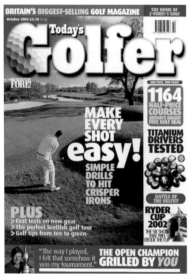

Figure 2.15

Brand	McDonald's Happy Meals	Date – Airdate	European delivery date – 1st Dec '00
Campaign Title	McD's Happy Meals – Bionic Bugs	Budget – Media	£200k
Date – Briefing	26.06.00	Budget – Production	£146k

WHY are we advertising?

To increase sales in McDonald's Happy Meals, by introducing & demonstrating to kids all the fun that can be had playing with and looking through Bionic Bugs.

WHO are we talking to, and what insights do we have about them?

Children aged between 3 and 8 years old.

They are familiar with McDonald's Happy Meals and the toys they get, but not Bionic Bugs and all the fun that can be had with them – yet.

Kids love things like bugs, worms, creepy crawleys etc. (pulling wings off them). In essence all the things that adults don't. They are fascinated with them. Perhaps because of an affinity with little things. Perhaps because they can do what they want with them without reprimand or because they can do it without being seen.

Kids also like to be the boss when they play in their imaginary worlds. Creating characters how they want, and building a world around them from their own unique view.

Looking at things from different angles, making them appear distorted in someway is highly amusing to kids (just like mirrors at a fair ground). It gives them an element of control to change what in reality they can't. Their Mums' faces, the size of their hands etc…

This personalising of the situation also translates to personalising the look of the characters in it, by "clicking and snapping" them together to make loads of combinations that they can show off to their friends. The bugs' 3 detachable body parts allow them to do just that.

WHAT SIMPLE, SINGLE THING DO WE WANT TO SAY TO THEM?

Get Bug Eyed at McDonald's.

HOW can we make this believable?

Every child that buys a Happy Meal will receive a Bionic Bug toy too. All 8 Bionic Bugs have a unique eye feature that if looked through, alters what you would normally see. So as well as playing with the bugs and making up new combinations from their 3 detachable body parts you can look through their eyes and literally see things as they do.

Cool Dude – With his special night vision eyes, everything looks green, including your straw.

Cryptic Bug – Be a super spy and find out what is written in the secret piece of paper that comes with this bug.

I.C.U – With his telescopic eyes, everything looks bigger, so you have an even bigger burger than your brother.

3D – With a special image attached, that you can see as though it were real (3D).

Hypno bug – with continuous spiralling eyes, you can mesmerise your teacher.

Angel eyes – creates holographic patterns on everything you see.

Multi Mate – with his multi-diamond patterned eyes, the view is fragmented.

Multi Miss – With her molded plastic circular eyes, the view is fragmented into a multi-circular pattern.

Figure 2.16 A Leo Burnett brief

ACTIVITY

The magazine *Marketing* produces an 'Adwatch' feature each week, which lists the top 20 TV commercials recalled by consumers.

List five adverts that you can recall. What do you think has made these adverts so memorable to you?

ADWATCH
The weekly analysis of advertisment recall
Q: Which of the following TV commercials do you remember seeing recently?

	Last week	Account	Agency/TV buyer	%
1	(1)	B&Q	BatesUK/Zenith Media	80
2	(10)	Sainsbury's	AbbottMeadVickersBBDO/PHD	67
3	(4=)	Woolworths	BatesUK/Zenith Media	66
4	(4=)	Terry's Chocolate Orange	BMP DDB/Zenith Media	63
4=		AOL	MortimerWhittakerO'Sullivan/ BBJ Media	63
4=		Skoda	Fallon/MediaCom	63
7	(12)	Comet	Saatchi & Saatchi/Zenith Media	54
8		Budweiser	DDB Chicago/OMD UK	50
9		MFI	Publicis/Optimedia	47
10=		NiQuitinCQ	Ogilvy & Mather/MediaCom	43
10=	(11)	WH Smith	AbbottMeadVickersBBDO/ Starcom Motive	43
12=		Currys	M&C Saatchi/WalkerMedia	42
12=		Lloyds TSB	Saatchi & Saatchi/Zenith Media	42
12=		Olay	Saatchi & Saatchi/Starcom Motive	42
15		Daily Mail	FCB Productions/MediaVest	28
16		Sharps Bedrooms	BCMB/MBS Media	22
17		Dolphin Bathrooms	BCMB/MBS Media	20
18		Waterstone's	Bds beechwood/PHD	13
10	(22=)	Meltus	McCann-Erickson/ Universal McCann Manchester	9

Adwatch research was conducted from January 18 to January 20 by **NOP Research Group** (020 7809 9948) as part of a weekly telephone omnibus survey among more than 500 adults. Copies of the Adwatch data and analysis are available from Victoria Black at NOP. Advertisements were selected by **Xtreme Information** (020 7871 8080) and **CIA UK** (020 7633 9999)

Figure 2.17   Adwatch in *Marketing*

Direct Marketing

Direct mail is advertising sent through the post, addressed to a person.

There has been a massive increase in direct mail in recent years as the information that companies hold about their customers has become more sophisticated. If you have a store card or a 'loyalty' card, your name and address plus what you tend to buy will be held on a database somewhere. This information may then be used by organisations to promote particular products or services to customers who they think will be interested in them.

The ability of direct mail to target precise market segments saves money (it is cost-effective) because it means that only customers who are likely to buy the product, receive the information.

The majority of direct mail is read by the recipient and organisations often combine direct mail with sales promotions, such as offers and competitions, to encourage a response.

Public Relations

Public Relations (PR) is the planned effort that an organisation makes to establish, develop and build relationships with the public. The public can include potential customers, employees and shareholders.

It takes a long time for a company to improve the way people think about its products and activities. The Millennium Dome never fully recovered from its launch evening, when many important people were left queuing for hours. Many newspapers criticised some of the Dome's activities and questioned whether the cost of the Dome was worthwhile. This public relations problem haunted the Dome for the entire year that it was open.

There are various types of PR activity including:

◆ **Press releases**. These tell stories of what is happening in the company, such as new openings, news stories, policy changes and so on.
◆ **Hospitality**. For instance, at Wimbledon and other major sporting events, large companies may entertain their customers, treating them to lavish meals and an opportunity to view the sport.

Creative Music opens at Xscape

Xscape are pleased to announce the opening of Creative Music – a totally new type of musical superstore.

Creative Music contains a permanent live performance area, DJ and vinyl bar and the Creative Juices coffee and juice bar. The whole emphasis is on giving the customer a 'hands on' experience with specialist staff allocated to each section and all displayed equipment available for audition in the acoustically-treated demo booths.

The permanent live performance area is in the centre of the shop and provides one of the focal points of the superstore, creating the venue not only for masterclasses and workshops, but also for the Creative Fame Academy. Employees from Creative Music were involved in the development of the BBC1 TV series aired in 2002.

So if you want to be the up and coming star of the future get in touch!

The superstore is open from 10.00 a.m to 8.00 p.m.

The contact phone number is 08718 728 2286

The web address is www.creativetechnologies.co.uk

Figure 2.18   Example of press release

Personal Selling

This is still an important part of promotion in leisure and tourism. Well-trained and knowledgeable sales staff are still valued by customers in this industry.

The death of the travel agency has been suggested ever since computerisation. However, customers still like the personal service from staff who know them and their tastes. Staff involved in face-to-face selling in leisure and tourism include:

◆ Travel agents
◆ Resort representatives selling excursions
◆ Cabin crew selling duty-free goods
◆ Leisure centre staff selling coaching and sports equipment
◆ Timeshare sales staff
◆ Ticket sales people in theatres, theme parks and tourist attractions
◆ Catering and accommodation staff

The aim of personal selling is to sell the customer something! It requires matching a customer's needs with the goods and services on offer. Many leisure and tourism organisations spend a large amount of money on personal selling. Think of the cost of employing sales people and training them. The next unit on customer care goes into selling in greater depth.

Displays

Displays can take various forms:

◆ **In-store displays**. For example, some travel agencies have cardboard advertising boards in the shop. These may hold leaflets promoting a particular service or they may be an additional advertising tool, telling you more about a product or service that the organisation sells.
◆ **Window displays**. Many leisure and tourism organisations with suitable premises will use window displays effectively – this is free advertising. They have already paid for the window and people passing by will notice any eye-catching displays promoting products and services. Travel agencies use window displays often to promote last minute deals or special offers on tour operator holidays.

Sponsorship

Sponsorship is a business arrangement where both sides aim to benefit. The organisation or sponsor will provide money for a person or event. In return, the sponsor's company will have its name or logo displayed.

An obvious advantage of sponsorship can be seen with football. The companies who sponsor football clubs have their company name or logo emblazoned on the shirts of players. These are viewed by spectators both at the pitch and watching their television at home. The football club receives money and the sponsor receives advertising which is seen by potential customers.

Sports sponsorship is the most common form of sponsorship. It can range from Flora advertising the London Marathon, to a small local business sponsoring the under 9s in the local youth football team. NTL sponsors a number of football clubs, including Scottish arch rivals Rangers and Celtic and the English club Newcastle United.

Can you list five sponsors and the sporting events that they are tied into?

Tobacco companies often sponsor sporting events because they are unable to promote their products in many other ways. There have been government discussions about curtailing this activity. Do you think tobacco companies should be allowed to continue sponsoring international sporting events?

Talk about...

Figure 2.19   British Grand Prix

Demonstrations and Visits

Because leisure and tourism involves the sale of so many 'intangible' services, it is difficult for customers to try something before they buy it. Leisure centres, golf and tennis clubs hold open days so that customers can try out different activities before committing themselves to join. Exhibitions enable the public to try out sports and leisure equipment or to taste the food of a particular country. Timeshare and overseas property companies invite potential buyers to view the accommodation, frequently providing transport and hotel accommodation to the resort. Travel agents are often invited on educational visits to look at resorts and accommodation – personal knowledge helps with personal selling. These 'educational visits' are greatly valued by travel agency staff.

Sales Promotion

Sales promotions are measures used to entice customers to buy. They include:

◆ two-for-the-price-of-one offers
◆ vouchers for money off or free entrance
◆ special discounts
◆ price reductions
◆ free gifts
◆ prize draws
◆ loyalty schemes.

Most sales promotion techniques are short term. That is, they are introduced for a limited time period to increase sales. For example, national newspapers like the *Sun* will team up with a theme park to offer vouchers that discount the entry price. Travel agencies might offer free insurance for holidays booked in the month of January. buzz airlines may run two-for-one seat offers in conjunction with *The Times* newspaper.

One long-term sales promotion method that has increased in popularity is the loyalty card scheme. A loyalty card allocates points when the customer makes a purchase. Some leisure and tourism organisations have their own loyalty cards. For instance, many airlines, including British Airways, Virgin and KLM, award points for air travel. These points can then be used to reduce the cost of a future flight (see Case Study overleaf).

Many other organisations are keen to use leisure and tourism as the customer incentive for accumulating points. Companies have responded to the wishes of their customers. 'Travel and leisure are by a long way the favoured incentive' said a Tesco spokesperson after it was announced that Tesco had seized the Air Miles reward brand from Sainsbury's.

Simply more **rewarding journeys**.

We've made Shell pluspoints easy – after all, you've got enough to think about when you're out on the road. Here's how it works:

• For every litre you buy at Shell, you earn one pluspoint.

• Plus, you get bonus pluspoints up to four times a year (depending on how far you drive) and statements showing your balance.

• Collect enough pluspoints, and exchange them for £10 shopping vouchers, Shell vouchers or AIR MILES. You can even use them to make a donation to charity.

So the more times you visit a participating Shell Service Station, the more pluspoints you'll earn – and the more rewards you can claim.

Drive for miles. **Earn AIR MILES**.

Why not swap the highways and byways of Britain for the freeways of America or the autoroutes of France? You can exchange your pluspoints for AIR MILES – so whether it's a short break, a package holiday, a treat for the family closer to home or a flight to any of hundreds of world-wide destinations, AIR MILES have it covered.

1,500 Shell pluspoints = 100 AIR MILES

EXECUTIVE CLUB BRITISH AIRWAYS   Alternatively, if you are a British Airways Executive Club member, you may wish to exchange your pluspoints for BA Miles.

1,500 Shell pluspoints = 1,000 BA Miles

Figure 2.20   Air Miles marketing information

Air Miles Loyalty Scheme

When Keith Mills founded Air Miles in the late 1980s, he recognised that it was a great way for British Airways to shift 9 million empty off-peak seats. However, if these seats were sold at rock bottom prices it could damage the brand name of British Airways. He also realised that free flights could be a powerful loyalty motivator for retailers. In other words, customers could be encouraged to buy more or shop more often if they were likely to be rewarded with a free flight. Sainsbury's, NatWest and Shell bought into Air Miles and based their loyalty schemes around them. In turn British Airways filled more seats.

Retailers quickly realised how these schemes could change customer behaviour and many copy-cat loyalty schemes have been introduced. Air Miles is still a well-known name and Tesco have recently acquired the Air Miles reward brand.

One leading loyalty consultant said, 'Going on holiday is an emotional purchase, a treat. So behaviour really does change and this is the holy grail for a successful loyalty scheme'.

Appropriate Promotional Techniques

Different promotional techniques are used by different organisations at different times. A national company might use a national television advertisement to establish its name and promote itself. Thomson Holidays, for instance, will advertise quite extensively from January to March when most people book their summer holiday. The aim is to bring their name to potential customers' minds when they are looking for brochures and planning their holiday. This is also a time when there are many holidays still available.

However, when it comes to the months of June and July and late bookers are trying to find the last remaining holidays for the summer, Thomson Holidays is more likely to advertise in newspapers. This is cheaper for the the company and it can also include more detail about specific holidays and any discounts available.

Companies currently based in one place, such as Xscape, will promote their products and services in regional newspapers and on regional television. This is cheaper and there is little point in advertising in Newcastle, when Milton Keynes is so far away. However, Xscape has found that its potential geographical catchment area to be much larger than anticipated. People now regularly travel from London for skiing sessions in the largest indoor ski slope in the UK.

If buzz wants to update Club buzz members on its new services, it will use direct marketing because it has the addresses on its database. This targets a market that has already shown an interest in buzz services, and should be a very effective promotional technique.

ACTIVITY

Identify the promotional technique that you would use for the scenarios outlined below. Explain why you chose this technique.

a) The local leisure centre wishes to advertise its new pilates exercise class.

b) A national tour operator is introducing a new brochure called 'Cookery Classes in Italy'.

c) A major restaurant chain has decided to sell some of its famous ingredients such as relishes and salad dressings, via the internet.

Effective promotional methods must reflect the target customer. In 2002, McDonald's ran the 'largest retail-based mobile marketing campaign ever carried out in Europe'. It ran a text messaging campaign mainly aimed at the 12–19 age group, who use text messaging as a major form of communication.

McDonald's in SMS movie deal

McDonald's is to run its first SMS (text messaging) campaign – a tie in with the UK opening of Disney's hit movie "Monsters, Inc.".

The mobile specialist 12snap, which has created the campaign alongside promotions agency The Marketing Store, claims it will be "the largest retail-based mobile marketing campaign ever carried out in Europe."

Breaking on February 8 and running for four weeks, it includes all 1,200 McDonald's restaurants in the UK. Millions of French fries boxes will have a "Monsters, Inc." peel-off door revealing one of six characters from the film, next to a special code and a text-in number. Consumers should received an immediate reply text letting them know if they have won a prize.

Prizes include 500 widescreen TVs, 2,000 DVD players, 5,000 MP3 players, 1,000 Toy Story DVD box sets and 370,000 ring-tones and logos.

Anne de Kerckhove, managing director of 12snap, says: "This project is a huge leap forward for the mobile medium."

The promotion is supported in restaurants, with nationwide TV ads and online at textamonster.co.uk, which goes live on February 8.

Source: *Marketing Week* 31 January 2002

Different Types of Promotional Material

The leisure and tourism industry uses a wide variety of promotional materials including the following.

1 Advertisements

These include adverts on television and in newspapers, on billboards, on bus shelters, in magazines, on the internet, radio and cinema, etc.

Figure 2.21

2 Brochures and Leaflets

When customers think of brochures, they think generally of holiday brochures. The tourism industry makes considerable use of brochures. They are expensive to produce and distribute, but they are the main selling tool for tour operators and travel agencies. A holiday is an 'intangible' product and so brochures with photographs and descriptions are the main way that travel companies can explain the benefits of their product to the customer.

Most brochures are produced in colour, on good quality paper and have excellent photography. Because this is the first opportunity to attract a customer, a brochure has to be visually appealing. A glance at any travel agency brochure rack will demonstrate the amount of competition there is. Tour operators have to ensure that their brochure is displayed well. Many will pay extra commission to travel agencies to ensure that their brochure is displayed in a prominent position (at eye level and about two racks in from the front door). Brochures are very expensive to produce and travel agents are rated by the tour operator according to the number of holidays they have booked in the past. The more they sell, the more brochures they will receive.

Leaflets are used to describe all types of leisure facilities and tourist attractions. They are distributed through tourist information centres, hotels, inside newspapers and at the actual attraction itself. Leaflets are generally cheaper to produce and can be changed more frequently than a large brochure.

When using leaflets as a promotional technique, you must ensure that they are placed in the correct locations. It is a waste for a small tourist attraction in Aberdeen to display hundreds of leaflets in a hotel in Wales because it is unlikely that this will target potential customers.

3 Merchandising

Merchandising involves producing products, such as pens, pencils, notebooks, mugs and diaries with a company's logo or image printed on them.

Quite often merchandise is given out as 'freebies' to people who could influence potential customers. The average travel agency will have a large number of mugs, pens, calendars, notebooks and mouse mats. T-shirts, travel bags, balloons and pencils carrying company logos are popular prizes in competitions and prize draws. If you are organising a fund-raising event it may be possible to get some of these items from leisure and tourism organisations to use as raffle prizes.

The large football clubs make a substantial income from merchandising material. They merchandise curtains, bed linen, mugs, pens and, of course, football strips. There is constant debate about the number of times that football clubs change the colour or design of strips and encourage fans to spend more money. In addition to raising money, merchandise does raise the profile of the club.

1 Contact two different football clubs to obtain their merchandising brochure and any other promotional material they have regarding the club. Use this material to identify the different types of customers that the club is trying to sell to.

2 Check out the easyJet website at http://www.easyjet.com and click on easyJet gifts. Find out the cost of five items and identify which types of customers they might appeal to.

Figure 2.22 Football club merchandise

137

4 Videos

Videos and DVDs are a growing resource used by the leisure and tourism industry. They are a good way for potential customers to view an 'intangible' product. The Disneylands in both Florida and Paris advertise their free videos in their television advertising. Tourist boards for different countries produce their own videos to promote the tourist aspects of their countries.

In the leisure field, videos have become a product in themselves. There are countless aerobics, pilates, yoga and diet videos aimed at getting our 'couch potato' nation in shape.

Football clubs sell videos about their recent successful games, while many sports sell videos produced by experts which aim to help improve the performance of customers. These may demonstrate new products, e.g. golf clubs and football boots, or introduce new sports, e.g. snowboarding.

Figure 2.23

5 Press Releases

Companies, perhaps after talking to a public relations consultant, will issue press releases in the hope that the media will use them.

Press releases can be used on various occasions:

◆ To advertise a new service, attraction or destination
◆ To announce changes in staffing or company name
◆ To draw attention to a closure
◆ To lessen the effect of bad news on the performance of the company
◆ To notify customers about forthcoming events, e.g. the appearance of a celebrity

Local newspapers are usually very happy to print press releases about local events and so smaller organisations and voluntary groups often gain free publicity in this way.

Unlike paid advertising which can be booked for a particular date, press releases depend on the other news which a newspaper or television news editor wants to print at a particular time – there is no guarantee that anything will be printed at all.

Press releases need to be very carefully written and presented. They should give the company name, address and 24-hour contact numbers. The copy should be double spaced with wide margins. The opening sentence must immediately attract attention and convey the message.

6 Internet Sites

Internet websites are a rapidly growing promotional technique for leisure and tourism organisations.

The booking procedures involved in organising a flight or holiday mean that the travel industry has long been at the forefront of any new technology. The internet has given many companies the opportunity for customers to book flights directly, without talking to an agent at all. This has saved the company money in staff costs and, in many instances, the company has passed at least some of these savings on to the customer. This provides an incentive for potential customers to visit the site and companies promote their services on the websites.

For example, buzz, at www.buzz.co.uk, uses its site to promote its destinations and the lowest fares. buzz also advertises Airport PLUS packages, which at an additional cost allow customers fast-track security clearance and access to a VIP lounge, amongst other things. buzz also advertises various sites and partners that provide accommodation.

easyJet, at www.easyjet.co.uk, uses many promotional news stories on its site, always emphasising how cheap and popular its airline is. In addition, easyJet advertises many other services, including car hire and currency exchange.

Xscape, at www.xscape.co.uk, provides information on all its facilities. Xscape also has Xscape TV, which consists of 20 plasma screens within the complex and a huge LED screen on front of the building. The website tells you how any company can advertise there. Xscape also sponsors athletes who represent the country in activities that are available in the complex. You can catch up on their activities on the website too.

Factors to Remember to Make Promotional Materials Effective

1 The material itself should be attractive and eye-catching. You want the reader to be interested and keen to find out about what is being advertised.
2 The timing of the campaign should be planned. There is no point in advertising Thorpe Park when it is closed!
3 The distribution of the literature should be planned carefully. Place it where your potential target market will find it.
4 If the organisation has received bad publicity because of an accident, for example, then any promotional campaign will struggle to make a positive impact on people.

SWOT Analysis

SWOT stands for Strengths, Weaknesses, Opportunities and Threats. A SWOT analysis focuses on the strengths, weaknesses, opportunities and threats facing a company and its products or services at a given moment. It includes both an internal and an external element. The internal element looks at current strengths and weaknesses of the organisation. The external element looks at the opportunities and threats present in the environment in which the organisation operates.

Inside the organisation (Internal)	Outside the organisation (External)
Strengths (Positive)	Opportunities (Positive)
Weaknesses (Negative)	Threats (Negative)

A simple SWOT analysis might show that a company has the following:

Strengths

◆ Good product
◆ Good relationship with customers
◆ Good management team

Weaknesses

◆ A small company which operates on a small scale
◆ Bank accounts can be low after creating a product and waiting for sales
◆ Small regional market

Opportunities

◆ New, growing market
◆ Meeting changing tastes of customers
◆ Could sell other related products or services

Threats

◆ Growing competition from other companies
◆ Recession, threats of war

In the case studies in this unit each company has carefully outlined their own SWOT analysis. Have a good look at these.

A SWOT analysis for McDonald's might look something like this:

Strengths Good brand name Good quality service Child-friendly facilities	Opportunities New product ranges based on chicken and fish Diversification into other markets, e.g. McDonald's is an owner of the sandwich shop Pret A Manger
Weaknesses Staff recruitment problems	Threats BSE scare with beef Growth in vegetarianism Increasing awareness of value of eating a low fat diet

ACTIVITY

In pairs choose two local leisure and tourism organisations and undertake your own SWOT analysis of both organisations.

Figure 2.24 Pret A Manger

Figure 2.25 McDonald's

How SWOT can be used

As a result of carrying out a SWOT analysis, an organisation should develop policies and practices that enable it to build upon its strengths, minimise its weaknesses, seize its opportunities and take measures that cancel out or minimise threats.

For example, McDonald's is constantly reviewing staff pay, benefits and progression, in order to encourage new employees. It is also a very flexible employer in terms of hours worked. McDonald's constantly trials new products, including salads and meals which use more chicken and vegetables. Its diversification into Pret A Manger means that it has spread its risks for maintaining its income and profit. Customers view Pret A Manger as a more healthy food option than McDonald's. The company uses high quality products and makes its sandwiches on the premises fresh every day. Any left over food at the end of the day is given to charities to distribute to the homeless. Pret A Manger has been named as one of the top ten employers in the UK. In fact, some of their sandwiches are laden with more fat and calories than a McDonald's burger!

If you look at the SWOT analysis that buzz produced, you can see that they viewed the increase in business travellers as an opportunity. Some of their recent product development and promotion work has been geared to ensuring that this increase continues. For example, the Airport PLUS packages allow priority check in, easy car parking and access to an executive lounge area and this service is aimed primarily at business travellers. The development of Club buzz means that the airline can communicate directly with frequent users, including business users, because they hold their names and addresses.

Producing a SWOT analysis for an organisation is a good starting point. This should be carried out before you analyse and assess the range of promotional techniques and materials that are produced for the company's different customer types (target markets).

ACTIVITY

Choose either Xscape or buzz. Study the SWOT analysis carefully. Now produce an item of promotional material for the organisation that advertises either an existing service or introduces a new one that you have devised.

Describe the market you are targeting for your campaign and justify how your promotional material will reach these particular people.

ASSESSMENT ACTIVITY

Undertake a SWOT analysis for the organisation that you investigated during your marketing studies in Section Two of this unit.

SECTION NINE

Promotional Campaigns

The success of promotional campaigns depends on thorough planning beforehand. Below are illustrations of the type of planning a company will undertake to ensure that its promotional campaign is a successful one.

What a Promotional Campaign Tries to Achieve

When a company launches a marketing campaign, it will usually have an objective or objectives that it is trying to achieve. For example:

◆ To raise the number of customers using the organisation, e.g. the Millenium Dome
◆ To promote a new location, e.g. Lunn Poly opening a new branch
◆ To promote a new product that the organisation is selling, e.g. Xbox
◆ To attract a new target market, e.g. buzz promoting its destination of Murcia through golfing magazines

Almost all private companies, and many public and voluntary ones, will also want to make more money for the organisation.

Who the Target Market Is

Once a company has decided the main objectives for its marketing campaign, it will need to decide who its campaign target market will be. For instance if Xscape wish to open a new skateboard facility, its target market will probably be young people aged from 9–19 years of

Figure 2.26

age. However, if buzz wants to expand its destinations and fly to the Algarve in Portugal, where golfing holidays are very popular, its target market will be people aged 35–60 years of age. A tour operator like Thomson Holidays could aim a campaign at travel agents, rather than directly at the customer.

What Promotional Techniques to Use

Once the target market has been identified, it is much easier to decide what promotional technique to use. This is because some forms of promotion will be very successful with one target market segment, whereas a completely different promotional campaign will need to be used for another.

If Xscape, for example, is trying to target young people aged 9–19 it might use text messaging because this age group is a high user of mobile phones. Xscape could put posters on billboards near schools and colleges. It might offer two people entrance for the price of one because this age group can be price sensitive and is far more likely to take part in an activity with a friend.

buzz, on the other hand, could promote its cheap flight to the Algarve through advertising in specialist golfing magazines. It could send leaflets to the Club buzz members who fall within its target market. buzz might link up with a golf course in the area and offer their passengers a free day of golf at a first-class golf course.

Thomson Holidays could send literature to travel agents to highlight the main things they want agents to remember. They might link this to a competition to win a holiday in order to motivate travel agents to read and remember the information.

Research must be undertaken before a promotional technique is decided upon to ensure that the technique will reach the target market identified.

What Promotional Materials to Use

Different age groups and/or sexes often respond to different words, phrases and language. When deciding on a campaign, the promotional materials should attract the target market that the organisation wants. One technique often quoted with regard to promotional materials is AIDA: Attention, Interest, Desire, Action.

First of all promotional materials should attract the attention of customers. How? This is not always easy! Sometimes humour, bright colours, music, celebrity pictures and interesting 'catch phrases' are used.

Next, the customers' interest must be retained. One way of doing this is to make the product relevant to the customer: show teenagers having fun skateboarding, if teenagers are the target market you want to attract.

The third phase is to instil desire. Skateboarding is an activity, but it also involves an element of excitement and the ability to demonstrate skill and agility to peers. A marketeer should aim to reinforce the connection between customers' desires and the benefits of the product or service.

The final stage should make it simple for the customer to take action. For example, by providing a phone number or tear off slip for further information. The easier a promoter makes it for customers to buy a product, the more likely they are to do so.

How to Monitor and Evaluate the Success of the Campaign

It is important to monitor a promotional campaign to ensure that the money spent has succeeded in helping the organisation to reach its objectives. There are many different ways that a company can try to monitor the effect of a promotional campaign:

◆ Companies may undertake surveys that ask customers if and how they have heard of the product they are promoting
◆ Companies can provide vouchers or coupons with a special offer, which can be counted when redeemed – this is an excellent way of monitoring the success of a campaign
◆ Companies may compare profit and/or sales of the current year with last year.
◆ Companies may compare the number of customers they have this year with last year

An evaluation should always be undertaken after a promotional campaign to look at what has happened and what could be improved for next time. The following questions should be asked:

◆ Was the campaign successful in informing potential customers?
◆ Did it raise awareness in a beneficial way?
◆ Did more people buy the product?
◆ Did it raise the profile of the product and/or the organisation in people's minds?
◆ Did the campaign attract new customers and help to retain existing ones?

> **Comparing sales and the number of customers year on year may show that a promotion has been successful, but what else might this indicate?**
>
> **Talk about...**

Promotional Campaign Check-list

Research

1 Carry out a SWOT analysis to help to focus the campaign. Build upon strengths, minimise weaknesses, seize opportunities and take measures to cancel out or minimise threats.

Planning

2 Set objectives for the campaign.
3 Work out the target market for the campaign.
4 Decide what promotional techniques to use.
5 Decide what promotional materials to use.

Preparation

6 Use AIDA to prepare promotional materials.

Implementation

7 Monitor to ensure that the campaign progresses as planned.

Evaluation

8 Did it inform?
9 Did it raise awareness?
10 Did it make customers buy?
11 Was the image improved?
12 Did it attract new customers and retain old ones?

ASSESSMENT ACTIVITY

For the organisation that you have been studying in depth (see Section Two), you now need to produce a well-structured and creative item of promotional material. This should demonstrate a good understanding of target marketing. Your material should show some evidence of matching the pictures, graphics and wording to the target audience (e.g. photographs of people taking part in an activity usually show people of a similar age to the target market). It should be clear how the selected material – its images and choice of words – is appropriate for the target market.

SECTION TEN
The Marketing Assignment

You are an independent marketing consultant. Choose an organisation that you would like to investigate. You will advise them on their latest marketing campaign. This will involve researching the organisation in depth and then producing a report for the organisation that includes the following:

a A description of the 4 Ps in relation to the selected organisation showing how they work together to meet the organisation's objectives.
b An assessment of the range of promotional techniques and materials that the organisation uses, including research methods used to identify target markets.
c A comparison between one of the organisation's promotional campaigns and the promotional campaign of one other leisure and tourism organisation.
d An item of promotional material that you have produced for the organisation, designed to attract a particular target market.

Tips for Success

◆ You may find that your research and analysis will be easier if you produce a SWOT analysis.
◆ Specify what market research methods the organisation uses and how these methods helped to identify their target markets.
◆ If you have been on a visit to learn about the marketing activities of a particular company or if you have had a guest speaker in your centre, refer to the notes you made to give you ideas.

For Top Marks . . .

1 Your work must describe, in your own words, the full range of prices available, including basic prices, special offers, concessionary rates and discounts. You should also fully explain how these products and services are made available to customers and how they are promoted. You must describe the organisation's objectives and give a clear explanation of how the 4 P's interrelationship (working together) enables them to meet the organisation's objectives.

2 Your material must be logically structured, it must show imagination by using original ideas and it must be fully suited to the target market. Materials should show some evidence of matching the images, graphics, wording and content to the audience (e.g. photographs of people usually show people of a similar age to the target market).

3 You must provide a detailed assessment of the range of promotional techniques and materials that the organisation uses and show how they work together as a strategy. You must be clear about the differences between techniques and materials.

For full marks, the assessment must relate to the following criteria:
◆ target market
◆ objectives
◆ quality of the presentation
◆ use of colour and images
◆ originality of design in the assessment of all techniques and materials presented

Your analysis of the market research techniques used should include an appraisal of methods used and how these can be used to identify target markets.

4 Your promotional comparison should be presented with a detailed description of the campaign activities to be compared. The considerations for planning a promotional campaign listed on page 145 should be described and compared in depth for both organisations. You should reach conclusions that you can back up from your descriptions and analysis.

UNIT 3

CUSTOMER SERVICE

Introduction

Figure 3.1

What is customer service and why is it important to the industry?

Have you heard people say, 'If you have one dissatisfied customer, it could mean losing ten more'? What does this mean?

If customers are unhappy with the service that they get from a company, they will go elsewhere. In the meantime they will tell anyone who will listen about the poor service they received. Word of mouth is a strong tool for either building or destroying confidence.

When you work for an organisation, which provides a product or service to the general public, you have a loyalty to that company to sell that product or service in the best way that you possibly can. Everyone who approaches the company to buy that product or service is a customer and everyone else is a potential customer – even you. You are part of the structure of the company and, therefore, what you do impacts on the customers. You can affect the profit or even the existence of the company.

It is important that all employees are *positive* in their dealings with customers and that they create a favourable impression, even when outside company time.

WHAT YOU WILL LEARN ...

Customer Service in Leisure and Tourism

From this unit you will gain knowledge and understanding of the benefits of good customer service for various organisations. It will be helpful if you can use the information in the unit to support your investigation into a leisure and tourism organisation in your area.

You will look at how organisations meet the needs of different customers, communicate with those customers and deal with a variety of situations. You will investigate the use of records and administrative procedures, which support customer service. You will also consider the importance of first impressions and personal presentation. The topics covered will explain:

- The different types of customers, both internal and external
- The benefits of customer service
- The different communication methods used in organisations
- The importance of personal presentation
- The importance of keeping accurate records
- How to deal with customers, including complaints

Activities

The activities at the end of each section link with your study programme and help to develop evidence for assessment and the final assignment.

Assessment Evidence

To achieve this unit, you will need to produce:

◆ a review of the customer service provided by a selected leisure or tourism organisation
◆ a record of your involvement in a variety of real or simulated customer service situations.

The assignments at the end of the chapter should enable you to provide sufficient assessable evidence to achieve the unit.

Case Study

Customer Service at Pleasurewood Hills Leisure Park

WEBSITE – http://www.pleasurewood.com

Pleasurewood Hills is a Family Leisure Park. It caters for 260,000 customers every year. Those customers bring in revenue by paying an inclusive entrance fee and spending on retail, catering and amusements.

Who are the Customers?

Customers at Pleasurewood Hills fall into two main categories:

1 Families with young children
2 Single people up to the age of 17

The park caters well for people with disabilities and people with other special needs.

Benefits of Customer Service

Pleasurewood Hills provides quality customer service, which leads to increased sales and an enhancement of the company image. They have to compete with other attractions in the area and they adapt the facilities to cater for the needs of a demanding public.

Case Study (cont.)

Communication

The Managing Director says, 'You never get a second chance to make a first impression.'

Positive communication with the public will lead to customer satisfaction, and the possibility of a return visit.

All employees at Pleasurewood Hills go through extensive Customer Care Training, where they are given the opportunity to learn communication skills and how to deal with the public.

During their time on the park, employees may have to deal with a variety of situations – some of which may involve disputes and complaints. It is important that the staff develop skills in listening and responding and how to deal with difficult situations. Training videos are used extensively to give instruction on how to deal with customers in a variety of settings.

Face to Face

The majority of people who work for Pleasurewood Hills come into contact with the customers. The first call might be the ticket booth or the Customer Advice Centre. There are supervisors on the rides and sales people in the shops.

Other Forms of Communication

The administration buildings house the offices and are central to the organisation. From here the Receptionist deals with customers on the phone, by fax and by e-mail. She communicates with other members of the organisation. There is a team approach to the running of the facility. All staff are aware that they themselves are internal customers working together to provide a service for the external customers.

Customer service

There is plenty of promotional material in the form of leaflets, posters and a website for the park. They all give information to customers on a variety of topics. The website lists the following:

- Planning the day
- Student information
- Educational visits
- Rides and shows
- Group visits
- Media relations
- Job opportunities
- Online tickets
- Park facilities
- Opening times
- Maps and directions

Case Study (cont.)

Keeping Records

Pleasurewood Hills, like any other business, has built-in procedures, which require record-keeping and form-filling. A database is used to store information on bookings and customers. Various files are kept including up-to-date information on:

- policies
- quality assurance
- health and safety
- codes of practice
- events
- marketing and promotion.

Forms

Pleasurewood Hills uses a variety of forms to support the administration procedures in the organisation:

- Application forms for jobs
- Pre-paid ticket forms
- Group booking forms
- Telephone message sheets, memos and letterheads
- Health and safety forms, following strict procedures

Health and safety regulations are an important part of the organisation's quality assurance system. Every care has to be taken when dealing with rides and attractions. All employees have to be competent to operate machinery. There are a number of records which have to be kept on all aspects of the health and safety procedure.

Case Study (cont.)

Schools booking form

School details

School name: [_____]

Address: [_____]

City: [_____]   Postcode: [_____]

Telephone No: [_____]   e-mail: [_____]

Organising teacher: [_____]   Date of visit: [_____]

Estimated time of arrival: [_____]

Ticket details

Number of children/students: [_____]   at £7.75 each = £ [_____]

Number of teachers free:
1 per 10 children/ students. [_____]   NIL

Number of additional teachers/helpers: [_____]   at £7.75 each = £ [_____]

Total number of tickets: [_____]   Total payment: [_____]

Do you require party catering details: [Yes ▼]

Payment details

I am enclosing a cheque payable to Pleasurewood Hills Limited along with my printed form. [ ]

I wish to pay by credit or debit card online and have entered my details below. [ ]

Please charge £ [_____]   to my   [Please select ▼]

If other please specify [_____]

Account number
Credit card only, 4 digits per box. [____] [____] [____] [____]

Switch or other debit card number: [_____]   Issue number. Only applies if you are paying by Switch. [_____]

Card expiry date: [_____]   Name on card: [_____]

I would like to collect my tickets from the administration office upon my arrival. [ ]

I would like my tickets sent to me by post. [ ]

From time to time we may wish to keep you up to date with developments at Pleasurewood Hills and would like to retain your details on our lists. We confirm that any information you may provide will not be passed on to other organisations. Please tick here if you would prefer not to receive future correspondence from us.

[ ]   [Submit] [Reset]

Case Study

Customer Service at The Forum

Norfolk and Norwich Millennium Library

WEBSITE – http://www.theforumnorfolk.com

Norfolk and Norwich Millennium Library is part of a new development called The Forum. The Forum houses a cafe, a restaurant, the tourist information centre and a Heritage visitor attraction called 'Origins'.

The Millennium Library

Who are the Customers?

The library caters for everyone and states its purpose as being there 'to support reading and learning for all'.

The library has:

◆ 120,000 books to suit all tastes
◆ 85 PCs with free internet, e-mail and office software
◆ Computer facilities for people with disabilities
◆ 220 study spaces
◆ Access to CD-ROMs and a community information database
◆ Newspapers and magazines
◆ Electronic guiding system to help you locate subjects via touchscreens
◆ Videos and DVDs
◆ CDs
◆ Music scores

The Forum building has been designed to provide easy access for people with special needs and there is a large car park beneath the library with lifts to the main reception area.

There is something at the Forum for everyone. It is open and free to people who want to browse, borrow, get information, use the technology or simply take in the atmosphere.

All libraries in Norfolk have

◆ Free Internet access
◆ Free email
◆ Word processing, spreadsheets and presentation software (desktop publishing and web editing software in selected libraries)
◆ Netways: its own guide to selected online sites for health, learning, under 5s, community information, ICT skills, family history and quick reference.
◆ Online Catalogue
◆ Access to its own CD-ROMS and online information resources
◆ Access to 'Picture Norfolk': images and scenes from Norfolk's towns, villages, people, buildings and rural life
◆ Community Information
The Norfolk Community database has details of local clubs, and associations. Also health, educational, charitable, political and many other organisations in Norfolk
◆ Access to digitised local newspaper archives at the Millennium Library Norwich

155

Case Study (cont.)

Benefits of Customer Service

The library knows that customer service is central to the success of the organisation. It wants people to use the facilities and it is aware of the needs of regular library users as well as new users. It wants to appeal to the new generation of readers and encourage participation.

The library hopes that by developing new ideas and innovations and by using technology, it will appeal to customers who, in the past, have not used the library service.

Discover Our Remarkable Origins

origins

The History Mix

THE AMAZING NEW INTERACTIVE
JOURNEY THROUGH TIME STARTS HERE
OPEN OCTOBER 2001

the forum

MILLENNIUM PLAIN NORWICH

Communication

A customer care team has been established and staff are trained to deal with people and to provide for different customer needs.

Customer care services are available throughout The Forum. The restaurants and cafés are open-plan and accessible. The Tourist Information Centre is at the front of the building, encouraging people to go in, and offering a wide range of information about Norwich and the surrounding area.

Visitors have the opportunity to visit 'Origins', a multimedia and interactive experience that looks at the history of Norwich and the surrounding area. The whole venture can be seen as a way of communicating with the public. There is a plethora of information and a variety of ways to explore and understand how the area has developed through the ages.

The first impression people get when they enter The Forum is a feeling of space and excitement. The building has been specifically designed to meet the needs of all visitors. Signing is clear and directs customers to the various services and attractions.

Face to Face

Because of the variety of organisations which make up The Forum, employees greet and deal with customers in very different ways. Customers are served face to face in the cafés and restaurant, at a desk in the Tourist Information Centre and at a Reception in the Library. There are people to help direct and support customers. Maps are available to give directions to the various parts of the library.

Customers are dealt with efficiently and effectively in an atmosphere that enables them to fully experience the facilities available.

Case Study (cont.)

Tourist Information Centre in The Forum

Other Forms of Communication

Leaflets and brochures are available for visitors. There is information on the Main Library, Norfolk Heritage Centre, The Business Library, The Children's Library, The express facility, Origins and of course the Tourist Information Centre.

The Tourist Information Centre gives out information on accommodation, visitor attractions, transport, bookings and tours, as well as selling a variety of books, cards and gifts.

An Educational/Information film is shown as part of the Origins experience. The film gives background information on Norwich and a tour of the most beautiful parts of the city and surrounding area.

The websites offer many opportunities to visit various areas and to explore the following:

◆ Plan and lay-out of the building
◆ Learning
◆ Questions and answers
◆ Visiting
◆ Playing and working

Visit: http://www.theforumnorfolk.com and
http://www.library.norfolk.gov.uk/millenniumlib.htm

'Ask a question' on the website gives information on:

◆ The lay-out and description of the services on offer
◆ The opening times
◆ Directions
◆ Who to contact for further information
◆ Vacancies

Case Study (cont.)

Norfolk & Norwich
Millennium Library

- **Business Library 650 - 659**
  - **Business Link Norfolk Information Service**
  - **Euro Info Centre**

- **Norfolk Heritage Centre**

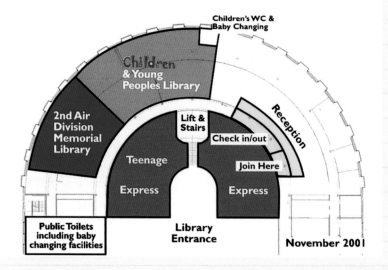

Business Library

Lift & Stairs

Norfolk Heritage Centre

First Floor Main Library
- Fiction & Non Fiction

Subject Areas

- **Arts & Recreation 635 - 649**
  700 - 799

- **Language & Literature 400 - 499**
  800 - 899

- **History People & Places 900 - 999**

- **Science & Technology 001 - 029**
  500 - 634
  660 - 699

Society 030 - 399

Science & Technology

History People & Places

Society

Lift & Stairs

Sound & Vision

Language & Literature and (Fiction)

Arts & Recreation

Spoken Word Arts

Ground Floor

- **Express**
- **Children's Library**
- **2nd Air Division**

Reception

- **New Members**

- **Book check in/out**

Children's WC & Baby Changing

Children & Young Peoples Library

2nd Air Division Memorial Library

Lift & Stairs

Reception

Check in/out

Join Here

Teenage

Express

Express

Public Toilets including baby changing facilities

Library Entrance

November 2001

Plan of The Forum

Case Study (cont.)

Keeping Records

Various records are kept throughout the facility. Technology plays a big part in the way that information is stored and retrieved. All reception desks have computers and the library computers list all of the books in the library with easy access for borrowers.

All customer records are kept and these include details of the people who belong to the library. This information is confidential and not available to the public. Library cards are issued which look very much like credit cards.

Forms

The library uses a number of forms and documents:

The Forum

◆ Customer comment forms
◆ Joining forms
◆ Library cards

Norfolk Library & Information Service

Please complete this form in block capitals and take it to your nearest library.

Surname | First names | Title Mr/Mrs/etc

Address - we will need to see one proof of your name, address and signature

Postcode

Home tel no | Daytime tel no | Extension

Date of birth   If under 16 please give the full name of your parent or legal guardian

Please tick if you are
○ receiving invalidity/incapacity benefit
○ registered blind or partially sighted (proof will be required)
○ housebound (unable to visit the Library in person)

Please sign this declaration if you are 16 or over, or signing as a parent or guardian

Declaration: I agree to be responsible for all items borrowed on the Norfolk Library and Information Service card issued to me. I will observe the Bylaws which are available for inspection in the Library and the Conditions of Use which have been issued to me. I understand that the information which I have provided will be held on the library computer systems.

Signature | **Date**

borrowdiscoverconnect borrowdis

Joining form

Case Study

Customer Service at De Vere Dunston Hall Hotel and Country Club

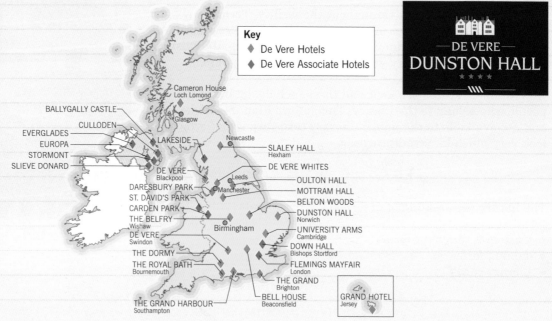

Location of De Vere hotels

WEBSITE – http://www.devereonline.co.uk

De Vere Dunston Hall is a large country hotel situated on the outskirts of Norwich.

It offers 130 bedrooms, nine conference rooms, a leisure club with swimming pool, sauna, steam room and fully equipped gym, and an 18-hole golf course. There is also a beauty salon.

There are several reception points for visitors to the hotel. The main reception area is situated off a courtyard at the entrance to the hotel. There are small reception points at the Carvery Restaurant, swimming pool, gym, beauty salon and a sale point at the golf shop.

Who are the Customers

The hotel caters for everyone; whether the visitor is interested in sport, business, relaxation or special events.

Sport

Hotel residents have free use of the leisure facilities at the hotel. There are fully qualified staff available to help customers to get the most out of their stay. Golfers can take advantage of the clubhouse and greens (green fees payable) and there is also a putting green and driving range. There are tennis courts and a football pitch.

Case Study (cont.)

Business

Conference facilities are available for large and small meetings. There is a day delegate package and a 24-hour delegate package.

Conference facilities

De Vere Dunston Hall

Dunston Hall works with other companies to offer a range of outside activities, such as hot air ballooning, quad biking, archery, laser shooting, go karting, croquet and bowls.

A combination of the conference facilities and activities are often used by companies to develop training packages for team-building and management programmes.

Relaxation

Customers demand a high level of service at Dunston Hall. Leisure break visitors are offered the opportunity to take part in all activities and to take advantage of all facilities. There are also a number of visitor attractions in the area and the hotel likes to give its customers advice on 'where to go' and 'what to do'.

Special Events

Dunston Hall offers a number of events for customers, including corporate golf, barbecues and dinners, private functions and wedding management or coordination. It is common to cater for 120 weddings a year. The building is large enough to cater for three weddings at once.

Case Study (cont.)

Benefits of Good Customer Service

The management believes that good customer service enhances their reputation and gains repeat business.

A great deal of time is taken to train staff and to make sure that there is a corporate approach to customer service and customer care. There is fierce competition in the area, which encourages all of the hotels to look carefully at the quality of their service.

Communication

There is an expectation that the reception staff will meet and greet customers with a high level of skill. The focus is on creating a friendly and efficient service. The staff are trained to deal with all situations and eventualities.

Face to Face

About 75 per cent of service in the hotel is face to face. This takes place at the reception desks, in the restaurants and bars and through porterage, housekeeping and conference support. The other 25 per cent of service goes on behind the scenes, dealing with customers on the telephone, preparing food, preparing rooms, and event organisation.

Other Forms of Communication

Hotel guests are contacted by telephone and in writing. E-mail is used for booking online and there is a website for the De Vere group. The website offers the opportunity to get information on all the hotels in the group. It lists the main categories of interest:

Dunston Hall

- ◆ Accommodation
- ◆ Business
- ◆ Dining
- ◆ Leisure
- ◆ Golf
- ◆ Directions
- ◆ Local interest
- ◆ Views

Keeping Records

Record-keeping is an important part of everyday work at the hotel. With so many functions, events, club activities and visitors to cater for, it is vital that everyone is clear about 'who is doing what'. Systems are in place to support the administration of all paperwork and database activity.

Case Study (cont.)

Forms

A number of forms are in use throughout the hotel:

◆ Registration forms
◆ Cancellation forms
◆ Maintenance reports
◆ Message forms
◆ Letterheads
◆ Complaint Action forms
◆ Spillage forms (guests' clothing)
◆ Conference and booking forms
◆ Lost property letters
◆ Laundry service forms

Health, safety and fire regulations are displayed throughout the hotel. Policy and procedure documentation are kept by management and form part of the quality assurance system. It is also a requirement to keep documents for security reasons. For example, the police might want information about someone who stayed at the hotel.

BOOKING

To make a booking request, please select a hotel below or call central reservations.

Please select your hotel below:

_____

Please Note: A Leisure Break is based upon two people sharing a twin or double room for a minimum of 2 nights.

◆ Central Reservations - Tel: **01925 639499**
◆ Central Reservations - Fax: **01925 403020**
◆ Brochure Hotline Service: **01925 639499**
◆ Click here for the Online Brochure Request
◆ E-Mail: reservations@devere-hotels.com
◆ Central Reservations are open Monday - Friday 9am-8pm. Weekends and Bank Holidays 10am-4pm.

If you would like more detailed information on any of our hotels or our wide range of business and leisure activities or breaks, please call the Brochure Hotline service above.

Online booking form

SECTION ONE

Customers

Internal Customers

It is important that an organisation has an effective and efficient workforce. This workforce is central to providing a service to all customers. Whether you work in a hotel, leisure centre or tourist attraction, it is the people around you who provide the structure necessary to meet the needs of the general public. You have a responsibility to each other to work as a team.

Internal customers are the people you work with both inside and outside the organisation. Customers can be your colleagues, your managers or your employees.

EXAMPLE

You work as a Hotel Receptionist. Who are your internal customers? Who provides you with a service?

The answer is the Junior Receptionist, the Accounts Clerk who prepares the bills, the Porters who carry the luggage to the rooms, and the people who answer the telephone in other departments and give you advice and information.

There may be a number of suppliers who, although they are not employees of the company, provide a service, which enables you to provide further service to external customers. These suppliers are also internal customers.

Employees may use the facilities of the organisation and, in some cases, receive discounts on products and services. Everyone is a potential customer.

External Customers

External customers are the people who come into your facility to buy products and services. These are the most important people to your organisation because they will pay for the service you provide. They will go away from the company and talk about it to friends and relatives. The results of good customer service will be seen through repeat business (customers return to use the facility or organisation again) and new business through recommendation (customers who have not visited the facility or organisation before).

Customers of the organisation come in many guises. They may come as individuals or as part of a group. They may be adults with children or adults with elderly relatives. They may come from different cultural backgrounds. They could be famous. You need to know how to cater for their individual needs and this takes a great deal of skill. Customer care training is important. Internal training is important to ensure understanding of the organisation in relation to customer needs.

Different Types of Customers

There is a wide variety of customer types – these will fall into the following categories:

- Individuals
- Groups
- People of different ages
- People from different cultures
- Non-English speakers
- People with specific needs (sight/hearing impaired, wheelchair users, young children)
- Business people

An individual might be:	a businessman/woman
He/she wants to:	Book a room Book a conference Attend a meeting Order a taxi Eat in the restaurant Book a flight Book accommodation Sell goods and services (rep) Inspect premises Report a complaint Check in, check out Use business facilities

THINK ABOUT...

What facilities would he or she use?

Figure 3.2

A group might be:	a group of tourists
They want to:	Book a tour Book accommodation Book flights Eat in the restaurant Arrange meetings/discussions Book taxis Ask for information Ask for directions Report or complain Visit local attractions

Would the tourists be different ages?
Would they be English speakers?
Would they come from different cultural backgrounds?
What specific needs might they have?

Talk about...

Figure 3.3

Customer Needs

There is no such thing as an average customer. People are individuals and they have individual needs and expectations. Each customer should be treated with care, consideration and sensitivity to make sure that they receive the best possible service from the organisation. Customers also need to feel confident that the organisation is providing a safe and secure environment.

General Needs

- Information and advice
- To ask for instructions and directions
- To complain
- To complete relevant documentation and records

Specific Needs

- Customers may use wheelchairs (accessibility/mobility problems)
- They may have language problems
- They could be hearing or sight-impaired
- They could have special dietary requirements

- ◆ They may have learning difficulties
- ◆ They may be from different cultural backgrounds
- ◆ They may need business services
- ◆ There may be needs relating to their age (children may need supervision or special equipment, the elderly may need support)

Looking at Customer Needs in Different Types of Facilities

Different types of facilities and organisations attract visitors with a variety of needs. It could be argued that all types of customers would at some point visit a facility. For example, a sports enthusiast might visit a library to find out about local clubs in the area.

It is important to remember that everyone who walks through the door is vital to the existence of the business. Whether they spend a great deal of money on entrance fees (perhaps as part of an organised group) or whether they call in to ask for directions, they are equally important in terms of service. The person asking for directions today may be the group organiser of tomorrow.

The Travel Agent

Who are the customers? Groups and individuals book holidays, use foreign exchange facilities, browse through the brochures and make general enquiries or ask for information.

The customers can contact the travel agent by telephone, in writing, by entering the travel shop or office, or through the website by e-mail.

Travel agents are used mostly by adults (men and women). Children would not be able to book holidays, although they may accompany their parents into the agency.

Figure 3.4 Travel agents

CUSTOMER NEEDS

The travel agent provides information through advertising campaigns, sometimes on the television and often in the press. The travel shops cater for customer needs by providing a variety of brochures which give detailed information about all kinds of holidays. Travel agents often have facilities for changing foreign currency and organising travel insurance.

Computers link to tour operators, airlines and other information sources, so that customers can get instant information about costs, availability and general detail on hotels and accommodation.

The Leisure Centre

Who are the customers? Groups and individuals use the facilities for swimming, racquet sports, clubs and societies, classes (i.e. aerobics, yoga, fitness).

The customer may be using the café, enquiry desk, collecting leaflets, booking the facilities or classes, collecting children or buying from the sportswear shop. Students may use the facilities for research when preparing work on vocational projects. Customers can contact the leisure centre by telephone, in writing, by entering the facility or through a website.

Leisure centres are used by people of all ages. Different leisure activities appeal to different age groups and to people with different lifestyles and interests.

The time of day affects the nature of the groups using the facilities. For example, more children use the facilities in the early evening, weekends and in the school holidays. Retired adults might use the facilities more during the day.

Figure 3.5 The leisure centre

CUSTOMER NEEDS

The leisure centre caters for customer needs by providing a variety of sports and leisure activities to suit all ages and levels of ability. It has facilities for the disabled and it caters for spectators as well as participants.

The leisure centre provides information in the form of leaflets and course descriptions. It displays timetables and posters to advertise activities. There are often notice-boards, signs and directions and there is usually an information or reception desk, which is always staffed.

The Museum

Who are the customers? Groups and individuals use museums. They may be on a family day out. They may be students researching for a wide variety of courses from GCSE to Degree level.

Schools and colleges may arrange visits to museums to support their study programmes. Some may be foreign students. Special interest museums might appeal to specific groups of people.

At large museums, customers can call into the museum shop or use the restaurant or the museum library. Both children and adults will buy souvenirs from museum shops.

Figure 3.6   The British Museum

CUSTOMER NEEDS

Museums cater for customer needs by offering a variety of services. Over the past few years, museums have developed ways of 'entertaining' customers so that the whole museum experience has become much more interesting. There are activities (often hands-on), lectures and demonstrations throughout the day, which provide visitors with more enjoyable experience and make learning fun for all who take part.

Information is given to the public in a variety of ways. There are often fact sheets and guide books. For younger children there are activity sheets, sometimes with gifts and prizes. In large museums there may be information points on different floors or in different sections.

Museums cater for people of all ages and there are usually facilities for people with disabilities. There are signs, directions and sometimes, for the larger buildings, maps on every floor. In addition to organised tours, taped commentaries are frequently available in different languages.

ACTIVITY

Look at the following list of facilities. Using the symbols, decide who the main customers are. Some facilities may cater for all categories.

KEY

 Holidaymakers/tourists/sightseers

 Students/education groups

 Activity groups/clubs

 Sports enthusiasts

 Home leisure users

 Local leisure users

What are the facilities?	Who are the main customers?
Example: Attractions (tourist)	🌴 📚 ♟ ⚽ 🖥 👫
Castles Churches/cathedrals Cinemas Clubs Community centres Conference centre Clubs Hotels and accommodation Leisure centres and health clubs Libraries Museums National parks Pubs, restaurants Seaside resorts and attractions Seaside towns Sporting venues Stately homes Theatres/arts venues Theme parks Tour operators/transport organisations Tourist Information Centres Travel agents Video rental shops Zoos	

THINK ABOUT...

When you have decided who the main customers are, think about:

a) What are their general needs?
b) What are their specific needs?
c) What types of customer are they?
d) Are they individuals or groups?
e) Are they different ages – how does this affect their needs?
f) Are they from different cultures – how does this affect their needs?
g) Are they English speaking?

ASSESSMENT ACTIVITY

Identifying customers and their needs

Choose an organisation in your area. It may be a leisure facility, hotel or tourist attraction. You will need to do some research via the internet or by contacting an organisation. You should use a variety of research methods to give you different and contrasting information.

If you cannot find an organisation, or you have difficulty with the research or you live in an area with few facilities, use one of the case studies at the beginning of the section. These companies will be happy to help you. You need to find the answers to the following questions:

- Who are the customers?
- Are they internal or external customers? What is the difference?
- What are their individual needs?
- How does the organisation meet those needs?

When you have researched your information, you may want to share this with other members of your group. You could do this in a number of ways:

1 Give a short talk on the company you have been researching.
2 Make a table of all the companies and their differences, in terms of the types of customers they attract.
3 Make a wall display that shows all organisations and lists their customers.

The Review

The information you have researched collected, discussed or displayed can be used to start your review.

The research you have done so far can form the introduction to a larger report which takes in all sections of this customer service unit.

Your review should be based on one organisation, although you can use others for comparison. Try to use as wide a range of examples as possible.

If you need to, use the following as a format for the report:

- The name of the organisation – are they leisure or tourism or linked?
- Where are they located?
- What do they do?
- Who are their customers? Individuals, groups, people of different ages, people from different cultures, non-English speakers, people

with specific needs (wheelchair users, impaired sight, young children), business people?

◆ What are their general needs?
◆ What are their specific needs?
◆ How does the organisation deal with the different needs of its customers?

SECTION TWO — Benefits of Customer Service

The Advantages of Providing Quality Customer Service

Most companies aim to provide a level of customer service which exceeds, not just meets, the needs of the customer. Once this has been achieved, there are enormous benefits to the organisation. No one can over-emphasise the importance of repeat business.

THINK ABOUT...

Use page numbers to keep your work in order. Use headings and paragraphs to help the reader to understand.

MEETING CUSTOMERS NEEDS

leads to

CUSTOMER SATISFACTION

which leads to

REPEAT BUSINESS

Figure 3.7

EXAMPLE

A family go into a travel agents to book a holiday. They want a range of activities to suit their individual needs and interests.

The agent goes through all of the options with them, making suggestions and checking bookings. It seems impossible to get everything in one package. A lengthy discussion takes place. The 'real' needs of the family are established. The family is told that the agent will do further research and get back to them with some ideas.

A holiday is found that not only meets their needs but offers a range of different activities for all ages. The holiday is called 'Pick and Mix'.

Their needs are met. The family are happy. They go on holiday – everyone in the family gets something. They come back satisfied and tell all their friends.

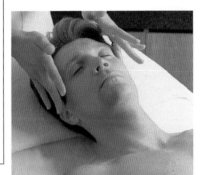

173

QUESTION

Where will the family book their next holiday?

Where will their friends book their next holiday?

Figure 3.8   A difficult customer

THINK ABOUT...

Was the family a difficult customer? How would you have dealt with the situation?

The travel agent was willing to put in time and effort to ensure that the customer service exceeded the needs of the customer. This resulted in customer satisfaction and, ultimately, in both *repeat* and *new* business. If a family holiday had been booked without taking into consideration the needs of all the family, the outcome would not have been so positive.

What happened here?

Talk about...

> **EXAMPLE**
>
> The family go into the travel agents to book a holiday and their needs are very different. The agent apologises and only gives them a list of options which partly meet their needs based on what the agent can find at the time.

LACK OF INTEREST IN THE NEEDS OF THE CUSTOMER

leads to

CUSTOMER DISSATISFACTION

which leads to

CUSTOMER COMPLAINT

which leads to

THE CUSTOMER GOING ELSEWHERE FOR BETTER SERVICE

Repeat Business

The reasons that companies obtain repeat business differ, but there is one common factor. No customer will return if they are dissatisfied with the service.

If complaints are dealt with in an efficient and effective way (see problem solving in Section Six, page 230), it is possible to turn a dissatisfied customer into a repeat customer.

If the customer leaves happy they will recommend the facility and this may result in new as well as repeat business.

Figure 3.9   Happy customers

A customer may have booked a series of golf or swimming lessons. The motives to return are to learn a new skill and to complete a series of sessions (money may have been paid in advance). The customer is likely to complete the first set of lessons but what will make them return for another set?

> Are you a repeat customer to leisure and tourism facilities? What makes you go back again and again?
>
> AND
>
> When have things gone wrong for you? What have you had to complain about? Did it put you off the facility?

Talk about...

Figure 3.10   Golfers at Dunston Hall

THINK ABOUT...

Because they paid up front, are the customers more likely to return? What reasons could there be for not returning?

All the ingredients need to be right to make sure that customers return. The best-case scenario for the organisation is if customers bring new business with them.

New Business

Whatever the circumstances, organisations cannot rely totally on repeat business. Therefore, they must establish ways of attracting new customers. Organisations need to 'move with the times' and adapt their products and services increasingly to meet the needs of a more critical customer.

Customers look for a good first impression of the company:

- Being greeted in a friendly and polite manner
- Being given the appropriate information, directions
- Being asked appropriate questions

Figure 3.11 A good first impression

Customers want a reliable service:

- Their queries answered effectively
- Information, products, services delivered effectively and where appropriate
- Getting what they want on time, where they want it and in the way they asked for it
- A quality product or service

Figure 3.12 A reliable service

The brochure did say all children under twelve travel free . . . .

Customers expect value for money:

- A product or service, which is 'fit for the purpose'
- A product or service, which is not overpriced and which is comparable with other organisations
- Offers, bargains and promotions – weekend breaks, leisure club activities, etc.

Figure 3.13 Value for money

Customers look for
satisfaction on departure:

◆ A friendly goodbye: 'We
hope to see you again'
◆ An enquiring goodbye:
'Was everything to your
satisfaction?'
◆ An offer, bargain or
promotion 'Would you be
interested in this offer?'
◆ A free gift: 'Please accept
this with the hotel's
compliments'

Figure 3.14 Satisfaction on departure

177

HAVING EXPERIENCED EXCELLENT CUSTOMER SERVICE

A SATISFIED CUSTOMER WILL LEAVE

WANTING MORE

A SATISFIED CUSTOMER IS A REPEAT CUSTOMER

THINK ABOUT...

What offers, bargains
and gifts might be
offered by the following
organisations to
encourage new
customers to come back
again:

leisure centres, travel
agents, restaurants,
tourist attractions,
hotels, video shops?

Remember the Internal Customers

One advantage of quality customer service is that the Customer
Service Team and their counterparts in all departments, will gain
satisfaction in their work.

HAPPY CUSTOMERS

lead to

JOB SATISFACTION

which leads to

HAPPY STAFF

Organisations have an obligation to give staff all of the help and support that they need to provide quality customer service. If the system works, the company makes a profit and everyone gains.

The advantages to the company of providing quality customer service		
New business	Increased sales	Staff retention
Repeat business	Improved company image	Staff satisfaction
	Competitive Advantage	

What does this mean?

Happy customers   Happy company   Happy staff

Companies that have a high rate of turnover in terms of customer service staff, may not be able to maintain the standard of their customer service. Their staff come and go too frequently. When staff are well trained, well motivated and have job satisfaction, they will promote the company in a positive way and therefore maintain the standard.

Increased Sales and Company Image

Company image is about how the organisation is perceived by people – those who use it, those who intend to use it and those who carry the image of what it might be like to use it. It is about reputation, standing and the quality of products and services.

When you first hear about a company your first impression is formed from its name and then from the information you glean from other people, articles, newspaper reports and the media in general.

The combination of the company image, the quality of the products and services and the customer service all lead to increased or decreased sales. It is important, therefore, to get these things right. The image of an organisation is fragile. The reputation of the organisation and how it is treated by the media is extremely important.

Figure 3.15 The Millennium Dome

Competition Across the Industry

Companies are always striving to gain the competitive edge. It is important for a leisure and tourism organisation to offer something different to its customers.

When there are a number of facilities offering the same product or service in a locality, you will often find that the facilities offer different services and specialise in different areas. The idea is to appeal to a different target market.

If facilities are exactly the same, competition is greater. This is where marketing and promotion play an important part in advertising what the company has to offer. Market research is an important marketing tool. It identifies gaps in provision and helps business to develop new products and services to meet the needs of an ever-changing customer base. For example, take two hotels, A and B:

HOTEL A – Bought when run down and in need of refurbishment. To gain a competitive edge the hotel added:

◆ a swimming pool
◆ a fitness suite
◆ a health spa
◆ a golf club.

The hotel can now offer:

◆ leisure and fitness breaks
◆ club membership
◆ golfing holidays
◆ coaching.

The Millennium Dome

What do you know about the Millennium Dome? What image do you get of the Dome? What is that image based on?

Talk about...

HOTEL B – Within 8 km of Hotel A – again bought when run down and in need of refurbishment. Hotel B knew what Hotel A had to offer. Hotel B built a conference centre to target the business market. The hotel added:

◆ computer links in all rooms
◆ a business centre – access to secretarial support
◆ conference rooms with all conference facilities, including large and small meeting rooms
◆ business management training programmes
◆ extra parking space for delegates
◆ separate entrances
◆ business coordination service.

180

A new hotel, is being built within 15 km of the other two. What can Hotel C offer that is different or complements the other two hotels?

Talk about...

ASSESSMENT ACTIVITY

The benefits of good customer service

In Section One of this unit you started to write your review of customer service. You will have selected a leisure or tourism organisation and you may have visited this organisation to gather information.

> **CHECK**
>
> In the first part of your review have you:
>
> 1 Described some of the ways in which the organisation meets the needs of its customers?
> 2 Looked at a wide range of needs in order to give plenty of detailed information in your review?

You are now going to write another section based on 'The benefits of customer service'. Ask the organisation:

◆ What are the benefits to your organisation of providing good customer service?
◆ How do you meet different customer needs and expectations?
◆ How does meeting these needs and expectations benefit the business?

Activity

Write in detail the benefits of customer service in relation to your chosen organisation – the focus should be on meeting the needs of a wide variety of customers.

Add this section to your review.

SECTION THREE

Communication

First Impressions

When a customer first approaches any organisation, the first impression will have a lasting effect. It is important that organisations take the opportunity to make that first visit or contact memorable in a positive way. Every first contact is an opportunity for business and for profit.

Reception entrances to companies do differ:

Figure 3.16   Hotel reception

Figure 3.17   Tourist Information reception

Figure 3.18   Museum reception

THINK ABOUT...

The leisure and tourism facilities in your area.

If you get an opportunity to visit different organisations you could investigate the following points.

Which of the above reception areas would attract you most if you were visiting?

Talk about...

1   When entering a facility or organisation, the customer will make judgements based on the following questions:

- ◆ Is the atmosphere friendly/welcoming?
- ◆ Is the entrance area clean, tidy?
- ◆ Is the signing/directions efficient? Do I know where to go?

2 Who is meeting and greeting?

◆ Is the person friendly/welcoming?
◆ Are they dressed appropriately?
◆ Do they smile as they greet me?
◆ Do they greet me appropriately?
◆ Have they got the time to serve me appropriately?
◆ Do they cater to my needs?
◆ Do they give the me the right information?

Remember, 'you never get a second chance to make a first impression'.

What do you expect when you walk into an organisation?

Leisure Centre

At the leisure centre there is a desk with a computer. Towels are neatly piled on one side of the desk. There is a telephone, some promotional material and a register for use of the gym. Doors lead from the reception area into the pool area and changing rooms. There are one or two people behind the desk. They are usually dressed informally in sweatshirts, which have the name of the organisation written across them. The same company logo is on the towels and on the signs in the reception area. Certificates are on show to tell the customer that the assistants are suitably qualified. Formality of dress may vary according to the rules and regulations of the organisation. Where a leisure centre is part of a hotel or more formal facility, it may be a requirement to wear a suit or smart/casual dress (see Figure 3.19).

Figure 3.19   Leisure centre reception

The atmosphere is cheerful, welcoming and informal. Visitors simply approach the desk, show their membership cards or their room keys (from the adjacent hotel) and enter.

The receptionist says: 'Hello, have you been here before? Please take a towel. If you need anything, come back to reception.' If the receptionist knows the person well (a long-term member), they may call them by name.

WHAT SORT OF COMPLAINTS MIGHT THE LEISURE CENTRE DEAL WITH?

Customer comments:

The equipment is not working.
The showers are not working.
The showers, changing and pool area are dirty.
There are no towels.
I have hurt my back using the equipment.
The drinks machine has broken down.
You have written a letter to me demanding money when I have already paid my subscription.

What do you think might happen if this last complaint is not dealt with efficiently

Talk about...

HOW ARE COMPLAINTS DEALT WITH INITIALLY?

What the receptionist/customer care assistant says:

'I am sorry the equipment is not working, I will make sure that I report it and I will put a sign on it to inform customers. I hope that it will be working on your next visit.'

'I am sorry there are no towels, I will get some brought up immediately.'

'I am sorry that you have had an injury. Please complete this injury form. I will inform the Leisure Centre Manager; he will want to speak to you.'

Museum

At the museum there are five people behind the reception desk. Three of the five take the entrance fees, give out maps and guidebooks and give general directions to the people who make their way into the impressive building.

The whole Customer Care Team are in uniform. Both the men and the women wear shirts (open collar for the women, ties for the men). They all wear navy blue blazers with the emblem of the museum on the pocket.

One of the Customer Care Assistants is behind the Customer Enquiry Desk. Here, the visitor can find more information on exhibitions, talks and activities. There are leaflets explaining special events, activities for school groups and timings.

The fifth member of the team is supervising and often works to the front of the desk, answering queries from customers in the queues. When it is very busy, he might help to guide people through and take up another position at the desk.

There are statues, artefacts and displays all around, helping to engage the interest of the visitor.

The atmosphere is quite formal. The building is quiet, considering the number of children visiting. The receptionists smile and politely give out directions and instructions.

The receptionist says: 'How many are there in the party? Here is a map of the museum, you start by going through that door [indicating]. The toilets and the restaurant are on the first floor.'

WHAT SORT OF COMPLAINTS MIGHT THE MUSEUM DEAL WITH?

Customer comments:

The signs and directions are terrible – we couldn't find the exhibition.

We have been queuing for an hour and it's only another hour before the museum closes.

You have overcharged me, my mother is a senior citizen and you have charged me the full rate for two adults.

The education department has run out of activity sheets and my children wanted to do the activity, this is what we came for, they are very disappointed.

HOW ARE COMPLAINTS DEALT WITH INITIALLY?

What the receptionist/customer care assistant says:

'I am sorry the signing is poor. This has been remarked upon before and reported. New signs and directions are being installed as soon as possible. Did you get a map?'

'I am sorry you have been overcharged, I will of course give you a refund.'

Travel Agent

At the travel agent there are six sales consultants behind the reception desk. All except one is seated. They are all wearing uniform, shirts and skirts/trousers.

There is a computer in front of each consultant and two seats placed on the other side of the counter.

The reception area is colourful with brochures on racks and posters of exotic destinations all over the walls. There are notice-boards advertising special offers and promotions.

The atmosphere is business-like. A great deal of detailed information is passed by the customer to the consultant, who is working at the computer and entering the information. The reception area is welcoming and friendly.

The consultant says: 'Would you like to sit down? My name is Simon, how can I help you? Can you give me your full name please?' He starts to input on the computer and then goes on to ask the relevant questions.

WHAT SORT OF COMPLAINTS MIGHT THE TRAVEL AGENT DEAL WITH?

Customer comments:

We have had a terrible holiday. I want my money back.

We are leaving for America next Tuesday and our tickets have not arrived yet.

When we booked our holiday we were given one price, but when the invoice came through it was £100 more.

I had my wallet stolen on holiday, what are you going to do about it?

HOW ARE COMPLAINTS DEALT WITH INITIALLY?

What the consultant says:

'I am sorry to hear that you've had a bad time on holiday. We need to complete some complaint forms and send them off to head office. Can you take a seat and I'll take down all the details?'

'I am sorry sir, I'll chase up what has happened to your tickets.'

'I am sorry that you had your wallet stolen. Have you got your insurance details with you? We will need to complete the insurance forms and send details of exactly what was lost in the wallet.'

Going Places
High Street

Brochures offered:
Jetset America & Canada
Cresta Worldwide
Airtours Far & Away

I was approached by a consultant immediately and asked if I needed any help. Details of my request were taken and a number of brochures suggested.

I was invited to take a seat and the consultant went through a Jetset brochure with me. She then offered to phone other operators to compare prices, but all were part of the MyTravel group which owns Going Places.

The consultant was friendly, willing to help and enthusiastic.

She said phoning operators would not necessarily result in a special deal, but she would find me the best possible price.

I was given a Jetset brochure, as well as a print-out of the best price found.

Every effort was made to tailor the holiday to my needs and I felt at ease.

The consultant handled the enquiry confidently. However, her poor knowledge about places of interest other than Graceland and the lack of special deals meant this shop did not score enough points to win a Top Shop certificate.

Travelcare
High Street

A consultant asked if I needed any assistance. My requirements were noted down, but no brochures were available so the clerk took my phone number.

Soon after leaving the shop, I received a call from the consultant and returned to the agency. This time a number of brochures were produced and quite a few accommodation options were suggested.

To help me choose, the clerk showed me a map of the state to illustrate where the towns were in relation to each other. Although she had no personal knowledge of the area, she did pass on feedback from previous customers who had used the operator being discussed.

No special deals were offered.

But the clerk did point out that a tour of Graceland would have to be booked independently unless I booked a package tour which included it.

Bailey's Travel
Worldchoice
The Bossard Centre

I was approached by a clerk who asked if she could help.

I explained my requirements and the clerk said she would have to get back to me after she had made enquiries about the flights and accommodation for the dates requested.

I asked for a brochure and was given a British Airways Holidays programme.

The agent was friendly and seemed quite helpful. However, I gained the impression that I had to work out on my own which option I wanted before I could return to discuss my choice.

The consultant did not offer to check availability during my visit.

Lunn Poly
Waterbourne Walk

A consultant asked if I needed any help. I told her what I was looking for and she offered me a brochure and pointed out the relevant pages.

She said I should take the brochure away and choose which hotels I was interested in. Only then would she provide me with any further details.

I asked if there were any special deals, but the consultant said the prices would be as listed in the brochure.

She had no personal knowledge of the destination, but one of her colleagues did eventually offer some first-hand advice.

Availability was not checked and I was told that any tours I wanted would have to be booked on arrival at the destination.

I left the agency with no details other than those in the brochure and with no idea about availability.

Figure 3.20

Source: *Travel Trade Gazette*, 29 April, 2002

Theme Park

At the theme park there are queues of people waiting to get in. There is a line of turnstiles, with a member of the Customer Care Team in each of the payment kiosks.

People walk through and pay their entrance fee. They are greeted on the other side by a variety of characters dressed in costume. The characters perform for the customers and give out balloons and sweets to the children.

Everyone entering the park is given a leaflet with a map and timings for shows and a publicity leaflet offering half price entry on the next visit. Two of the characters move up and down the queues, talking to the children and having photos taken.

There is a Customer Service Centre to the right of the turnstiles. Inside, a number of customers are making general enquiries. The person behind the desk is dressed in uniform and is surrounded by publicity materials and leaflets.

The atmosphere is very informal and very noisy. There is music playing in the background from a live band. There are many young children running around. The receptionist in the Customer Advice Centre is dealing with enquiries in a very quiet and professional manner, but the people in the payment kiosks are chatting and making conversation with the customers.

The receptionist (in the Customer Advice Centre) says: 'My name is Sarah, can I help you? I have a map of the park here; if you go to the supervisor just inside the gate they will be able to get you a wheelchair and show you where the facilities for people with disabilities are, should you need them. I will also mark them on the map for you. Come back and see me if you need anything.'

The girl in the kiosk says: 'How many are in your party? Please take this map and I hope you have a lovely day.'

Figure 3.21 Theme park kiosk

WHAT SORT OF COMPLAINTS MIGHT THE THEME PARK DEAL WITH?

Customer comments:

The food in the restaurant has been microwaved and is cold in the middle.

There are wasps all around the bins in the play area – these bins are overflowing – can't they be emptied, our children are frightened?

There are some young teenagers on the park who are behaving badly and swearing at other guests.

Your charges are too high, we were all charged full price at entry and that family over there got in for half the price.

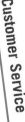
the receptionist/customer care assistant says:

orry about the food. Please take this voucher and get
r meal anywhere in the park.'

et the bins emptied immediately, thank you for letting us
know.'

'I will send security to find the teenagers, thank you for informing
us.'

'Have you seen the family ticket rate? I think you have been
overcharged – I will of course, give you a refund.'

Communication Techniques and Development of Skills

Use of Language

When dealing with customers it is important to ascertain their needs
and cater for those needs as quickly and efficiently as possible.

When approached by a member of the public, the receptionist or host
must be able to communicate in a way that impresses instantly,
responds to needs and is confident in their ability to deal with the
situation.

This is not always easy when dealing with complaints. It is important
to give the impression of confidence and calmness, whatever the
situation.

DO NOT	DO
Swear	Be polite
Be insensitive	Be kind
Giggle	Take the customer request seriously
Be overfamiliar	Be friendly
Joke	Be professional
Make bland statements	Be clear
Give inaccurate information	Give clear guidance and information
Make personal judgements	Be sensitive to special needs

It is important to be clear and responsive to customers when speaking to them face to face. There is nothing wrong in saying that you do not have the answer to their question, but you must follow through the response and get back to them. This might mean going to a supervisor or finding out some information and returning to the customer at a later date.

The tone of your voice can be important when dealing with customers face to face. You should consider how you are seen and heard by other people.

DO NOT	DO
Sound angry, but be friendly and supportive towards the customer.	Listen – if you are tired it is easy to miss what the customer is saying to you.
Be aggressive – the customer does not need to be bullied.	Speak clearly – the customer may be too embarrassed to keep asking you to repeat your instructions or directions.
Be boring – a single tone to the voice can be annoying. It may be that it has been a long day and you are bored but do not let the customer see that.	Be cheerful – a cheerful voice will help to put the customer at ease and an instant relationship will develop.
	Take your time – give yourself time to think about what you are saying or to listen effectively. You can then respond appropriately. Keep the communication going so that pauses and silences do not make the customer feel uncomfortable.

Questioning and Response

During a normal working day you may be asked hundreds of questions without even realising it. In time you will naturally develop your questioning technique. It is important that you use techniques which put customers at their ease while achieving your aim to acquire the information you need. You should develop the use of 'open' and 'closed' questions to gain information and clarify understanding.

Some customers will go on and give further explanation or information from a closed question, but they are more likely to respond in a positive way to open questions.

If a closed question is used in error and gets a 'Yes' or 'No' response, it is advisable to follow up with another more open question to obtain further information.

Most open questions begin with:

When
Where
What
Why
Who
(Remember – words beginning with 'W')
and How

Some closed questions begin with:

Are
Could
Does
Have
Has
Was

Closed questions	Closed answer
Is your name Mr Brown?	Yes.
Are you happy with the service?	No.
Would you like to see the equipment?	Yes.
Do you need help?	No.
Was everything to your satisfaction?	Yes.

Open questions	More detail given
How may I help you?	Can I book a room for the night?
What kind of holiday are you looking for?	We'd like to hire a villa in the sun.

Customers at the Travel Agents

Q: Hello, I want to book a holiday.

A: I'll need more information than that.

WRONG

A: Yes sir, if you would like to take a seat, I'll take some details . . .

RIGHT

THINK ABOUT…

Consider the questions opposite. How would you respond? The answers give just one or two examples of a correct response and depend on a knowledge of products and services. Try to think of several answers to the questions. Remember, customers do not have all the information that you have. They do not always know the questions to ask. Remember also that you are there to sell a product or a service. Do not let the customer get away – follow up the questions.

Q: Have you brochures on weekend breaks in the UK?

A: They are somewhere on the shelves (pointing in the direction).

WRONG

A: Yes, we have. There are a number of brochures (take customer to brochures and ask further questions while selecting appropriate material).

RIGHT

Q: How much will it cost to fly to Florida?

A: It's about £200.

WRONG

A: Whereabouts in Florida are you going? What dates do you want to travel? There are a number of options available, if you would like to take a seat we'll have a look at availability and take more details.

RIGHT

Q: I need to speak to someone about a complaint, I'd like to talk to the manager.

A: Sorry if you want to complain you'll have to put it in writing.

WRONG

A: Yes sir, I'll go and find her and let her know that you are here.

OR

A: Yes sir, the manager is not available at the moment, can I take the details and see if I can help?

RIGHT

Customers at the Leisure Centre

Q: Could you hurry up on the telephone please, I am waiting to be served?

A: Put the phone down and deal with them (unless it is a personal call).

WRONG

A: Turn to a colleague and ask them to deal with the customer.

OR

A: Say excuse me to the person on the phone, turn to the customer and say; 'I'm sorry madam, please take a seat and I will be with you in a moment'.

RIGHT

Q: Have you got any information on exercise classes?

A: Yes, we do but we are out of leaflets at the moment and I don't know what is running.

WRONG

A: Yes madam, we have a number of classes running at the moment. What are you interested in doing? (Show a number of leaflets based on the response from the customer pointing out the different times etc.)

RIGHT

Q: Have you got a leaflet about joining the gym?

A: No sorry, you'll have to come back in a week when they have been printed.

WRONG

the facilities.

A: I'm sorry, we haven't got a leaflet at the moment but the details are . . . Would you like to have a tour of the gym? One of our instructors would be happy to show you around

RIGHT

Body Language

To give customers a positive impression, you need to use your body language to its best advantage. If you are dealing with complaints, your body language can show how confident you are in dealing with the situation.

Body language is mainly about positioning, meeting, greeting and closing. You need to take account of all of the following:

◆ Opening the conversation
◆ The position of the body
◆ Facial expression
◆ Eye contact
◆ General movements and gestures
◆ Personal space
◆ Appearance
◆ Stance and posture
◆ Closing the conversation

When dealing with customers face to face:

◆ Smile
◆ Lean forward
◆ Use open expressions with hand gestures

If the customer is friendly, outgoing and positive, mirror the body language. This will give the impression that you are thinking alike. Do not mirror closed body language.

If the customer draws back, folds his or her arms or frowns, try the professional approach with a smile and always be polite. If customers seem unfriendly this is likely to be the result of something outside your organisation – do not take this personally.

When dealing with a group of people, always concentrate on the leader. He or she is likely to come forward to offer information. If this does not happen, ask politely if there is a group organiser.

If you are dealing with people from other countries or cultures, be careful that your body language does not give out the wrong impression or cause offence.

ACTIVITY

Look at the following pictures. Pick out:

a) Three which give a positive impression.
b) Three which give a negative impression.

Figure 3.22 Positive and negative body language

Personal Space
Everyone regards the 1 metre space around them as their own personal space. Some customers will feel that you are invading if you enter this space. It is important to give customers space so that they feel at ease. A reception desk, counter or table between you and the customer will help to achieve this.

Look at the pictures on pages 181–2. Take note of how many different reception areas there are. The majority of places which receive visitors have some kind of reception desk or counter. This is useful for many purposes:

◆ To lean on to fill out forms etc.
◆ To display promotional material
◆ To display general information
◆ To house services, such as telephone, key collection, storage, booking forms
◆ To house a computer

The counter or table puts a barrier between the customer and the receptionist. This can be positive or negative depending on how it is used. Most people like the distance that the barrier gives – it means that their personal space is not invaded. In some cases it is appropriate to help customers by greeting them on their side of the barrier.

EXAMPLE

The travel agent may start by meeting and greeting the customer from behind the counter, but may then take them to the promotional stand to help them choose the most appropriate brochure.

Different Forms of Communication

Figure 3.23   Travel agent

Using the Telephone
Although using phones is commonplace, using the telephone at work is different. It requires a different set of rules and skills.

In large organisations, it may be someone's sole responsibility to answer the telephone or there may even be more than one person answering. An example of this might be a central booking system for a chain of hotels.

Other organisations may have several lines with different telephone numbers for different departments. For instance, a large conference centre with leisure facilities and a hotel may have three different booking systems and three different telephone numbers.

Answering the Telephone

Following a set of simple procedures will help you to answer the telephone with ease and confidence. Always imagine the person on the other end of the phone can see you. People can tell if you are smiling and a cheerful and friendly voice will put everyone at ease. Use your natural voice and speak clearly.

Ten tips for answering the phone

1 State the name of the company as you answer.

This tells the customer that he or she has the right number.

2 Ask if you can help – and make sure that you take down the caller's name.

This immediately opens up the lines of communication.

3 Listen.

This will give the customer an opportunity to tell you what it is they need.

4 Answer the query, if you can.

Some queries are simple and straightforward.

5 Direct the call if appropriate.

It is important that you understand how the telphone system works and can transfer calls effectively. Nothing annoys a customer more than getting cut off or hanging on to a dead or ringing line.

6 Apologise if the respondent is not answering.

Pay close attention to the system to make sure that callers have got through. If there is a problem, apologise and either pass them on to someone else or take a message.

---

7 Take messages effectively.

It is important that messages are passed on and can be understood. If you do not understand what the customer is saying, ask them to repeat it.

8 Close the call.

Thank the customer for calling.

9 Deliver the message and follow through.

If a message has been left, it is important that it gets to the right person and is acted upon. Remember the customer is waiting for a reply – the result of poor service could be loss of business. It is a good idea to say to the customer when they are likely to receive a reply.

10 File and/or record.

Some organisations require that calls are recorded. You may have to record other information. For example, a customer may call for a brochure and this information has to be put onto a database.

Messages

You should always make sure that there is a pad and pencil near the phone so that you can write down any messages or make notes. Most organisations have special message pads for this purpose. Messages can be taken for a number of reasons and depend on the type of organisation or facility. Generally, messages are left to:

◆ Ask someone to call back
◆ Inform someone of something (instruct, direct)
◆ Confirm something

You may also be asked to pass on personal messages and these should be treated as confidential.

TIME RECEIVED _____	DATE _____
FROM _____	
_____	
MESSAGE _____	
_____	
_____	
RECEIVED BY _____	

Figure 3.24 Message form

Leaving messages on voice mail or answering services

It is easy to become nervous when you are making a call and there is an answer service on the other end. However, following a simple procedure will help you to leave an appropriate message.

When the machine message plays, take a deep breath and wait for it to finish. When the tone sounds to tell you to start your message, wait for just a second and then say, for example, the following:

1 Hello, my name is Sarah, I am calling from Fairweather's Fun Day Theme Park.
2 A purse has been found on the park and we think it may belong to you.
3 Can you please call me back on 02039–9393–292?
4 Thank you – goodbye.

Keep the message short and to the point, and always give your name and telephone number.

ACTIVITY

If you have a message machine or answering service at home leave a message then listen to the recording. If not use role-play with audio tape.

a) Did you speak clearly?
b) Did you understand the message?
c) Did you make sense?
d) Did you leave the correct details – name, telephone number, information?

Writing Letters and Memos

The main difference between letters and memos is that one is external (letter) and one is internal (memo). There are of course exceptions to this rule, for example when an internal candidate has applied for a job within the organisation and he or she will be formally written to.

Accuracy

When preparing documents for external customers, whether a poster, leaflet, brochure or letter, accuracy is extremely important. One error in a letter will give a poor impression of the organisation. If you are responsible for writing letters, it is a good idea to get them proofread before they leave the organisation.

Memos

Memos are much less formal than letters and can take the form of a written note. Companies often have set memo sheets which are designed specifically for the purpose and portray the company logo.

MEMORANDUM

To   Mrs L Critchley (Conference Coordinator)
          Mrs M Ollerton (Chef)
          Mr B Thomas (Reception)
          Mr D Kirkham (Accommodation)

From   Mrs L Hobson (Conference Manager)

Date   1 July 2002

Subject   NEWBY CONFERENCE – 5 August 2002

Please note that the conference booked by NEWBY LEISURE has been so popular that
we have 20 extra delegates to cater for.

Can you please let me have confirmation of accommodation (David), catering (Mick) and
meeting and greeting arrangements (Bill).

If you foresee any problems, please get in touch with me as soon as possible.

Len

Figure 3.25   Memo sheet

Why might you write letters?

- To confirm bookings
- To answer complaints
- To send out general information (activities available)
- To send out itineraries
- To send out tickets
- To send for payment (invoice)
- To inform about future events
- To inform of closure or cancellation
- To send information about special events
- To send out information about educational links
- To inform the media
- To advertise jobs

1 Using the above list, think about how the organisations
   below could use letters to communicate with customers.

conference centre   museum
country park   theme park
health farm/club   Tourist Information Centre
hotel   travel agents
leisure centre
library

Activity continued overleaf

ACTIVITY

> EXAMPLE
>
> **Sending out tickets**
>
> The conference centre might send out tickets for a special event that they are organising – a trade show for the leisure industry.
>
> The travel agent might send out travel tickets to a family going on holiday.
>
> The country park might send out tickets for a special event – a horse-riding competition.

2 Select three organisations and write appropriate letters using situations selected from the list.

Writing a Letter

Organisations often have set layouts for letters. These are used across the organisation and designed to show the company letterhead to the best advantage.

Most organisations follow a 'block' style letter with open punctuation. This lay-out is used because it is straightforward, time efficient and looks professional. Study the example opposite and note the main points:

1 The letterhead is centred on the page. Letterheads vary (see the examples above). Some are blocked to the right, some to the left and some are centred. Some have elaborate logos, others are simple and straightforward. It is important to an organisation that the letterhead is instantly recognisable, particularly in a selling situation. The letterhead should also have the contact details of the organisation, for example the telephone number, fax number and e-mail address.

THE HOBSON LEISURE CENTRE
The Mall
Hoddertown
HOP 2RU

Telephone 0174-234-548
Fax 0174-234-552
E-mail – HobHod@w.com

26 June 2002

Mr M Stott
23 Upton Street
Hoddertown
HOP 4JE

Dear Mr Stott

I am writing in reply to your letter of 21 June 2002.

I was sorry to hear that you have been having problems with your direct debit payments and that the money has been taken from the account twice this month, resulting in a double payment. I am assured that the payment was returned to your account this week.

If you have any further queries or find that the issue has not been resolved, please call me on my direct line 0174–234–512. Can I take this opportunity to apologise for the inconvenience caused and I look forward to seeing you at the centre in the future.

Yours sincerely

Mrs Katie Burgess
Manager
The Hobson Leisure Centre

Figure 3.26   Example of a letter

2 **The date.** In a letter, the date is usually written in full with the month and the year. This is blocked to the left-hand side. Sometimes a reference is given, set above the date, again on the left-hand side.

3 **The addressee** (the person the letter is going to). The address should be set below the date on the left-hand side and should include the name of the addressee and his or her full address and postcode. This address will be repeated on the envelope and, when word-processed, most software will print the envelope for you. Note that punctuation (full stops and commas) are not used in the address. This is called open punctuation. The body of the letter, however, should be punctuated throughout.

4 **The greeting.** This is where you would open the letter. Common examples are: *Dear Sir, Dear Madam, Dear Mr Brown, Dear Mrs Patel.*

Remember, if you are opening with *Dear Sir* – you must end with *Yours faithfully.*

If you are opening with *Dear Mrs Patel* – you must end with *Yours sincerely.*

5 **The body of the letter.** This part of the letter contains the information. There should be no need for more than three paragraphs in most letters.

Paragraph one should contain the introduction to the letter (why you are writing). For example:

I am writing to inform you . . .
I am writing in response to your . . .
I am writing to apologise . . .
I am writing to confirm . . .

Paragraph two should contain the information you want to give. For example:

Details of membership to clubs.
Details of bookings for events and conferences.
Details of holidays.
Including tickets for theatre, events, concerts.

Paragraph three should close the letter. For example:

Thank you for your support and we look forward to seeing you again.
I must apologise again for the inconvenience caused.
Please get in touch if you require any further information.

6 **Closing the letter.** This is where you close the letter. Common examples are: *Yours faithfully* and *Yours sincerely*. Again please note that *Yours faithfully* goes with *Dear Sir* and *Yours sincerely* goes with *Dear Mrs Patel.*

The first letter of *Yours* is upper case, but *faithfully* and *sincerely* start with a lower case 'f' and 's'.

7 **The signature.** You need to leave space between the close of the letter and the printed name for the signature as follows:

Yours sincerely

H Wright

Mr H Wright
Leisure Centre Manager

Electronic Mailing

It is now more common to use e-mails as part of the communication system, both internally and externally in organisations. E-mailing is quick, efficient and effective.

Letters, confirmation and advertising can also be written via the internet and through communication systems.

It is important that if letters and memos are sent by e-mail, they are still given the same quality checks as any other form of communication. Remember – once sent it is impossible to retrieve an e-mail.

DO NOT	DO
Use slang or be overfamiliar (you do not know who will read the e-mail).	Always be polite.
Send replies automatically without checking the address (you may wish the reply to go to just one of the senders).	Make sure that all detail is included.
Be too informal in a formal situation (it is better to send attachments in some cases).	Proofread and spell-check.
Send the wrong attachments (always check).	Check the address and use an address book efficiently.
Send out without proofreading.	Read the e-mail as if you were the recipient.
	Use Dear Sir, Madam and Yours faithfully/sincerely when sending out to a customer.
	Use attachments rather than write letters on the system (this is much more professional).
	Take your time – it is easy to make a mistake with e-mail.

ASSESSMENT ACTIVITY

Communicating with customers

In Sections One and Two of this unit you have started to write a review of customer service based on a chosen leisure or tourism organisation. You will have written about the ways in which the organisation meets the needs of its customers and the benefits of good customer service.

The next section of your review will be based on methods of communication. You will need to investigate:

Activity continued overleaf

1 How staff in the organisation communicate with their customers.
2 The different methods of communication.
3 How they deal with complaints.

Try to include as many examples as possible to support your investigation and try to list five examples of different types of complaint and how they were dealt with by the organisation. (See Section Six of this unit for more information on dealing with complaints.)

Ask the following questions:

◆ Do you have a reception area?
◆ Who has first contact with customers? What do they say?
◆ Is there a complaints procedure?
◆ How do you deal with complaints? Can you give some examples?
◆ What different ways do you communicate with customers?

ACTIVITY

Add to your review a section based on communication. Use the following headings. It may help to interview the person in the organisation who has the most contact with customers.

Staff deal with customers in the following ways.	(Give 5 examples)
Staff use the following communication methods.	(Give 5 examples)
Staff deal with complaints in the following ways.	(Give 5 examples)

ACTIVITY

Read carefully through the work you have done so far and prepare a presentation based on:

Recommendations for Improvement to Customer Service in the Organisation

1 Use overhead projectors or PowerPoint to list the main points and present these points to the group.

2 Give a demonstration of how to deal with an awkward customer who is complaining.

3 Try to reach straightforward, well-reasoned conclusions. If you can, give clear reasons why you came to the conclusions and justify the recommendations you are making.

4 Ask your teacher or another student to video the presentation.

SECTION FOUR

Personal Presentation

Contact with Customers

When coming into contact with customers, the first thing they see is you. They will notice everything about you, how you are dressed, your hair, your make-up, your jewellery and your attitude towards them.

It is important, therefore, that you dress appropriately and take care of the way you present yourself. No matter what your job is in the organisation, you are a representative of the company and need to make a positive impression.

Front of House

If you work 'front of house' it is likely that you are one of the first people that a customer sees as they walk through the door. It is imperative that you are clean and tidy and take pride in your appearance.

If you have a different role in the organisation, but still come into contact with customers it is equally important that you take your appearance seriously and avoid giving a bad impression.

General Attitude and Behaviour

After the first impression when a customer has noticed your general appearance, they will then note, very quickly, the way they are treated. It is important to think about your general attitude and behaviour. No matter how expensive your suit, if you scowl, shrug or are rude to a customer, your smart dress will pale into insignificance and you will give a negative impression to the customer.

It is the combination of dress, personal hygiene, personality, attitude and behaviour that gives the overall impression. Your aim is to get people to like and respect you for your efficiency and good manners.

Figure 3.27

Dressing Appropriately

Uniforms and dress codes are becoming more common. This can make it easier because you know what to put on in the morning and can stick to a routine way of dressing. The uniforms are often chosen in consultation with staff and, where there is a dress code, this is often closely monitored.

Dress and appearance can be mentioned at appraisal and if there have been any complaints or problems you will be notified. This can be embarrassing and a difficult situation for any manager or supervisor to handle.

Figure 3.28 Casual wear in the sports shop

Figure 3.29 Uniform on board

Your local area

What do they wear in travel agents? What do they wear in leisure centres? What do they wear in tourist attractions?

When you went on holiday abroad what did the staff wear at the airport? Did different travel companies or airlines have different uniforms?

Talk about...

Dress Codes

Where dress codes exist, companies see this as a way to improve quality and to encourage staff to have a more consistent approach. A great deal of work goes into choosing a uniform that matches the expectations and enhances the company image. Some companies employ top designers to provide outfits that will suit all ages, shapes and sizes. It is not appropriate for all companies to specify what people should wear and the cost has to be taken into account.

Choosing an Outfit for Work

If you are going to work for the first time, it is difficult to decide what to wear. It is acceptable to ask for advice at the interview or you may be told by your employer. You may have followed some sort of dress code throughout your school life and work is no different. The type of work you do, will affect your dress code.

Look at what other people are wearing in the organisation. You should try to strike a happy medium between showing your individuality and fitting in with the system. What do you buy?

- ◆ Avoid buying too much to start with, just in case you get it wrong
- ◆ Avoid extremes in fashion – work is not a fashion show and you should not look as though you are dressed for an evening out
- ◆ Girls should avoid short skirts, too many accessories and extremes in colour
- ◆ Boys should avoid very bright shirts, shirts worn outside trousers and trainers
- ◆ Buy a smart dark suit in a modern classic line and it will last you forever

ACTIVITY

Different components of the leisure and tourism industry will look at dress in different ways. For example, if you worked in a gym, leisure centre or sports club it is likely that you would wear sportswear rather than a suit.

What would you wear if you were a 'frontline' employee in the following organisations?

LEISURE	TOURISM
Leisure centre	Travel agency
Library	Airline (ground)
Cinema	Airline (cabin crew)
Theatre	Tourist Information Centre
Pub	Tourist guide organisation
Restaurant	Ferry company
Community centre	Tour operator (in resort)
Museum	Conference centre
Football stadium	Hotel
Theme park	

Personal Hygiene

Any job which involves working in close contact with the general public, requires that you take care of yourself and are aware of not only your dress, but of your health and well-being. It is important that you are clean and tidy and take care of your general hygiene as well as your hair, hands, skin and feet.

Smoking is becoming an anti-social habit. If you are working in a leisure centre or any organisation which promotes health and fitness, you should be aware that most people do not smoke. Everyone will know if you smoke because you will smell of cigarettes.

Figure 3.30

◆ More customers in hotels are asking for non-smoking rooms
◆ More customers in restaurants are asking for non-smoking areas
◆ Airlines have non-smoking policies
◆ Airports are non-smoking zones
◆ Railway stations are non-smoking zones

Companies take into account the needs of their employees and of their customers. There are rules and regulations which forbid smoking in the immediate area of the organisation If you want to work with customers or in health and fitness and you smoke, now is the time to consider giving up smoking.

Body odour can be an issue at times, particularly if you work in a tense, hot and busy atmosphere. Avoid this by:

◆ Showering before work
◆ Wearing natural materials in shirts and changing your shirt, underwear and socks every day
◆ Using an effective deodorant

Mouth odour can be embarrassing and cause offence to customers. This can be avoided by:

◆ Regular check-ups at the dentist
◆ Cleaning teeth and flossing regularly
◆ Keeping a toothbrush at work to use during the day after meals
◆ Avoiding spicy foods and garlic
◆ Having a good diet with plenty of fruit and vegetables
◆ Using a mouth spray

Foot odour is a common problem, but can be remedied with a small amount of care and attention:

◆ Always wash your feet every day
◆ Wear well-fitted shoes – avoid some synthetic materials
◆ Change socks and tights daily – natural fibres are best
◆ Use foot products (there a number of sprays on the market)
◆ Visit a chiropodist if you have any corns, callouses or verrucas

Regular foot care is often ignored, but if you spend much time on your feet, it is extremely important that you look after them and treat them with some respect.

Wear shoes which are the right size, low heeled, comfortable and appropriate for the workplace. Keep shoes clean and avoid extremes in fashion.

Hair and hands should be kept neat and tidy. Nails should not be too long; trim to an appropriate length. Your hands will be on show all the time. It is important that men, as well as women, keep nails neat and well manicured. If varnish is used, avoid bright colours and use colours which complement your dress and look professional.

Hair should be kept clean. There are many products on the market to help style hair. There may be set regulations regarding hairstyle at your work. If you have long hair it may have to be tied back and, if you ever come into contact with food, a hat or hairnet may be worn.

Attitude and Behaviour when Dealing with Customers

When you choose a career that involves dealing with customers or the general public, you have to think about whether you have the right personality to do the job.

Your personality is individual to you. It is part of your character and is very difficult to change. You can, however, work to improve your skills and develop ways to show the positive side of your nature.

Smiling at customers as you greet them gives an instant message that the customer is welcome and that you are willing to serve them. Your face changes when you smile and a customer will usually smile in return, showing that you are communicating in a positive way.

To deal effectively and efficiently with customers, you need to have patience, good communication skills in listening and responding and a good sense of humour.

To prepare yourself for the workplace, finding a part-time job, which involves dealing with customers, would be a good grounding. It would give you firsthand experience of dealing with difficult situations.

ACTIVITY

Complete this exercise and then pass it to a friend – let them use a different colour to mark where they think you score. Then give it to your teacher and let them mark in a different colour where they think you score.

The result will be three different colours against each statement. This will give you a good idea of areas where you need to improve.

What are your strengths? – Self-assessment

Strengths and weaknesses – highlight the appropriate number:

1 = Poor   10 = Excellent

	1	2	3	4	5	6	7	8	9	10
I get on well with people										
I smile a lot										
I am outgoing and friendly										
I am patient										
I am supportive										
I cope well under stress										
I am a good listener										
I am helpful										
I dress well										
I am well organised										

Behaviour in the Workplace

Unlike your personality and character, your behaviour can change. You can choose how to behave and you can choose the way that you are perceived by others. Generally, if you are friendly to people, they are friendly and supportive in return.

When you work in the leisure and tourism industry, you are likely to work as part of a team. You will have worked as a team during your school or college life. You know that in order to work as a team you have to share responsibilities. Sometimes you will be asked to do things which you do not like.

If your behaviour is **positive** you:

◆ work as a team with your colleagues
◆ share the jobs everyone hates to do
◆ make an effort to be pleasant.

This behaviour will help you gain the respect of your colleagues and line manager. If you are treated with respect your job will be more fulfilling and worthwhile and you will be happier.

If your behaviour is **negative** you may:

◆ refuse to do some kinds of work
◆ be aggressive, rude and unpleasant to colleagues
◆ turn up for work late
◆ not dress appropriately
◆ treat rules and regulations as unnecessary.

You will lose the respect of colleagues and management with this type of behaviour and this will make you unhappy.

Promoting a Positive Image of Yourself

◆ Smile
◆ Be helpful to customers and to colleagues
◆ Take a turn in doing the jobs that everyone hates
◆ Never say 'No that is not my job'
◆ If you have a genuine grievance, discuss this with your line manager
◆ Do not be aggressive or dismissive
◆ Do not shout or swear in public places
◆ Dress appropriately
◆ Be professional
◆ Do not gossip
◆ Try to be understanding of colleagues' and customers' problems
◆ Be patient when things do not go to plan
◆ Be patient with customers
◆ Treat every customer as an individual
◆ Take time with people
◆ Leave your worries and personal problems at home
◆ Be welcoming
◆ Most of all, be yourself

Do not pretend to be someone you are not. Develop your own character and personality and build on the positive things about yourself.

ASSESSMENT ACTIVITY

Personal presentation

In the previous sections of this unit you have looked in detail at how organisations provide customer service. In this section and the next two sections, you will have the opportunity to apply your customer service skills in practical activities. The overall activity for the three sections will involve:

1 setting up a reception area*
2 designing a set of forms for recording information*
3 dressing appropriately
4 dealing with customers, including dealing with complaints.

(*optional)

ACTIVITY

Work in groups of three or four. Visit as many leisure and tourism organisations as possible. This can include any that are listed in the previous sections. You may have already visited some facilities and you can draw on your past experience. Most organisations will have some sort of reception area for visitors.

The theme park will have a visitor centre or administration centre.
The cinema will have a payment counter.
The bowling alley will have a payment desk and shoe hire counter.
The library will have a reception desk.
The travel agent will have a line of reception desks.
The leisure centre will have a reception desk for the pool or gym.

Research

♦ What does the reception area look like?
♦ How are visitors dealt with?
♦ Who has first contact with the customer?
♦ What do they say?
♦ How are they dressed?

SECTION FIVE

Keeping Records

Administration Systems

All organisations, regardless of their size, have an office base. This administration centre plays an important part in the company, forming a central structure and supporting the departments in the company. Without it, the organisation or facility would not function.

The organisational structure shows the position of everyone in the company and their lines of responsibility. The administration system is central to all departments within that structure.

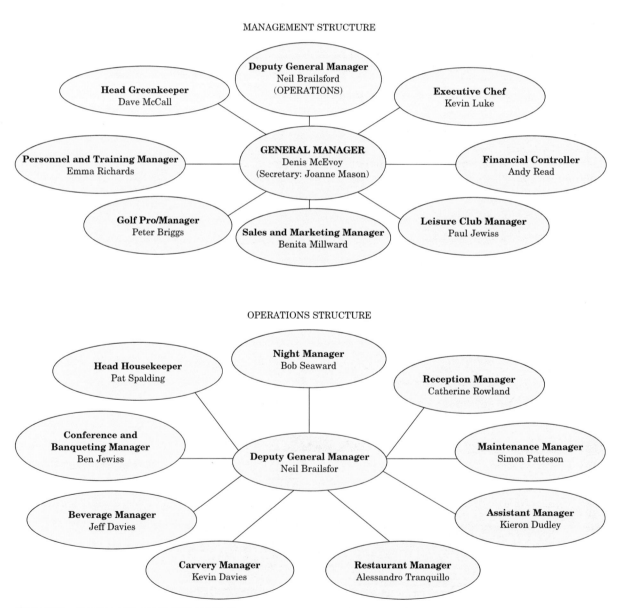

Figure 3.31 Dunston Hall organisation structure

What Happens in the Office?

The office can be one room or a suite of rooms, depending on the size of the organisation.

In a small hotel, the office may be a space at the back of the reception desk. In a large hotel, there may be a central office which deals with all accounts, bookings and conference organisation and a number of smaller offices dealing with housekeeping, leisure facilities and catering.

In a travel agency, the office is often open-plan with most of the records on show or computerised. There are frequently files at the back of a long reception area, which house all the paper-based documents. There are usually separate offices for management and supervisors who have to deal with the day-to-day running of the organisation and who may be involved in confidential work.

In a tourist attraction there are office buildings either on or off the main site, which house all of the administration staff. On a large site there are sometimes smaller offices dealing with catering, cleaning and customer support. There is often a small office specifically for customer care.

If you are in a theme park look out for Customer Information or Customer Service. You will often find a kiosk or small office with a desk and evidence of computerised or paper-based records and documentation.

ACTIVITY

Compare reception areas in different types of organisations and identify the similarities, e.g. they all have seating areas.

Figure 3.32   Tourist information centre at Pleasurewood Hills theme park

As new technology progresses, more and more information is kept on computer. This alleviates the need for large office space. In most organisations, however, there is a mixture of computer- and paper-based records and documents. In some cases it is important to keep paper copies of records as a backup. Computerised systems can break down and this can cause problems.

When an office is run effectively and records are kept in an organised and efficient way, the organisation can rely on the systems in place to support their customers.

ACTIVITY

1   What might an office look like in the following organisations?

◆ Museum
◆ Health club
◆ Heritage site (e.g. a castle)
◆ Countryside visitor centre
◆ Library
◆ Video shop

2   Answer the following questions.

a) Who would work in the office?
b) What would their job be?
c) What sorts of things might you find in the office?
d) What furniture would you expect to find?
e) What equipment would be used?

Figure 3.33

Record-keeping and Form Filling

All leisure and tourism organisations use forms and documents to record information about customers. Accurate records are an essential part of good customer service.

Records are kept for a variety of reasons:

◆ For health, safety and security procedures, all organisations need to know who is on the premises
◆ To ensure and improve the quality of customer service
◆ To help organisations monitor visitor numbers
◆ For marketing and promotion purposes

Different organisations use different forms and they are usually designed specifically for the company. Forms may have the company logo or heading and they may have specific information, which only relates to that company. However, there are a number of forms in common use and, although the design may vary, they can be used by any company.

Most organisations use some sort of booking form, reservation form and complaints form and keep records of customers' names, addresses contact details.

What forms and other methods are used to record customer details?

1 Booking forms

◆ Booking a holiday
◆ Booking a room in a hotel
◆ Booking a class in a leisure centre
◆ Booking tickets (travel, theatre)
◆ Booking a table at a restaurant
◆ Booking a tour
◆ Booking a concert or event
◆ Booking a conference or seminar
◆ Booking a sports activity (participant)
◆ Booking a sports activity (spectator)

2 Cancellation forms
3 Complaints forms
4 Customer service monitoring forms
5 Message forms

THE BOOKING FORM

Booking forms are used in hotels, travel agents, airlines, leisure centres and tourist attractions, as well as in many other organisations.

borrow discover **connect**

Please

let us have your

comments

on the

Norfolk & Norwich
Millennium Library

Figure 3.34 The Forum customer comments form

BOOKING FORM

Guest Name:	Arrival Date:
(Title & Init.)	Dept. Date:
Children's Names & Ages:	No. of Nights: No. of Guests
Company:	Type of Room(s)
Address:	
	Rate:
Post Code: Phone No:	A/C Instructions:
Special Requirements:	Cr. Card No: Exp:
Club De Vere No:	Arrival Time: Dept. Time:
Dinner Reservations:	Contact:

How did you hear about the Hotel?: Recommended .... Existing Client ....

Teletext .... Newspaper .... (which one) .... Other ....

Taken by: Date: Cnf #

Figure 3.35 De Vere hotel booking form

Leisure Estates INTERNATIONAL

Property Rental Booking Form - 2002

Please complete, sign and return to our sole UK agents:

Leisure Estates International, I Angel Court, High Street, Market Harborough, Leicestershire. LE16 7NL

OPTION/BOOKING REF.

CONTACT DETAILS

Name:
Address:
Postcode:
Telephone (Home):
(Office):
(Mobile):
(Fax):
E-mail address:

PROPERTY BOOKING DETAILS

Resort:
Property Type (as described on price grid)
Property Name/Number (if relevant)
Arrival date:
Departure Date:
Duration (nights)
Number of persons (Adult)
(Children) (Infs)
No. of cots High Chairs
Telephone required (if available) YES/NO

GUEST NAMES

Please complete the following information for you and all members of your party.

Mr/ Mrs Mast/Miss	Initial	Surname	Age (if under 16)	Insurance Required*
1.				Yes
2.				Yes
3.				Yes
4.				Yes
5.				Yes
6.				Yes
7.				Yes
8.				Yes
9.				Yes
10.				Yes

Special Requests:

TRAVEL INSURANCE

You will all be automatically insured unless "Yes" is *deleted in the Insurance Req'd box.

Please indicate with a tick if you require Individual ( ) or Family ( ) Cover.

We cannot accept your booking if you do not have adequate travel insurance against all risks. If you do not take our Travel Insurance please give details of your equivalent alternative insurance cover.

Insurance Company: Policy No:

DECLARATION

I have read and agree to the terms & conditions of booking this property as set out on pages 72 & 73 (General Information and Our Booking Conditions) of this brochure, on behalf of myself and all other persons named on the booking form.

I enclose the appropriate deposit(s) as set out in the general information on page 72 plus any travel insurance premiums

If Leisure Estates International have also booked flights, I enclose the flight payment required as advised at the time of booking and agree to accept the flight operators booking conditions.

Property rental deposit £
Total insurance premiums £
Flight payment £
Total £

Alternatively tick ( ) if you have already authorised payment of the above by credit or debit card.

Please make cheques payable to:
Leisure Estates International Ltd.

Signed:
Print Name:
Date:

CAR HIRE

Hire Date:
Period of Hire (days):
Group of Car:
Preferred Model:
Airport collection (Yes/No):
If not delivery address:

FLIGHTS

To ensure that your accommodation and/or car hire is ready for your arrival please acknowledge below ALL flight details confirmed to you at the time of booking (whether we have booked your flights or not).

Date	Time	From	To	Flight Number

One call does it all - book your villa or apartment, flights, car hire and insurance with Leisure Estates

Reservations Centre ✆ 01858 - 828060 or www.leisure-estates.co.uk

Booking Form

75

Figure 3.36 Leisure Estates brochure booking form

In a hotel, booking forms record:

- Guest's name
- Address
- Postcode
- Arrival and departure date
- Dinner reservations
- Type of room
- Room rate
- Orders for early calls and newspapers
- Date and signature
- Some research data – 'How did you hear about the hotel?'

In a travel brochure, booking forms record:

- Customers' names, address, contact details
- Booking details
- All customers' names, ages
- Insurance details
- Car hire details
- Flight details
- Payment details
- Date and customer's signature

Booking forms contribute to good customer service in the following ways:

- They give details of who is on a hotel's premises in case of emergency.
- They are a written record of what was said at the time of booking.
- They contain details which can be used at a later date.
- The information can be used to contact customers at a later date.
- They give customers a sense of confidence in the system.

THE CANCELLATION FORM

Cancellation forms can vary in detail, depending upon the type of activity being cancelled. They are used by any organisation which books rooms, events, activities, holidays and travel.

The cancellation may be taken over the telephone, in writing, by fax or by e-mail. It is important that the detail is recorded accurately because, in some cases, a great deal of money can be involved.

Companies often have clear procedures and cancellation policies to guard them against misuse when booking events, holidays and accommodation.

In its simplest form a cancellation form might detail:

1 name, address, contact details
2 booking details
3 date, time, person taking cancellation
4 any follow-up procedures.

Cancellation forms contribute to good customer service in the following ways:

- They are a written record of what was said at the time of cancellation.
- They support the customer by recording the date and time of cancellation in case of follow up, e.g. for an insurance claim.

◆ They give an opportunity for the customer to give the reason for cancellation.
◆ They reassure the customer that the cancellation has been formalised in writing.

CANCELLATION FORM

Guest Name:		Arrival Date:	
Contact:		Type of Room:	
Company:		No. of Nights:	
Telephone No:		Cancellation No: Verbal	System
Taken By:		Date:	Cnf #:

Another Date?

Figure 3.37 Cancellation form

Is the customer always right?
How do you complete the form while the customer is obviously upset?

Talk about...

THE COMPLAINTS FORM

The complaints form is used by most leisure and tourism organisations. Its purpose is to record the details of the complaint. It is extremely important that the information is recorded accurately and that the person dealing with the complaint gives a positive impression to the customer while completing the form.

The complaints form includes the same information, regardless of the organisation. However, the format and design of the form may be different. In a large organisation the form may relate to different departments (see Figure 3.37). The form will show:

◆ the name and address of the person complaining
◆ the details of the complaint
◆ the outcome of the complaint (what is going to be done)*
◆ follow-up details
◆ signature.

*When completing the outcome of the complaint, you should make sure that this is read and agreed by the customer. This also applies to any follow-up procedure.

Complaints forms contribute towards customer service in the following ways:

◆ They are a written account of the complaint, recording the reason and the outcome.

◆ They serve as a contract between the customer and the company regarding any further action.
◆ They help to improve customer service by giving detailed information which can be stored and compared with other complaints.
◆ They support the quality assurance system in the company.
◆ They ensure customer confidence and contribute to repeat business.
◆ They help to alleviate any negative messages which might result in loss of customer support.

Ref No ☐

De Vere Dunston Hall Hotel
Complaint Action Form

Date of Complaint .... Duty Managers Name ....

Name .... Room Number ....

Address ....

.... Postcode ....

Telephone Number .... Dates of Stay ....

Area of Complaint

Carvery	☐	La Fontaine	☐	Reception	☐
Leisure Club	☐	Room Service	☐	Main Bar	☐
Reservations	☐	Conference	☐	Bunkers Bar	☐
Golf Club	☐	Accommodation	☐		

Other ....

Reason for Complaint ....

....

....

....

....

....

Outcome of Complaint ....

....

....

....

Compensation Offered	Yes ☐	No ☐	Amount ....
Follow up call required	Yes ☐	No ☐	Date of call ....

Duty Managers Signature .... ☐

Figure 3.38 Complaints form

THE CUSTOMER SERVICE MONITORING FORM

One of the most common ways of monitoring customer service is to ask guests, visitors or members to fill in a form which gives information on the quality of the service they have received.

These forms improve the quality of the service by picking up common issues raised by customers. They contain the following:

◆ Name, address, contact details
◆ A list of departments with rating of service
◆ A comments box for all departments
◆ Overall comments
◆ Improvements to customer service

EXAMPLE		Good				Poor
How did you find the service in the restaurant?		1	2	3	4	5
How did you find the accommodation?		1	2	3	4	5
How did you find the service at reception?		1	2	3	4	5

Other comments forms ask for a variety of information and are designed specifically for the facility or organisation.

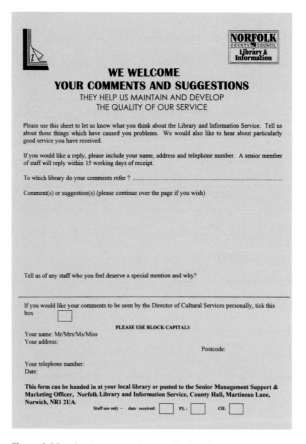

Figure 3.39 Customer service monitoring form

Monitoring forms contribute to good customer service in the following ways:

◆ They give the customer the opportunity to feedback about specific areas of concern.
◆ They give the organisation feedback on their services and where improvements need to be made.
◆ They are user-friendly and can be filled in at any time during the visit.
◆ They are in confidence.
◆ They help to identify common problems in the organisation.

MESSAGE FORMS

Message forms are often simple, but it is important that they are completed accurately and that the message is delivered to the right person. If a customer does not receive an important message it can lead to complaints. If a colleague does not receive a message, important information about arrangements could be missed and this could also lead to a complaint, e.g. failure to provide a service such as special meals.

Message forms should detail:

◆ the time and date of message
◆ who the message is for
◆ who the message is from
◆ who received the message
◆ the message itself (this may be just to return a call or may contain detailed and/or confidential information).

Message forms contribute to good customer service in the following ways:

◆ They show that the organisation is giving individual attention to customers.
◆ They show that the organisation can keep the customer informed and that there is a quality service.
◆ Delivering a message effectively and efficiently shows the quality of the customer service staff.
◆ They prevent complaints arising.

MESSAGE FORM

PLEASE USE THIS FORM TO RECORD ALL MESSAGES. PLEASE COMPLETE
ACCURATELY AND DELIVER PERSONALLY TO THE APPROPRIATE PERSON

DATE ....   TIME ....

MESSAGE FOR ....
DEPARTMENT ....

MESSAGE FROM ....

(MESSAGE)

RECEIVED BY ....   TIME ....

Figure 3.40   Message form

DESIGN A FORM

Choose from one of the following:

a) Joining form for a tennis club.
b) Health form for a gym and fitness studio.
c) Lost property form for a railway company.

Make sure that the form includes all the necessary customer details.

When you have designed the form, get another student to complete it. How does your form contribute to good customer service?

ACTIVITY

Filing

Where paper-based systems are used, you may have to log details and/or file forms, records, accounts and customer details. The most important thing to remember about filing is that you need to be able to retrieve the information.

It is essential that everyone who uses a paper-based system for recording and retrieving information understands the system and uses it efficiently and effectively.

◆ Have respect for other employees – put records back in the right place when not in use
◆ Always remember to keep paperwork tidy and in order. Trays can be used for pending files (files which are being attended to, but are not yet complete)
◆ Use indexes when there are a large number of records

◆ Old records should be cleared out periodically to make space and to keep paperwork up to date

Use of Computers

Figure 3.41 Using computers

It is now usual to use a computer database to keep customer records and contact details. Databases are used to mail existing customers and to contact new customers. They can also contain details of special requirements and details of a specific nature relating to an organisation. For example, if you looked at records on a health club database, you might see details of a fitness programme, visit log and medical details. Remember that information kept by companies on individuals is confidential and should not be passed to a third party.

The advantages of using computers to keep customer records are:

◆ Information is secure
◆ It is time-effective to save and retrieve information
◆ It saves space – paper-based systems are bulky
◆ It is easy to use after minimum training
◆ It is quick for accessing files and information
◆ Once the system is set up it can be used for a number of different purposes – databased customer records can be used to mail customers, link accounts and billing systems and to identify target groups for marketing
◆ It is becoming commonplace to e-mail customers direct for an instant response

The disadvantages are:

◆ The initial inputting of the information takes a long time

◆ Computers can break down and this can cause problems, particularly if they are linked to several systems in an organisation
◆ Backup systems are needed in case of breakdown
◆ It often means that there are two systems in place – paper-based and computerised
◆ Training is needed

Systems are improving and becoming more complex all the time and increasingly organisations are relying on computers for customer records.

Watch out for computers which are:

◆ used to book holidays in travel agents
◆ used to check in at airports
◆ linked to switch card facilities for entry to gyms, health clubs
◆ linked with cameras for security in large hotels, entertainment centres, libraries and video shops
◆ linked to games in amusement arcades, bowling alleys and tourist attractions

---

Completing Forms Online

It is now more commonplace to complete booking and complaints forms online. This is an easy process which takes a few minutes and saves both time and effort in booking. When you are using websites, look to see if they have computerised systems in place to deal with customer service.

ACTIVITY

Let's look at a website

Work in twos – follow the instructions carefully and ask your teacher if help is needed.

ANGLIA RAILWAYS

a) Enter address http://www.angliarailways.co.uk or enter Anglia Railways in the search engine.
b) Click on 'leisure traveller' in the profile box.
c) On the top menu click services.
d) Click 'if things go wrong' on the left-hand side.
e) Read the details on the page (take note of the information for customers).
f) Click on 'compensation form' (in the text).
g) Complete the form – make up the information.
h) When complete, click 'submit'.
i) Print off form and keep (you can go back into the form and change the information and reprint).

Look at some of the websites listed in the appendices and see if any other organisations have forms that you can complete online.

The Need for Accuracy

Accuracy in record-keeping and form filling is essential if an organisation is to function effectively.

It is often the case that customers will be required to fill in forms. However, you cannot rely on the customer to complete all of the details and it is always necessary to check forms before they are filed away or passed to a third party.

If you are inputting information on to a computer, you should check all details with the customer. The customer will not mind you asking twice – it is important that the information is correct. With computers it is possible to make a very big mistake by pressing a single key on the keyboard.

> What do you think are the advantages of completing forms online?
> Do you think Anglia Railways provide good customer information on the site?

Talk about...

What could go wrong:

◆ A holiday is booked for the wrong number of people
◆ The wrong hotel is booked
◆ The name is incorrect
◆ A letter is mailed to the wrong customer

If you get it right first time, you will save yourself work later on.

Form Filling

If you are filling out forms for customers, it is vital that the information is written correctly. You need to think about:

◆ your handwriting – it must be legible
◆ your spelling
◆ reading the instructions carefully if the form is complicated (you may have little experience with a particular form)
◆ dates, times and details – make sure they are written clearly and accurately
◆ deleting, if appropriate, Mr/Mrs/Ms

◆ making sure the form is complete – do not leave blanks on forms. It is appropriate to put N/A which means Not Applicable.
◆ remembering to get the customer to sign the form – you may have to sign it too
◆ asking the customer to print their name under the signature. This is useful just in case you cannot read the signature at a later date.

ACTIVITY

Reception areas need sets of customer records.

Identify:

◆ what records an organisation might need?
◆ which of the following are needed:
  ● Booking forms
  ● Cancellation forms
  ● Customer service monitoring forms
  ● Message forms
  ● Reception tracking records, i.e. wallcharts
  ● Index cards
  ● Database records?

ASSESSMENT ACTIVITY

The written work you did in Sections One, Two and Three should include detailed information on how the organisation used customer records in different situations.

The review

For Sections One, Two and Three you investigated a selected leisure or tourism organisation. Now, add to that review by completing the following exercise. Relate your answers to your selected leisure or tourism organisation.

a) Write descriptions of situations that require staff to have contact with customers.
b) Describe the types of customer records used in each situation (list content, use and location).
c) Write an explanation of why each record contributes to good customer service.

SECTION SIX

Dealing with Customers

Face to Face with the Customer

Figure 3.42   Dealing with customers

Previous sections have given information on dealing with customers in face-to-face situations, using the telephone and in writing. In this section we look at how to apply the theory, and the activity is based on actually dealing with customers.

Before undertaking the practical Assessment Activities, you need to practise to make sure that you understand how to:

◆ Listen to the needs of the customer
◆ Explain and clarify
◆ Solve problems
◆ Apologise
◆ End the discussion
◆ Follow up any outstanding issues
◆ Use the support of supervisors and/or colleagues

The following sections will test your ability to deal with difficult situations, including customer complaints.

Listening to the Needs of Customers

To show that you are listening to customers, look at them and gain good eye contact. Try not to make judgements about people; it is sometimes easy to make assumptions based on appearance, attitude and demeanour.

Lean towards the customer. If you do not catch their first words, ask them politely to repeat the question or statement. 'I'm sorry madam, would you mind repeating that?' Let the customer complete the sentence and give a full explanation. If you interrupt before a customer has finished, you may misunderstand what they are trying to say. If they are giving a long explanation, perhaps a complaint, they will want to be heard in full. Nod your head in agreement and use appropriate body language to show that you are following their words.

Do not be intimidated if the customer is angry, but try to remain calm and objective. The most important thing to remember is that you have the answer to the problem. You will be able to help if you follow the procedures set down by your organisation. Most companies have complaint procedures or a set of guidelines to help staff to deal with difficult customers.

ACTIVITY

Work with a partner or your teacher. Decide which kind of organisation you are going to be employed by:

◆ Airline
◆ Hotel
◆ Leisure centre
◆ Library
◆ Restaurant
◆ Travel agency

One person should stand behind a desk and the customer should approach and complain about some aspect of the service in the facility. The receptionist should not say anything until the end but show that he or she is listening to the complaint.

Take it seriously. Even in a 'real' situation it is sometimes difficult to listen and some situations are genuinely funny – never giggle.

You should aim to get through the exercise without interupting, shrugging, scowling, lifting eyebrows or giggling.

Explanation and Clarification

When you have listened to the first explanation from a customer you may need further explanation and clarification. At this point you should write down anything which is important. For example, the names of any staff involved, times, dates, and the reason for the complaint or general enquiry.

Queries will not always be complaints. A customer might ask for directions to some of the local tourist attractions. You may have to listen to find out where the customer wants to go and then ask for clarification. For example, you could ask 'Will you be driving?'. You may have to explain something to the customer with regard to the tourist attraction such as, 'I'm sorry sir, the attraction closes on

Face to Face Complaint Procedures
Complaint received by a member of staff

Depending on the severity of the complaint the member of staff can do their best to solve the problem eg if given the wrong drink they can change it
If they solve it they will make their Supervisor aware of the problem
If problem is more severe they will notify their Supervisor/Manager

The Supervisor/Manager speaks to the customer as they have more authority eg can deduct items from bills etc
If they solve the problem they will make the Duty Manager aware
If they still cannot solve the problem or if requested the Duty Manager will be called
Problem solved to the customer's satisfaction

Note of what has happened, complainant's name/room number/outcome etc will be recorded in the department and Duty Managers handover

At the 9.30am Meeting the problem will be discussed and if the person is still staying they will be listed as a V.I.P to look after

Telephone Complaint Procedures
Complaint received by a member of staff

Depending on the severity of the complaint the member of staff may be able to solve the problem eg require more towels
If they can solve it they will make their Supervisor aware
If they cannot solve it they will get some basic details and get their Supervisor/Manager.
If they cannot easily find their Supervisor they will get a number for us to call them back

The Supervisor/Manager will speak to the customer and solve the problem, if they can they will make the DM aware

If the call is directly to a Duty Manager they will follow a similar format in getting to the bottom of a problem and offering apologies/compensation if applicable

The call will be followed up with a letter detailing the conversation, apologising and offering any compensation if applicable

The complaint will be recorded in departmental/DM books detailing problems/outcome etc. if the guest is still to come to the hotel, a trace will be put on their booking so everyone is aware of the problem

Figure 3.43   Complaints procedures from Dunston Hall

Mondays'. Perhaps the customer has special needs (for instance, uses a wheelchair).

You need to be aware of what is available in the local area and to be fairly knowledgeable about different aspects of the work you do. It is likely that you will need help and support from colleagues, particularly if you are new to the job. When you become more used to dealing with queries and complaints, you will be more aware of the procedures and it will become easier to know what to say.

Work with a partner or your teacher as before, but this time take the opposite role. Decide what kind of organisation you work for; it would be good to use different organisations from the first activity:

◆ An airline – as cabin crew
◆ A museum
◆ A theme park
◆ A video shop
◆ A golf club
◆ A children's activity centre

One person should stand behind a desk and the customer should approach and complain about some aspect of the service in the facility.

This time you are going to listen to what the customer has to say and then follow through by asking for further explanation while recording (writing down) the main points of what has been said.

Try to get through the exercise without interrupting the customer.

Problem Solving

In order to solve a problem, you have to be clear about what the problem is. Having asked the customer to clarify the complaint and asked for further explanation, you have to decide whether it is your responsibility to deal with the issue or whether you need to ask for support.

Never:
◆ be frightened to ask for help
◆ say you can do something when you do not intend to
◆ try to do anything when you are not sure if you are capable
◆ make management decisions
◆ say you will follow up a problem and fail to do so.

Always:
◆ be sympathetic, whatever the problem
◆ apologise if appropriate
◆ address the customer by name
◆ follow up the problem
◆ make sure that the customer knows exactly what you are going to do.

Dealing with problems and customer complaints is never easy, but it is part of customer service. In a large organisation this is likely to be part of daily routine. Remember – a problem solved is no longer a problem.

What is a Problem?

- The pool attendant has forgotten to put clean towels by the pool at the health club.
- A newspaper has not been delivered to a room at the hotel.
- A customer complains that someone has been smoking in a non-smoking room.
- A customer is short changed at the entrance to the theme park.
- A customer with disabilities has arrived at the museum and all the wheelchairs are already on loan to other customers.
- A waiter spills soup into the lap of a customer.
- A family arrives at the travel agents to complain about their holiday.

It is not always appropriate to offer compensation – think of other ways to solve the problem.

What would you do about the above?

Talk about...

Taking the Problem Forward and Ending the Discussion

When discussing a problem or complaint with a customer, try to see the issue from the customer's point of view. This will help you to show understanding and make the customer feel that you are on their side. Once the problem has been fully explained and you are aware of all the details, you can now take steps to solve the issue.

If the problem is so complicated that it requires you to pass the responsibility to your line manager, you should do so without delay. Remember to tell the customer what you are doing.

Some customers will demand to see the manager themselves. If this happens, contact your line manager to report the problem. If the manager is available he or she may see the customer straight away and take the problem out of your control.

If the issue is something simply rectified, deal with it as quickly and efficiently as possible.

If a customer becomes aggressive or difficult in any way, call for help.

Our Customer Charter

Our commitment

London Underground aims to deliver the best possible service for all our customers. You want a quick, frequent and reliable train service, a safe, clean and welcoming station environment with up-to-date information and helpful, courteous staff. This means a continuous, demanding programme of improvements to meet rising expectations.

Our refund pledge

If a journey you make is delayed by more than 15 minutes or as set out in the current London Underground Customer Charter, for reasons within our control, we will refund you with a voucher to the value of the single delayed journey. Please claim by filling in this form within 14 days of the delayed journey that you experienced. If you make a journey but suffer a delay for reasons beyond our control or that of our contractors, such as security alerts, third party action or freak weather, refunds cannot be paid. The same applies where changes to services have been advertised in advance, for whatever reason.

Refunds for industrial action are not payable under the Customer Charter. If services are disrupted by an industrial dispute, special rules apply for claiming ticket extensions or refunds. These special rules will be advertised at the time on notices at stations. They are also available from the London Underground Customer Service Centre.

Your feedback

If you have any complaints or suggestions on how we can improve our service, please contact us. Send all written correspondence to: **Customer Service Centre, London Underground Ltd, 55 Broadway, London SW1H 0BD. Telephone: 0845 330 9880. Fax: 020 7918 4093. Email: customerservices@email.lul.co.uk.** The address and telephone number of your local Customer Service team is also displayed in the ticket hall and further contact details are also available from station staff. Please do not use this form to send us correspondence.

Data Protection Act 1998

The data on this form will be retained by London Underground Ltd for the purposes of administering the Customer Charter Scheme. The data may be passed to associated companies and organisations for the purposes of the administration of the Scheme, and to law enforcement agencies where criminal activity is suspected.

The data may also be disclosed to companies and organisations associated with London Underground Limited for related marketing and survey purposes. Please tick the box if you do not wish your information to be disclosed for these purposes. ☐

Figure 3.44 Anglia Railways Passenger's Charter

Figure 3.45 London Underground customer charter

Ending the Conversation

Some customers will repeat the problem over and over because they have a need to make their concerns known. You may have to end the conversation or pass on the responsibility. It takes skill and experience to end a conversation and to remain on good terms with the customer. Firstly, wait for a break in the conversation, then say:

'I am sorry sir, but I need to speak to my line manager so that we can deal with your problem as quickly as possible. Would you mind taking a seat?'

You could also offer to bring the customer a cup of coffee, particularly when you feel they have good reason to complain. This will give you time to think about what to do next. Keep calm and under no circumstances argue with the customer.

Even when you have ended the conversation, the problem may still exist and will have to be resolved. It is important that issues are finalised and that the customer is notified (often in writing) of the outcome.

ACTIVITY

This time you are going to try to solve a problem.

1   Write down five problems or customer complaints that you might come across in different leisure and tourism facilities. Swap them with your partner's. Now try to answer the problems in front of you. What would you do?
2   Now practise being the customer. Choose one of the problems and practise with your partner. Remember what you did in the first two practice sessions.

   ◆ Listen
   ◆ Allow the customer to explain
   ◆ Deal with the problem or complaint
   ◆ Take the problem forward
   ◆ End the conversation
   ◆ Follow through
   ◆ Write a letter to the customer explaining the outcome

How to Apologise

At some time during your working life you will have to apologise to a customer. You may, at times, have to apologise when it is not really the organisation's fault.

An apology goes a long way to putting things 'right' between you, or your organisation and the customer. It is probable that the apology will follow a complaint of some kind and that it will be given at the end of the discussion. The apology may be an indication that you are going to take the matter further.

EXAMPLE

I am sorry ...

I am sorry this has happened, I will deal with it straight away.

I am sorry about the delay, I will check what is happening and get back to you.

I am sorry that you have been inconvenienced and I enclose a voucher to the value of ...

There are three main ways to communicate an apology:

◆ By telephone
◆ Face to face
◆ By letter

The approach is slightly different, depending on the communication method. It is important that you are confident when you approach the problem. You should always take responsibility in the short term, but ask for help if needed. Take charge of the situation, be confident, helpful and polite and most of all show that you care.

On the Telephone

When apologising on the telephone, you must always sound convincing and sympathetic to the customer's needs.

You may be simply apologising for being unable to provide a product or service:

'I am sorry madam but we do not allow children into the pool on Wednesday afternoons.'

You may be returning a call to answer a complaint:

'I have checked the outstanding balance with accounts and you have been wrongly charged for your meal in the restaurant, we will credit the amount to your card immediately. I am so sorry that this happened and I hope that this will not deter you from using the facility again.'

You may answer the telephone and have an angry customer on the other end of the phone.

'Can I please have all the details, sir [write it down] and then I will check out your complaint and get back to you by the end of the morning.'

Never pass the blame to someone else, this will not solve the problem.

Face to Face

Figure 3.46

It is difficult to face a customer and apologise for making a mistake or to apologise for some shortfall in customer service. You not only have to sound convincing, but your body language will show the customer exactly how confident you are about dealing with the problem.

You may have to deal with issues where it is not your fault but you are getting the blame. Never say 'This is not my fault'. It is better to say 'I am sorry this has happened, I will deal with the problem and get back to you'.

Remember – patience is a virtue: You must always stay calm. Never argue with the customer and always sound apologetic when there is a genuine reason for complaint. Customers have different needs and what may seem like a minor problem to you can be a major problem for others.

You have the company image to sustain and your aim is to make sure that the customer in front of you is a repeat customer. Most of all you want he or she to give a positive message to other prospective customers.

You work as part of a team of ground crew personnel for a small airline company. You have worked for them for six months and this is your first week dealing with customers at 'check-in'.

A passenger has turned up at the airport with too much baggage. You explain that it is over the weight allowance and you tell the passenger the cost involved. The passenger is not happy and insists that it is your fault and that you are being unreasonable. The passenger also states that they have carried this much baggage before without any problem.

1   What would you do?

   A   Say – 'No, I am sorry but these are the rules and you either pay or I will not check-in your baggage.'
   B   Offer the passenger the opportunity to talk to a supervisor.
   C   Pass it through anyway.
   D   Call for the help of another crew member to ask their advice.
   E   Shout back at the customer saying that it is not your fault that the rules exist.
   F   Tell the customer that you agree with him, the restrictions are too severe and you think the company should change their check-in policy, going on to tell him about all your problems with your employers.

2   Is there more than one answer?
3   What difference do you think it would make if you were more experienced at dealing with customers?

In Writing
If a customer leaves the organisation with an unresolved problem, it is important that this is followed up and that there is a 'closing' of the complaint or issue.

A letter of apology is one way of closing the communication between the organisation and the customer. The letter should explain how the issue has been resolved and what the company is going to do to make sure that the problem does not arise again.

The letter may give some compensation in the form of vouchers, credit notes, tickets or refund. It is normal for the company to make an offer of a repeat visit. The reason for this is that it means instant repeat business and the secondary spend which comes with that. It also gives the company the opportunity to show the customer that the complaint has been taken seriously. Customers may have a completely different experience on a second visit to a facility. It is up to the organisation to make sure that the problem is not repeated on the second visit.

Dear Mr and Mrs Brown

I am writing to apologise for the inconvenience caused when the leisure facilities were closed during your recent visit to our resort.

As you are probably aware, we suffered a minor fire during June and due to various technical problems we were not able to open the swimming pool, health spa and beauty therapy centre until the middle of July. During the refurbishment we were able to improve our facilities by building a fully-equipped gym and exercise studio.

I am enclosing a voucher for a 'weekend break' at the Sunsea Resort and hope that you will be able to visit us sometime during the autumn or anytime during the next year at your convenience.

I apologise again for the distress caused during your holiday with us and hope that the voucher will go some way to compensating for the disappointment.

Please do not hesitate to get in touch if you need further information.

Yours sincerely

H Fairweather
Customer Services Manager
Sunsea Resort

Figure 3.47   Example letter of apology

Dealing with customers, including complaints

You will need a variety of recording documents, samples of which can be obtained from different organisations or your teacher.

Now is the time to deal with customers

Role-plays are not the same as dealing with real customers. The best experience comes from working with customers in the workplace, on work experience or on a work-based assessment activity. However, role-plays are very good for practice. They will prepare you for when you deal with real customers in the workplace.

Write a scenario for a role-play activity.

ACTIVITY

Activity continued overleaf

ACTIVITY

In groups, make up some customers. You can decide:

- who they are
- what their needs are
- why they are visiting the facility
- what they have to say
- what the likely outcome will be
- now the problem or query is solved.

You need to write role-plays for five different customers in five different situations.

Customers can be:

- individuals
- groups
- people of different ages
- people from different cultures
- non-English speakers
- people with specific needs, for example sight and hearing impaired, wheelchair access, facilities for young children
- businesspeople.

Situations can include:

- providing information
- giving advice
- receiving and passing on messages
- keeping records
- providing assistance
- dealing with problems
- dealing with dissatisfied customers
- offering extra services.

Two of the five situations should be complaints.

All of the situations should require recording information, if only notes or messages.

ACTIVITY

Now you have written your role-play exercises, it is time to try them out. Using a video, if possible, act out the role-plays – everyone should take a turn at being the customer and the employee. You will need to evaluate if the role-plays are appropriate for use in the final activity.

Are they:

- appropriate to the organisation (you would not want someone trying to book at room at a leisure centre)?
- appropriate in terms of content (they need to include plenty of information so that they test the skills of the receptionist)?
- complex enough in terms of the complaint?
- appropriate to the records being used (you need a lost property form if someone has lost a purse)?

Watch the video.

- Evaluate your own performance and the performance of others.
- Make notes on any improvements which can be made to the role-plays.
- Obtain any additional records which may be needed.
- Ask your teacher for advice and his or her comments.

ASSESSMENT ACTIVITY

Now it is for real

For formal assessment of the role-play situations, you must have clear evidence of dealing with at least four customers in different situations, including complaints. It would be useful if a video was used. Your teacher should complete observation records on your performance.

Each of you should take a turn behind the reception desk and deal with a variety of customers in different situations.
Use a video – it will help to improve your skills if you do not reach the required standard the first time.
You should:

- dress appropriately for the chosen situation or organisation
- deal with customers showing your skills in communication, using computerised records, using paper-based records and dealing with a complaint
- always be helpful and friendly towards all the customers, irrespective of their needs.

Assessment Activity continued overleaf

The rest of the group do not have to watch you doing this. You would not have a critical audience in a real situation, although other customers (internal and external) might be listening to your conversation.

NOTE: You can do this exercise more than once if needed. You may not reach the required standard the first time. Watch the videos and talk to your teacher about how you can improve your skills.

SECTION SEVEN

The Customer Service Assignment

For this section you need to produce a review of the customer service provided by a selected leisure or tourism organisation – Assignment One.

You also need to produce a record of your involvement in a variety of real or simulated customer service situations – Assignment Two.

Assignment One

The review links to the assessment activities at the end of sections One, Two, Three and Five.

Assessment Activity Section One   –   Who are the customers?
Assessment Activity Section Two   –   The benefits of customer service
Assessment Activity Section Three   –   Communicating with customers
Assessment Activity Section Five   –   The review

You work for the National Tourist Board and you have been asked to produce a review of customer service in a specific organisation. The review will be part of a larger report on a number of organisations, and this will be published and used for evaluation and training.

The organisation can be local or national but should be large enough to give you all the information you need.

You are one of a team of researchers and you will all choose different organisations.

You will need to:

1 Describe the situations that require staff to come into contact with customers and describe the type of customer records that need to be completed.

2 Include an assessment of:

- the ways in which the chosen organisation meets the needs of its different customers
- the methods of communication used by the staff
- the ways used to deal with complaints.

3 Evaluate the appropriateness of the customer service provided by the organisation.

Assignment Two

The practical activity links to the assessment activities at the end of Sections Four, Five and Six   Assessment Activity Section Four   –   Personal presentation   Assessment Activity Section Five   –   Designing and completing records   Assessment Activity Section Six   –   Dealing with customers, including complaints

Having completed your review of customer service, you have been asked to make a video to promote good customer service in leisure and tourism organisations.

You will need to include evidence of your dealings with a variety of customers and the outcomes from your handling of a customer complaint.

Tips for Success

Assignment One
- Structure your work carefully
- Choose an appropriate organisation
- Use as many examples as possible
- Describe as wide a range of customers as possible

Assignment Two
- Dress appropriately and, using the reception desk, deal with a variety of customers, including complaints
- Take the role-play seriously
- Plan carefully and practise dealing with customers before the formal Assessment Activity
- Make sure that you deal with a wide variety of different types of customers in different situations, including complaints

For Top Marks

1 Your work must be well structured and include detailed descriptions of all customer service situations (detailed on page 150). Headings, sub-headings and numberings should be used appropriately and attention should be paid to spelling, punctuation and grammar.

2 All work should relate directly to the organisation being investigated.

3 Customer records should be described in relation to all of the customer service situations. Each record needs to be detailed, including content, use and location. Records must relate to the organisation being investigated. The description should include an explanation of how each record contributes to good customer service.

4 You should provide detailed descriptions, including examples, of a wide range of different kinds of customer, including both internal and external customers.

5 You should provide an accurate description of a range of communication methods, including the strengths and weaknesses of each method used. You should give a detailed assessment of the communication methods used by the staff in the organisation.

6 There should be clear evaluation of the customer service provided by the organisation. You should analyse the strengths and weaknesses and give examples, with justification for all conclusions. You should also look at the organisation's policy on customer service and assess how this is put into practice.

7 For full marks you must reach substantiated conclusions, provide recommendations for improvements and fully justify all recommendations given.

Appendices

Please note that these statistics are predominantly for 2000. They
are given to you as relevant background material for you to start
to research the importance of the leisure and tourism industries
and to identify different trends affecting the industries. You will
note that statistics for admissions to major attractions for both
2000 and 2001 have been included to provide comparisons for a
year when the Millenium Dome was operational.

You should always find out the latest information available at the
time you carry out any activities related to statistics, from
publications and websites related to the leisure and tourism
industries.

Visitor Attractions 2000

It is estimated that there are 6,800 visitor attractions in the UK, which in 2000 attracted 413 million visits, resulting in revenue of £1.4 billion and providing employment for 130,000.

Sector structure and visits in 2000

The following analysis is based on attractions responding to the Survey of Visits to Visitor Attractions 2000. Information from attractions which responded in previous years but not in 2000 has not been included this year.

Region	Attractions	Visits
	%	%
England	70	81
Northern Ireland	5	3
Scotland	20	13
Wales	6	3
UK	100	100

70 per cent of UK attractions are in England. With a higher proportion of large attractions than elsewhere in the UK, England attracts 81 per cent of all visits. Across the sector overall the average number of visits per attractions in the UK in 2000 was around 82,000.

Region	Attractions	Visits
	%	%
England	70	81
Cumbria	2	2
Northumbria	4	3
North West	4	9
Yorkshire	6	7
Heart of England	16	14
East of England	9	7
London	5	19
South West	10	7
Southern	5	6
South East England	8	7

London received the majority of visits recorded in the survey in 2000 (19 per cent) although it represents only five per cent of sample attractions. The Heart of England and the North West are the next two regions to have received most recorded visits to visitor attractions in 2000.

Source: www.staruk.org.uk, sponsored by the National Tourist Boards of England, Scotland, Northern Ireland, Wales and the Department for Culture, Media and Sport.

Household Expenditure 1974–2001

Based on underweighted, adult-only data

Year	1992	1994 –95	1995[1] –96	1995[2] –96	1996 –97	1997 –98	1998 –99	1999 –2000	2000 –01
Grossed number of households (thousands)				24,130	24,310	24,560	24,660	25,330	25,030
Total number of households in sample	7,418	6,853	6,797	6,797	6,415	6,409	6,630	7,097	6,637
Total number of persons	18,174	16,617	16,586	16,586	15,732	15,430	16,218	16,786	15,925
Weighted average number of persons per household	2.5	2.4	2.4	2.4	2.5	2.4	2.4	2.3	2.4

Commodity or service	Average weekly household expenditure (£)								
1 Housing (net)	58.60	54.70	55.10	55.60	54.60	55.50	59.80	58.70	63.90
2 Fuel and power	16.10	15.30	14.70	14.60	14.80	13.50	12.20	11.70	11.90
3 Food and non-alcoholic drinks	59.00	59.40	60.40	61.70	62.60	61.60	61.60	61.40	61.90
4 Alcoholic drink	13.70	14.50	13.00	14.00	14.60	15.30	14.60	15.80	15.00
5 Tobacco	6.70	6.60	6.70	6.70	6.90	6.80	6.10	6.20	6.10
6 Clothing and footwear	20.30	20.20	19.60	20.30	20.90	21.90	22.70	21.60	22.00
7 Household goods	27.10	26.70	26.80	27.20	29.70	29.10	31.00	31.60	32.60
8 Household services	16.60	17.80	17.30	17.30	18.00	19.10	19.80	19.50	22.00
9 Personal goods and services	12.60	12.70	13.20	13.40	13.20	13.70	13.90	14.30	14.70
10 Motoring	44.10	42.60	42.20	43.60	47.00	51.00	54.10	54.10	55.10
11 Fares and other travel costs	8.90	7.80	7.00	7.60	8.60	9.30	8,70	9.40	9.50
12 Leisure goods	16.50	16.40	15.70	16.50	17.60	18.70	18.60	19.10	19.70
13 Leisure services	34.10	36.70	36.60	37.40	39.00	42.60	43.90	45.30	50.60
14 Miscellaneous	2.20	2.70	2.70	1.40	1.10	1.20	1.30	1.50	0.70
1–14 All expenditure groups	336.40	334.00	330.90	337.30	348.50	359.20	368.40	370.20	385.70

Average weekly expenditure per person (£)									
All expenditure groups	137.30	141.60	135.60	141.00	139.40	149.70	153.50	160.90	163.90

	Average weekly household income (£)[3]								
Gross income (£)	427.60	447.00	434.80	444.80	450.30	463.10	478.00	494.20	502.50
Disposable income (£)	349.20	361.30	350.20	357.50	367.90	377.30	387.80	402.70	409.20

1 From 1974 to this version of 1995–96, figures shown are based on unweighted, adult-only data.
2 From this version of 1995–96, figures are shown based on weighted data, including children's expenditure.
3 Does not include imputed income from owner-occupied and rent-free households.

Source: Social Trends.

Household Expenditure by Age of Head of Household

Based on weighted data and including children's expenditure

		Under 30	30 and under 50	50 and under 65	65 and under 75	75 or over	All households
Grossed number of households (thousands)		2,670	9.940	6.220	3.190	3.010	25.030
Total number of households in sample		687	2.598	1,646	956	750	6.637
Total number of persons in sample		1,620	7,989	3,617	1,622	1,077	15,925
Total number of adults in sample		1,132	4,802	3,243	1,602	1,073	11,852
Weighted average number of persons per household		2.3	3.0	2.2	1.7	1.4	2.4
Commodity or service		**Average weekly household expenditure (£)**					
1	Housing (net)	78.70	84.00	56.80	34.80	30.30	63.90
	Percentage standard error	*3*	*2*	*3*	*3*	*5*	*1*
2	Fuel and power	9.90	12.30	13.00	11.80	10.00	11.90
	"	*7*	*1*	*2*	*2*	*2*	*1*
3	Food and non-alcoholic drinks	55.00	73.60	67.10	47.00	34.70	61.90
	"	*2*	*1*	*2*	*2*	*2*	*1*
4	Alcoholic drink	18.70	17.90	17.40	7.90	4.90	15.00
	"	*5*	*3*	*4*	*6*	*8*	*2*
5	Tobacco	7.50	6.90	7.20	3.90	1.80	6.10
	"	*6*	*4*	*5*	*8*	*13*	*3*
6	Clothing and footwear	25.00	29.80	21.10	12.20	5.80	22.00
	"	*6*	*3*	*4*	*6*	*8*	*2*
7	Household goods	28.20	37.30	37.80	28.90	14.40	32.60
	"	*7*	*4*	*5*	*10*	*9*	*3*
8	Household services	20.80	26.90	21.70	17.60	11.80	22.00
	"	*9*	*3*	*4*	*11*	*6*	*2*
9	Personal goods and services	16.40	17.00	15.70	11.20	7.50	14.70
	"	*8*	*3*	*4*	*7*	*7*	*2*
10	Motoring	52.00	67.30	67.60	32.70	15.40	55.10
	"	*6*	*3*	*4*	*5*	*9*	*2*
11	Fares and other travel costs	12.00	11.80	10.10	5.40	2.50	9.50
	"	*12*	*6*	*10*	*21*	*20*	*5*
12	Leisure goods	18.80	25.60	19.60	14.20	7.30	19.70
	"	*10*	*4*	*5*	*11*	*8*	*3*
13	Leisure services	38.30	6.120	60.80	34.90	22.40	50.60
	"	*7*	*4*	*5*	*5*	*10*	*2*
14	Miscellaneous	0.60	1.20	0.60	0.20	0.10	0.70
	"	*15*	*8*	*11*	*16*	*26*	*6*
1–14	All expenditure groups	381.70	472.80	416.40	262.60	169.10	385.70
	Percentage standard error	*3*	*1*	*2*	*3*	*3*	*1*
		Average weekly expenditure per person (£)					
	All expenditure groups	167.40	160.20	187.80	154.60	118.90	163.90

Source: Social Trends.

Major Paid Admission Attractions in the UK

Attraction	Location	Country	Visits 2000	Visits 1999	% Change
Millennium Dome	London	England	6,516,874 E	N/A	N/A
British Airways London Eye	London	England	3,300,000 E	N/A	N/A
Alton Towers	Alton	England	2,450,000	2,650,000	−7.5
Madame Tussaud's	London	England	2,388,000	2,640,000	−9.5
Tower of London	London	England	2,303,167	2,428,603	−5.2
Natural History Museum	London	England	1,577,044	1,696,725	−7.1
Chessington World of Adventure	Chessington	England	1,500,000 E	1,550,000 E	−3.2
Legoland Windsor	Windsor	England	1,490,000	1,620,000	−8.0
Victoria & Albert Museum	London	England	1,344,113	1,251,396	7.4
Science Museum	London	England	1,337,432	1,483,234	−9.8
Flamingo Land Theme Park & Zoo	Kirby Misperton	England	1,301,000 E	1,197,000 E	8.7
Canterbury Cathedral	Canterbury	England	1,263,140 E	1,318,065 E	−4.2
Westminster Abbey	London	England	1,230,000	1,260,000	−2.4
Edinburgh Castle	Edinburgh	Scotland	1,204,285	1,219,720	−1.3
Windermere Lake Cruises	Newby Bridge	England	1,172,219	1,140,207	2.8
Windsor Castle	Windsor	England	1,127,000	1,280,000	−12.0
Chester Zoo	Chester	England	1,118,000	1,065,000	5.0
St Paul's Cathedral	London	England	937,025	1,068,336	−12.3
Roman Baths	Bath	England	932,566	918,867	1.5

Note: 2000 data excludes one attraction where operator did not authorise figures for publication. The table above only contains data on attractions which responded to the Survey of Visits to Visitor Attractions and gave permission for their information to be published.

Major Free Admission Attractions in the UK

Attraction	Location	Country	Visits 2000	Visits 1999	% Change
Blackpool Pleasure Beach	Blackpool	England	6,800,000	7,100,000	−4.2
British Museum	London	England	5,466,246 E	5,460,537 E	0.1
National Gallery	London	England	4,897,690 E	4,964,879 E	−1.4
Tate Modern	London	England	3,873,887	N/A	N/A
Pleasureland Theme Park	Southport	England	2,600,000 E	2,500,000 E	4.0
Adventure Island	Southend-on-Sea	England	2,500,000 E	2,000,000 E	25.0
York Minster	York	England	1,750,000 E	1,900,000 E	−7.9
Pleasure Beach	Great Yarmouth	England	1,500,000 E	1,500,000 E	0.0
Tate Britain	London	England	1,204,147 E	1,822,428 E	−33.9
National Portrait Gallery	London	England	1,178,400	999,842	17.9
Kelvingrove Art Gallery & Museum	Glasgow	Scotland	1,003,169 E	1,051,050 E	−4.6
Chester Cathedral	Chester	England	1,000,000 E	1,000,000 E	0.0
Clacton Pier	Clacton-on-Sea	England	1,000,000 E	1,000,000 E	0.0
Birmingham Museum & Art Gallery	Birmingham	England	735,994	714,613	3.0
World Famous Old Blacksmith's Shop Centre	Gretna Green	Scotland	697,226 E	651,005 E	7.1
Tate Liverpool	Liverpool	England	653,789	674,929	−3.1

Note: 2000 data excludes four attractions where operators did not authorise figures for publication. The table above only contains data on attractions which responded to the Survey of Visits to Visitor Attractions and gave permission for their information to be published.

Source: www.staruk.org.uk, sponsored by the National Tourist Boards of England, Scotland, Northern Ireland, Wales and the Department for Culture, Media and Sport.

Major Cathedrals & Churches in the UK

Attraction	Location	Country	Visits 2000	Visits 1999	% Change	Admission
York Minster	York	England	1,750,000 E	1,900,000 E	−7.9	F
Canterbury Cathedral	Canterbury	England	1,263,140 E	1,318,065 E	−4.2	P
Westminster Abbey	London	England	1,230,000	1,260,000	−2.4	P
Chester Cathedral	Chester	England	1,000,000 E	1,000,000 E	0.0	F
St Paul's Cathedral	London	England	937,025	1,068,336	−12.3	P
St Martin in the Fields	London	England	600,000 E	575,000 E	4.3	F
Truro Cathedral	Truro	England	500,000 E	500,000 E	0.0	F
Exeter Cathedral	Exeter	England	450,000 E	410,000 E	9.8	F
St Giles Cathedral	Edinburgh	Scotland	386,400 E	N/A	N/A	F

Note: 2000 data excludes one attraction where operator did not authorise figures for publication.

Major Country Parks in the UK

Attraction	Location	Country	Visits 2000	Visits 1999	% Change	Admission
Strathclyde Country Park	nr. Motherwell	Scotland	4,808,590 E	4,891,287	−1.7	F
Sutton Park	Sutton Park	England	2,500,000 E	2,500,000 E	0.0	F
Ashton Court Estate	Long Ashton	England	1,500,000 E	1,500,000 E	0.0	F
Heaton Park	Prestwich	England	1,200,000 E	1,000,000 E	20.0	F
Carsington Water	Ashbourne	England	1,100,000 E	1,200,000 E	−8.3	F
Bradgate Country Park	Newtown Linford	England	1,000,000 E	1,000,000 E	0.0	P
Blaise Castle Estate	Henbury	England	800,000 E	700,000 E	14.3	F
Dunstable Downs	Dunstable	England	750,000 E	1,000,000 E	−25.0	F
Pugneys Country Park	Wakefield	England	700,000 E	700,000 E	0.0	F

Note: 2000 data excludes one attraction where operator did not authorise figures for publication.

Major Farms in the UK

Attraction	Location	Country	Visits 2000	Visits 1999	% Change	Admission
Cannon Hall Open Farm	Cawthorne	England	350,000 E	330,000 E	6.1	P
Callestock Cider Farm	Penhallow	England	285,000	330,000	−13.6	F
Temple Newsam Home Farm & Estate	Leeds	England	245,005 E	273,918 E	−10.6	F
Godstone Farm	Godstone	England	221,900 E	232,300 E	−4.5	P
Folly Farm	Begelly, Kilgetty	Wales	204,489	203,407	0.5	P
Amerton Farm	Stowe-by-Chartley	England	185,000 E	185,000 E	0.0	F
Odds Farm Park	High Wycombe	England	157,624	168,000	−6.2	P
Woodside Animal Farm	Slip End	England	150,000 E	150,000 E	0.0	P
Fishers Farm Park	Wisborough Green	England	130,000 E	120,000 E	8.3	P

Note: 2000 data excludes one attraction where operator did not authorise figures for publication.

Source: www.staruk.org.uk

Major Gardens in the UK

Attraction	Location	Country	Visits 2000	Visits 1999	% Change	Admission
Kew Gardens	Richmond	England	860,340	864,269	−0.5	P
Botanic Gardens	Belfast	Northern Ireland	650,000	650,000	0.0	F
Wisley Garden	Wisley	England	613,987	615,034	−0.2	P
Royal Botanic Gardens	Edinburgh	Scotland	609,838 E	609,488 E	0.1	F
Glasgow Botanic Gardens	Glasgow	Scotland	400,000	400,000 E	0.0	F
Wakehurst Place	Ardingly	England	304,890	292,883	4.1	P
Ventnor Botanic Garden	Ventnor	England	298,524 E	250,000 E	19.4	F
Stourhead Gardens	Stourton	England	253,833	272,816	−7.0	P

Note: 2000 data excludes two attractions where operators did not authorise figures for publication.

Major Historic Houses & Castles in the UK

Attraction	Location	Country	Visits 2000	Visits 1999	% Change	Admission
Tower of London	London	England	2,303,167	2,428,603	−5.2	P
Edinburgh Castle	Edinburgh	Scotland	1,204,285	1,219,720	−1.3	P
Windsor Castle	Windsor	England	1,127,000	1,280,000	−12.0	P
Warwick Castle	Warwick	England	793,300	793,000	0.0	P
Hampton Court Palace	Hampton Court	England	618,710	699,218	−11.5	P
Leeds Castle & Gardens	Nr Maidstone	England	527,594	569,505	−7.4	P
Chatsworth	Bakewell	England	490,000 E	470,000 E	4.3	P
Tatton Park	Knutsford	England	441,896 E	480,256 E	−8.0	P
Stirling Castle	Stirling	Scotland	430,362	416,070	3.4	P

Note: 2000 data excludes one attraction where operator did not authorise figures for publication.

Major Historic Buildings in the UK

Attraction	Location	Country	Visits 2000	Visits 1999	% Change	Admission
Roman Baths	Bath	England	932,566	918,867	1.5	P
Stonehenge	Amesbury	England	799,742	836,294	−4.4	P
HMS Victory	Portsmouth	England	317,459	319,255	−0.6	P
Mary Rose Ship Hull	Portsmouth	England	239,718	245,436	−2.3	P
HMS Warrior	Portsmouth	England	221,074	229,310	−3.6	P
HMS Belfast	London	England	221,000 E	220,000 E	0.5	P
Cutty Sark Clipper Ship	London	England	166,597	159,480	4.5	P

Note: 2000 data excludes three attractions where operators did not authorise figures for publication.

Source: www.staruk.org.uk

Major Leisure & Theme Parks in the UK

Attraction	Location	Country	Visits 2000	Visits 1999	% Change	Admission
Blackpool Pleasure Beach	Blackpool	England	6,800,000	7,100,000	−4.2	F
Pleasureland Theme Park	Southport	England	2,600,000 E	2,500,000 E	4.0	F
Adventure Island	Southend-on-Sea	England	2,500,000 E	2,000,000 E	25.0	F
Alton Towers	Alton	England	2,450,000	2,650,000	−7.5	P
Pleasure Beach	Great Yarmouth	England	1,500,000 E	1,500,000 E	0.0	F
Chessington World of Adventures	Chessington	England	1,500,000 E	1,550,000 E	−3.2	P
Legoland Windsor	Windsor	England	1,490,000	1,620,000	−8.0	P
Flamingo Land Theme Park & Zoo	Kirby Misperton	England	1,301,000 E	1,197,000 E	8.7	P
Thorpe Park	Chertsey	England	925,000	926,000	−0.1	P

Note: 2000 data excludes one attraction where operator did not authorise figures for publication.

Major Museums and Art Galleries in the UK

Attraction	Location	Country	Visits 2000	Visits 1999	% Change	Admission
British Museum	London	England	5,466,246 E	5,460,537 E	0.1	F
National Gallery	London	England	4,897,690 E	4,964,879 E	−1.4	F
Tate Modern	London	England	3,873,887	N/A	N/A	F
Natural History Museum	London	England	1,577,044	1,696,725	−7.1	P
Victoria & Albert Museum	London	England	1,344,113	1,251,396	7.4	P
Science Museum	London	England	1,337,432	1,483,234	−9.8	P
Tate Britain	London	England	1,204,147 E	1,822,428 E	−33.9	F
National Portrait Gallery	London	England	1,278,400	999,842	17.9	F
Kelvingrove Art Gallery and Museum	Glasgow	Scotland	1,003,169 E	1,051,050 E	−4.6	F

Note: 2000 data excludes one attraction where operator did not authorise figures for publication.

Major Steam/Heritage Railways in the UK

Attraction	Location	Country	Visits 2000	Visits 1999	% Change	Admission
North Yorkshire Moors Railway	Pickering	England	272,079 E	277,870 E	−2.1	P
Severn Valley Railway	Bewdley	England	227,204	228,010	−0.4	P
Bluebell Railway	Sheffield Park	England	184,235	168,477	0.4	P
Swanage Railway	Swanage	England	168,092	152,276	10.4	P
Lakeside & Haverthwaite Railway	Ulverston	England	160,000 E	159,000 E	0.6	P
Romney, Hythe & Dymchurch Railway	New Romney	England	154,443	154,906	−0.3	P
West Somerset Railway	Minehead	England	154,421	153,832	0.4	P
North Bay Miniature Railway	Scarborough	England	150,000 E	96,155	56.0	P

Note: 2000 data excludes two attractions where operators did not authorise figures for publication.

Source: www.staruk.org.uk

Major Visitor Centres in the UK

Attraction	Location	Country	Visits 2000	Visits 1999	% Change	Admission
World Famous Old Blacksmith's Shop Centre	Gretna Green	Scotland	697,226 E	651,005 E	7.1	F
Cadbury World	Bournville	England	480,467	496,456	−3.2	P
Lulworth Cove Heritage Centre	Wareham	England	406,911 E	440,899 E	−7.7	F
Our Dynamic Earth	Edinburgh	Scotland	398,790	295,959 E	34.7	P
Giants Causeway Visitor Centre	Bushmills	Northern Ireland	395,247	433,745	−8.9	P
East point Pavilion Visitor Centre	Lowestoft	England	312,236 E	326,778 E	−4.5	F
Dalby Forest Drive & Visitor Centre	Low Dalby	England	307,842	302,427	1.8	P
New Lanark Visitor Centre	Lanark	Scotland	306,000 E	311,000 E	−1.6	f
The Former Royal Yacht Britannia	Leith	Scotland	304,395	415,297	−26.7	P

Note: 2000 data excludes one attraction where operator did not authorise figures for publication.

Major Wildlife Attractions & Zoos in the UK

Attraction	Location	Country	Visits 2000	Visits 1999	% Change	Admission
Chester Zoo	Chester	England	1,118,000	1,065,000	5.0	P
London Zoo	London	England	930,000	1,000,057	−7.0	P
London Aquarium	London	England	780,000 E	650,000 E	20.0	P
Lotherton Hall Estate	Aberford	England	650,000	750,000	−13.3	F
Edinburgh Zoo	Edinburgh	Scotland	522,279	526,000 E	−0.7	P
Twycross Zoo	Twycross	England	482,058	475,174	1.4	P
Bristol Zoo Gardens	Clifton	England	449,552	459,721	−2.2	P
Paignton Zoo	Paignton	England	444,936	421,094	5.7	P
Colchester Zoo	Stanway	England	406,415	396,657	2.5	P

Note: 2000 data excludes one attraction where operator did not authorise figures for publication.

Major Workplaces in the UK

Attraction	Location	Country	Visits 2000	Visits 1999	% Change	Admission
Colony Country Store	Ulverston	England	260,000 E	261,160 E	−0.4	F
Glass Studio	Eastbourne	England	250,000 E	250,000 E	0.0	F
Jorvik Glass	York	England	213,000 E	215,000 E	−0.9	F
St Aidan's Winery	Holy Island	England	200,000 E	200,000	0.0	F
Belleek Pottery	Belleek	Northern Ireland	193,672	190,113	1.9	P
Adrian Sankey Glass	Ambleside	England	181,953	154,255	18.0	P
Stuart Strathearn Crystal	Crieff	Scotland	165,811	238,163	−30.4	F

Note: 2000 data excludes three attractions where operators did not authorise figures for publication.

Source: www.staruk.org.uk

Major Paid Admission Attractions 2001

Attraction	Location	Visits 2001	Visits 2000
British Airways London Eye	London	3,850,000*	3,300,000*
Tower of London	London	2,019,210	2,303,167
Eden Project	St Austell	1,700,00	498,000
Natural History Museum	London	1,696,176	1,576,048
Legoland Windsor	Windsor	1,632,000	1,490,000
Victoria & Albert Museum	London	1,446,344	1,344,113
Science Museum	London	1,352,649	1,337,432
Flamingo Land Theme Park & Zoo	Kirby Misperton	1,322,000*	1,301,000*
Windermere Lake Cruises	Ambleside	1,241,918*	1,172,219
Canterbury Catherdral	Canterbury	1,151,099*	1,263,140*
Edinburgh Castle	Edinburgh	1,127,389	1,204,285
Chester Zoo	Chester	1,060,433	1,118,000
Kew Gardens	Richmond	989,352	860,340
Westminster Abbey	London	986,354	1,241,876
Royal Academy of Arts	London	910,276	760,800
London Zoo	London	906,923	930,000
Windsor Castle	Windsor	904,164	1,126,508
Roman Baths	Bath	864,989	932,566
St. Pauls Cathedral	London	837,894	937,025

Major Free Admission Attractions 2001

Attraction	Location	Visits 2001	Visits 2000
Blackpool Pleasure Beach	Blackpool	6,500,000	6,800,000
National Gallery	London	4,918,985*	4,897,690*
British Museum	London	4,800,938	5,466,246*
Tate Modern	London	3,551,885	3,873,887
Pleasureland Theme Park	Southport	2,100,000*	2,100,000*
Claction Pier	Clacton-on-Sea	1,750,000*	1,000,000*
York Minster	York	1,600,000*	1,750,000*
Pleasure Beach	Great Yarmouth	1,500,000*	1,500,000*
National Portrait Gallery	London	1,269,819	1,178,400
Poole Pottery	Poole	1,063,499	1,129,419
Kelvingrove Art Gallery & Museum	Glasgow	1,031,138*	1,003,169*
Tate Britain	London	1,011,716	1,204,147*
Cannon Hill Park	Moseley	950,000*	950,000*
Chester Cathedral	Chester	900,000	1,000,000*
Flamingo Family Fun Park	Hastings	900,000*	860,000*
National Museum of Photography, Film & Television	Bradford	874,000*	1,017,373*
The Lowry	Salford	774,577*	688,600*
Carsington Water Visitor Centre	Ashbourne	750,000*	825,000*
Somerset House	London	700,000*	450,000*
St. Martin-in-the-Fields	London	700,000*	600,000*

Note: *Estimates

Source: www.staruk.org.uk, sponsored by the National Tourist Boards of England, Scotland, Northern Ireland, Wales and the Department for Culture, Media and Sport.

Suggested reading

Caterer & Hotelkeeper	Reed Business Information	01444 445565
Conference and Incentive Travel	Haymarket Marketing Publications	0208 845 8545
Core Geography: Leisure (Martin &Whittle)	Hutchinson	0171 9739000
From Tourist Attractions to Heritage Tourism	Elm Publications	01487 773254
Group Leisure	Yandell Publishing Ltd	01908 613323
Hospitality: The Journal of the Hotel and Catering International Management Association	Reed Business Information	0208 772 7426
Hotel Report	Martin Information Limited	0208 240 4479
Intermediate GNVQ in Leisure and Tourism (2002) (Vranic)	Hodder & Stoughton	01235 827720
Intermediate Leisure and Tourism GNVQ (Vranic)	John Murray & Sons	0207 4934361
Introduction to tourism (Likorish & Jenkins)	Butterworth Heinemann	01865 311366
Leisure and Hospitality Business	Centaur Publishing Ltd.	020 72923750
Leisure and Tourism GNVQ (Trigg)	Butterworth Heinemann	01865 311366
Leisure Management	The Leisure Media Company	01462 471932
Leisure Manager	Institute of Leisure and Amenity Management	01491 874855
Leisure Opportunities	The Leisure Media Company	01462 431385
Marketing for tourism (Holloway and Plant)	Pitman Publishing	01279 623623
Providing accessible tourist attractions	English Tourism Council	0870 606 7204
Providing Service for all in Education	English Tourism Council	0870 606 7204
The Business of Tourism, (JC Holloway)	Addison Wesley Longman Ltd.	01279 623623
The Leisure Environment (Colquhoun)	Pitman Publishing	01279 623623
Tourism (Davidson)	Pitman Publishing	01279 623623
Tourism and Hospitality in the 21st Century	Butterworth Heinemann	01865 311366
Travel and Tourism (Lavery)	Elm Publications	01487 773254
Travel and Tourism, (Youell)	Pearson Education Limited	0207 20744720
Travel GBI	Travelscope Publications	0207 729 4337
Travel Trade Gazette	United Business Media	0207 8616109
Travel Weekly	Reed Business Information	01444 445566

Websites

	Name	Description	Website
1	Arts Council of England	Independent body supporting the arts, lottery funding	www.artscouncil.org.uk
2	Arts Council of Northern Ireland	Responsible for funding and development of the arts	www.artscouncil-ni.org
3	Arts Council of Wales	Responsible for funding the arts, lottery grant distribution	www.ccc-acw.org
4	Association for Conferences and Events	Event organisers' information centre	www.martex.co.uk/ace
5	Association of British Travel Agents (ABTA)	Leading trade organization for travel agents and tour operators in UK	www.abtanet.com
6	Association of Independent Museums	Improving standards in the private and voluntarily run museum sector	www.museums.org.uk/aim/
7	Association of Independent Tour Operators (AITO)	Organisation representing top independent specialist tour operators	www.aito.co.uk
8	Association of Leading Visitor Attractions	Trade Association	www.alva.org.uk
9	Association of Scottish Visitor Attractions	Trade Association	www.asva.co.uk
10	British Airports Authority	Owner of major UK airports	www.baa.co.uk/
11	British Association of Conference Destinations	Represents and assists in promotion of over 3000 venues	www.bacd.org.uk/
12	British Holiday & Home Parks Association	Trade Association	www.bhhpa.org.uk/
13	British Hospitality Association	Trade Association	www.bha-online.org.uk
14	British Incoming Tour Operators Association (BITOA)	Official trade body for incoming tour operators and their suppliers	www.biota.co.uk
15	British Olympic Association (BOA)	Body responsible for supervision of British Olympic team	www.olympics.org.uk
16	Business in Sport and Leisure	Trade, lobby and umbrella organisation	www.bisl.org
17	buzz	Budget airline	www.buzz.co.uk
18	Civil Aviation Authority	Leads the development and economic regulation of British aviation	www.caa.co.uk
19	Coach Tourism Council	Promoting coach travel and tourism	www.coachtourismcouncil.co.uk/
20	De Vere Hotels	Hotel chain	www.devereonline.co.uk
21	Department for Education and Skills	Responsible for education, training and development	dfes.gsi.gov.uk
22	Dept. for Culture, Media and Sport	Responsible for leisure and tourism policies	www.culture.gov.uk/
23	Dept. for Transport, Local Government and the Regions	Responsible for environmental issues, countryside	www.detr.gov.uk/
24	easyJet	Budget airline	www.easyJet.co.uk
25	English Association of Self Catering Operators	Trade Association	www.englishselfcatering.org
26	European Tour Operators Assocation (ETOA)	Inbound and intra-European tour operating organisations	www.etoa.org
27	Exhibition Venues Association	Provides information on venues and undertakes research	www.martex.co.uk/eva/
28	Expobase	Provides information on 20000 tradeshows worldwide	www.expobase.com
29	Further Education Development Association (FEDA)	Organisation offering support for all qualifications	www.feda.ac.uk
30	Holiday Care	Charity enhancing travel possibilities for elderly and disbled.	www.holidaycare.org.uk
31	Institute of Leisure and Amenity Managers (ILAM)	Trade Association	www.ilam.co.uk
32	International Air Transport Association (IATA)	Represents the airline industry	www.iata.org/

	Name	Description	Website
33	International Association of Amusement Parks and Attractions	Setting professional standards	http:208.247.232.62/
34	Meetings Industry Association	Trade Organisation for Conference Industry	www.meetings.org
35	Museums Association	Represents interests of museums and galleries employees	www.museumsassocation.org
36	National Caravan Council	Trade Association	www.nationalcaravan.co.uk
37	National Piers Society	Pier Preservation Group	www.piers.co.uk
38	National Trust	Voluntary body concerned with preservation of national heritage	www.nationaltrust.org.uk
39	Norfolk and Norwich Millennium Library	Tourist Information Centre, heritage attraction and library	THEFORUMNORFOLK.com
40	Northern Ireland Hotels Federation	Trade Association	www.nihf.co.uk/
41	Northern Ireland Museums Council	Supports and promotes museums in Northern Ireland	www.nimc.co.uk
42	Office for National Statistics	Source for statistics	www.ons.gov.uk
43	Pleasurewood Hills Leisure Park	Theme Park	www.pleasurewood.com
44	Qualification and Curriculum Authority (QCA)	Government body responsible for curriculum quality and standards	www.qca.org.uk
45	Resource (formerly Museums and Galleries Commission)	Works with and for museums on collaborative projects	www.resource.gov.uk/
46	Scottish Arts Council	Body responsible for channeling government funding	www.sac.org.uk
47	Scottish Museums Council	Aims to improve museum and gallery provision in Scotland	www.scottishmuseums.org.uk
48	Sport Council for Northern Ireland	Promotion of sport in Northern Ireland	www.sportni.org/
49	Sport England	Sports development body	www.English.sports.gov.uk
50	Sport Scotland	Promotion of sport in Scotland	www.sportscotland.org.uk/
51	Springboard UK	National organisation promoting careers in travel and tourism	www.springboarduk.org.uk
52	SPRITO	National training organisation for sport and recreation	www.sprito.org.uk
53	StarUK	UK Tourism research liaison group	www.staruk.org.uk
54	Sustrans	Charity promoting walking and cycling to reduce motor traffic	www.sustrans.org.uk/
55	The British Association of Leisure Parks, Piers and Attractions	Trade Association	www.balppa.org/
56	The Ramblers Association	Voluntary organisation for ramblers	www.ramblers.org.uk
57	The Sports Council for Wales	Promotion of sport in Wales	www.sports-council-wales.co.uk
58	The Tourism Society	Representing professionals in tourism	www.toursoc.org.uk
59	Theme and Leisure Parks Guide	Annual list of Major Theme Parks in UK and rest of Europe	www.themeandleisure.com
60	Tourism for All	Consortium which creates, develops and supports accessibility	www.tourismforall.org.uk
61	UK Sport	Overview of sports in UK	www.uksport.gov.uk
62	UNESCO	World Heritage sites	www.unesco.org
63	Vocational Learning Organisation	Learning Skills Council site for interactive and other resources	www.vocationallearning.org.uk
64	Worktrain	Dept. for Education and Skills site for jobs and training	www.worktrain.gov.uk
65	Xscape	Entertainment and leisure centre	www.xscape.co.uk

Index